The Iowa C

The Iowa Caucuses

First Tests of Presidential Aspiration, 1972–2008

JOHN C. SKIPPER

McFarland & Company, Inc., Publishers
Jefferson, North Carolina, and London

John C. Skipper is also the author of numerous works
of baseball history, published by McFarland, including
A Biographical Dictionary of the Baseball Hall of Fame (2d ed., 2008)

LIBRARY OF CONGRESS CATALOGUING-IN-PUBLICATION DATA

Skipper, John C., 1945–
   The Iowa caucuses : first tests of presidential aspiration,
1972–2008 / John C. Skipper.
      p.   cm.
   Includes bibliographical references and index.

   ISBN 978-0-7864-4001-6
   softcover : 50# alkaline paper

   1. Primaries — Iowa — History.   2. Presidents — United
States — Nomination — History.   I. Title.
JK2075.I82S55   2010
324.273'1520977709045 — dc22   2009037449

British Library cataloguing data are available

On the cover: Barack Obama in Iowa, 2008; photo ©2010 Shutterstock

Manufactured in the United States of America

McFarland & Company, Inc., Publishers
   Box 611, Jefferson, North Carolina 28640
   www.mcfarlandpub.com

For Bob Link

Table of Contents

Preface

It was about 9 o'clock on a crisp night in April 2007 when Barack Obama walked into a small office, just off of the gymnasium at North Iowa Area Community College in Mason City, Iowa. In two years, he would be president of the United States. On this night, he was the junior senator from Illinois — the "first-term senator," as the local newspaper pointed out.

Obama had spent the day campaigning all over Iowa and was tired after finishing off with a speech to a crowd that was a mix of staunch Democrats, ardent Obama supporters and curious onlookers who just wanted to take a look at this political novice who was creating quite a buzz. Obama had one more commitment before calling it a night — an interview with the local newspaper reporter.

When he opened the door and came in the office, suit coat draped over his shoulder, he had a bit of a bounce in his step, a glide to his walk that belied the fact he had been on the go for 14 hours. In build and in the way he carried himself, Obama reminded the newsman of Ozzie Smith, the retired Hall of Fame shortstop of the St. Louis Cardinals whom the reporter had recently interviewed and was struck by how smooth and athletic he looked for a man of his age, even in street clothes. Obama had that same way about him as he sauntered in.

He shook hands with the reporter as they introduced themselves and then sat down across a table from the writer, within arm's length of him. As the reporter began to ask his first question, the future president raised his hand as if to say, "Stop!" He looked at the man with the pen in his hand and said, "Before you begin, I just want to tell you one thing." He paused for a moment and then said, "You are the only thing standing between me and dinner!" Then he flashed a big grin and encouraged the reporter to fire away with his questions.

Eight months later, on the day after Christmas, the same reporter had the opportunity to meet with Obama again. This time, it was a week before the Iowa caucuses and Obama was no longer just the "first-term senator" from Illinois. He was mounting a serious challenge to defeat Senator Hillary Rodham Clinton of New York, the former first lady who had been the odds-on favorite for months not only to win the caucuses but to capture the Democratic presidential nomination.

On this day, Obama gave a speech in the gymnasium of Newman High School in Mason City. His aides had once again arranged for the reporter to have a little one-on-one time with him after his speech. The setting for this interview was in a practice gym not far from where Obama had spoken. The writer wondered if all the attention the candidate had gotten in the past several months had changed his personality and style.

Obama came into the practice gym, once again with his suit coat over his shoulder. He tossed the coat on the floor, picked up a basketball and started shooting baskets. He went all around the three-point line, starting from the right baseline, gradually moving to the top of the key and ending at the left baseline.

Every time he shot, Tommy Vietor, his press secretary, retrieved the ball and tossed it back to him as he moved a few feet and shot again. The reporter had been told he had 10 minutes to do the interview, so there was no other option but to trail along side the future president, with pen and notebook in hand, and conduct the interview, jump shot after jump shot.

"How was your Christmas?" The shot went up.

"Great. I got the present I wanted most—a good night's sleep."

"What do you hope people realize about you now that they might not have known six months ago?" *Swish*—the ball went cleanly through the hoop.

"That I'm more than just a man who made a good speech," he said, dribbling to his left and launching a shot that glanced off the rim. (He was referring to his keynote speech at the 2004 Democratic convention that provided him with a national television audience who may never have seen or heard of him before, and knew little about him afterwards until he announced his candidacy for president.)

"As we get to these final days, what do you want voters to think about? Why should they vote for you rather than one of your opponents?"

The change in his pocket rattled as he tossed up another shot. "I have been opposed to the war from the beginning. I can restore the respect other countries have for us and I can bring about the changes we so badly need." *Swish*. He hit another one.

Then he rolled the ball into the corner of the gym, picked up his coat, shook hands with the reporter, smiled and said, "Gotta go."

Incidents like these were the genesis for what you are about to read. The Iowa caucuses, wacky as they are to many outside observers, provide a unique brand of retail politics, a dying brand in the age of multi-million dollar advertising blitzes and a smothering national media. The following pages provide insight into how the Iowa caucuses came to be what they are today, the first testing ground for men and women who aspire to be president of the United States.

You will read about candidates doing extraordinary things to try to impress Iowa voters. They've dyed their hair, they've changed their wardrobes to try to look more Iowan, they've posed for pictures in front of sculptures made out of butter, they've flipped pancakes at charity breakfasts, and they've given speech after speech after speech. If you live in Iowa, residents will tell you, you have the opportunity to meet the next president. But you won't know at the time who the next president will be so you have to meet about 20 candidates along the way. This pattern is repeated every four years.

As you read this book, you might get the impression that Mason City, Iowa, is the center of the universe because there are so many references to it. There are two reasons for its prominence on these pages. It is where the author lives and works, he being the reporter in the aforementioned events with President Obama. It has been the picture window that has provided him with a panoramic view of grassroots presidential politics.

But you could live almost anywhere in Iowa and experience the same thing. That's the point, because in the sense that presidential politics in Iowa has been a mission for so many candidates over the years, Mason City, like dozens of other cities in Iowa, has been a mission field for most all of them. So it is a good place to put the point of the compass as we examine the first roads on the journey to the White House.

It has not only been the setting for hand-shaking, baby-kissing, picture-posing, "how-ya-doing" retail politics, but also for the backroom strategizing, the efforts to make every well-planned moment seem spontaneous and fresh.

It is where Pat Buchanan's handlers were seen ordering that several rows of chairs be taken out of a room where the candidate was to speak because they wanted to make sure he spoke to a standing-room-only crowd.

It is where Hillary Clinton's people had throngs of reporters line up, like schoolchildren waiting for their turn at the drinking fountain, and then, one by one, each was ushered in to an alcove and granted five minutes with Mrs. Clinton.

It is where one of Lamar Alexander's assistants came into a meeting room and chose a man in the audience — a middle school social studies teacher — to be the designated clapper, the person who would lead others in applause when the candidate entered the room.

It is where Senator Chris Dodd's people called the newspaper office and pleaded for some interview time with their man after he had gone virtually unnoticed by the public during a stroll through a downtown mall.

The second reason that Mason City is showcased on many of these pages is to demonstrate one of the fascinating aspects of presidential politics. Mason City, population 28,000, and cities like it throughout Iowa, take on tremendous importance to men and women who want to be president.

Jimmy Carter was the first candidate to recognize this. With most of the other would- be candidates in 1976 scrambling to get in front of a microphone in Washington, D.C., Carter theorized, "I likely would be the only presidential candidate that day in Sioux City." He might just as easily have said Mason City or Dubuque or Waterloo or Council Bluffs. Carter wanted to be the first candidate in Iowa so he could start early on the path to win the first presidential test that might just result in his nomination and his election. As it turned out, he was right on all counts.

In order to understand how the caucuses evolved into the dynamic political force that they've become, it is useful to reach back into history to a time when Americans were crying out for reforms in the presidential selection process so more people could have more of a say — from blacks in Mississippi in 1964 to women and young people and war protesters in 1968. The reforms that were enacted spelled an end to a system where powerful political bosses dictated who the candidates would be, an end to "to hell with what the people wanted."

What emerged was a system emphasizing primary elections and caucuses where delegates would be elected — not selected — and those delegates would ultimately determine the nominees of their party. And out of all of that, little Iowa became first, quite by accident as it turned out.

The author is indebted to the many writers who have chronicled the events over the years; they have made the research not only possible but also utterly enjoyable. They include Theodore H. White, Jules Witcover,

Jack Germond and Walter Shapiro, whose books on various campaigns have been witty and insightful.

Professor Hugh Winebrenner of Drake University produced the first in-depth study of the enormous media impact on the caucuses. His work and his counsel have been extremely helpful.

Understanding the personal relationships between candidates and the folks they have met is an integral part of understanding the dynamics of the caucus season. The author has talked to hundreds of voters over the years whose thoughts and actions are indelibly etched into the pages of this book even if their names are not specifically mentioned. Their contributions to this work cannot be overstated.

But special thanks go to Gloria Goll, a widowed farmwife in the little town of Klemme (pronounced Clem-ee) who taught Senator John Kerry of Massachusetts some of the finer points about pigs; to Marilyn Garst, who, in 1975, was an ardent Democrat with a new car, ample qualifications to be chauffeur to Jimmy Carter, a former Georgia governor whose Iowa experience became the role model for generations of other politicians; to Garst's daughter, Becky Greenwald, a county Democratic chairwoman and candidate for Congress who suggested her mother would be a good source: she was right; to Steve Lynch, an accountant for a food company who helped Gary Hart through some Iowa blizzards; and to Chuck Laudner, a Republican stalwart who provided both food and food for thought for Steve Forbes.

Colleagues past and present along the campaign trail deserve special mention for sharing their observations. They include Mark Manoff, the former *Philadelphia Daily News* reporter who offered perspective from outside the corn beltway; to John Jaszewski and Bill Schickel, two former television newsmen who later became politicians; and especially to David Yepsen, political writer and columnist for the *Des Moines Register* for 32 years who graciously provided the author with insights about candidates and the caucuses themselves, never mentioning that he too was planning to write a book about the caucuses.

John Stone, a veteran political observer, spent much time schooling the author on the finer points of Democratic caucuses, including the unusual procedure in which candidates are eliminated from consideration if they don't represent 15 percent of the total vote of the caucus. When asked, "What do supporters of those candidates do?" Stone gave the answer as if it was a battle cry. "Realign," he said, in a General Patton–like tone. The sharing of his expertise was essential to this work.

A special note of gratitude to Jennifer Skipper, veteran television news producer, for sharing her broadcast knowledge and her suggestions on valuable resources; and to Michael Grandon for his many stories, his insight, his friendship and his interest in this work.

Thanks also to Richard Bender, an aide to Senator Tom Harkin of Iowa, who, 38 years ago, was one of the architects of the Iowa caucus system. He graciously gave of his time to provide the author with much pertinent information on how the present-day caucuses came to be and have survived despite widespread criticism and ridicule.

Photographs for this book would not have been possible without the help of Andrew Hampton, Terry Harrison and Arian Schuessler. Thanks also to Schuessler for his interest in the project as a whole and being a sounding board for the author. He can probably rightfully say that he heard the book before he got a chance to read it. Also, the author is indebted to Howard Query, publisher of the *Mason City Globe Gazette*, for his support of this project.

A book like this could not have been attempted without the help of the many politicians who have been interviewed by the author over the years and whose thoughts and insights were invaluable in putting all the pieces together. They include two former Iowa governors, Terry Branstad and Tom Vilsack and, at this writing, the present governor, Chet Culver; two U.S. senators, Chuck Grassley and Tom Harkin; and the parade of candidates, a parade that stretches not in miles but in years, and includes President Barack Obama, Vice President Joseph Biden, former presidents George H.W. Bush and George W. Bush and former vice presidents Al Gore and Walter Mondale.

Also, candidates Lamar Alexander, Gary Bauer, Bill Bradley, Sam Brownback, Pat Buchanan, Wesley Clark, Hillary Clinton, Howard Dean, Christopher Dodd, Bob Dole, Michael Dukakis, Pete DuPont, John Edwards, Steve Forbes, Richard Gephardt, Phil Gramm, Rudy Giuliani, Gary Hart, Orrin Hatch, John Kerry, Bob Kerry, Alan Keyes, Dennis Kucinich, Richard Lugar, John McCain, Bill Richardson, Mitt Romney, Paul Simon, Tom Tancredo, Fred Thompson, Tommy Thompson and Paul Wellstone.

This is their story; this is their song.

Introduction

"Can I shovel your walk for you?"

At this moment, someone in the United States is thinking about running for president. He or she may be meeting with fund-raisers, conferring with advisers or having a heart-to-heart talk over the dinner table with family members. There are all sorts of scenarios for how the process begins, but there is a common denominator in all of them.

If you're thinking about running for president, wherever you may be, you're thinking about Iowa. Georgetown University adjunct professor Christopher Hull makes that observation in a detailed study he conducted on the importance of tiny Iowa in presidential politics.[1]

The dual thoughts seem preposterous. Iowa and the presidency? How does one connect with the other?

Iowa is hardly representative of the rest of the nation. At 2.9 million, it is 30th among all the states in population; in fact, there are three U.S. cities that have as many or more people than Iowa — New York, Los Angeles and Chicago.

Most people in other states make their living in ways different than Iowans do. The state's economy depends heavily on pigs, corn and soybeans — and manure is a precious commodity. By many government standards, *every* business in Iowa would be considered a small business.[2]

Iowa is no melting pot of racial, ethnic and generational diversity. Nearly 93 percent of its people are white and only Florida and Arizona have more senior citizens per capita.

And then there's the matter of who actually participates in these unusual town-hall type of meetings that are the fabled Iowa caucuses. As one critic said, "The majority of the people in these tiny little caucuses in

Iowa that exert such extraordinary influence in choosing successive presidents are ... retired farmers and their wives who have time to sit with senators, governors and vice presidents who would be president, getting commitments about the security of the Medicare and Social Security programs."[3]

In short, by most people's standards, Iowa is hardly representative of the nation as a whole.

The attraction of Iowa for presidential candidates is its status of being the first testing ground for voters because its precinct caucuses occur before any other primaries or caucuses. So candidates who want to get out of the starting gate quickly come to Iowa — sometimes years in advance of the elections.

Yet historically, Iowans have a dismal track record for picking presidents. Aside from incumbents, the state has picked only three winners since 1972 — Jimmy Carter in 1976, George W. Bush in 2000 and Barack Obama in 2008 — and Carter actually finished second to uncommitted.

But caucus results have littered the political landscape with the broken dreams of presidential hopefuls, most recently former Vermont governor Howard Dean in 2004 and former Massachusetts governor Mitt Romney in 2008. And there were many more before them. As one veteran county courthouse pundit put it, "If the Iowa caucuses meant anything, we'd all be talking about President Gephardt." The reference is to former Missouri congressman Richard Gephardt who was the winner of the Iowa Democratic caucus in 1988. The same could be said for former Arkansas governor Mike Huckabee who did the same in 2008. They both won in Iowa but were not able to sustain the momentum.

Since 1972, the likes of Pierre DuPont, Reuben Askew, Alan Keyes, Gary Bauer and Bob Smith (yes, there really was a Bob Smith) and dozens of others have come to Iowa with ambition and hope and left with humility and enough gas in their vehicles to at least get them home to lick their wounds. Pat Buchanan skipped the Iowa caucuses once, competed twice and, after the second loss, continued his campaign as a third-party candidate.

In their caucuses, Iowans don't even vote like most people do. Instead of holding a primary, where polls are open for 10 to 12 hours and voters can go to the polls at their convenience, Iowans gather in their caucuses on a cold winter night, almost always in January, at 7 p.m. — a time that might interfere with their work shift, bowling night, PTA meeting, or when they could be home in front of their televisions watching college basketball.

Caucuses are, in essence, neighborhood meetings. About 2,000 of them are held throughout the state, all at the same time, in church basements, fire stations, school gymnasiums, and even around kitchen tables. Participants don't vote. They separate into groups, with supporters of Candidate A going to one corner of the room while those for Candidate B gather by the drinking fountain or pencil sharpener and supporters of Candidates C, D and E move to whatever free space they can find. Each group represents a presidential preference.

In most instances, time is allotted for a spokesperson from each group to extol the virtues of the candidate they support, hoping to lure the undecideds into their corner.

When the supporters of the various candidates have formed their groups, the chairman of the caucus, usually a local elected official, counts the number of people in each group to determine which candidate has the most support. To the unschooled observer, the process seems bizarre. There are no secret ballots. Everything is out in the open.

The Republicans treat it as a straw poll. They count heads and add up the totals. The Democrats have a more complicated process. If supporters of a particular candidate don't represent 15 percent of all the people participating, the candidate they represent is not considered viable. Supporters of other candidates then flock to their corner, trying to woo them. When the wooing ends, another vote is taken. The process continues until all candidates are viable.

This is a huge difference from normal voting procedures and, critics claim, hugely undemocratic, because the unviable candidates are eliminated as if they had no support at all. Complicating things further is the fact that a candidate who was unviable at one precinct caucus could have been the leading vote-getter at another caucus. Democrats say this never happens and that the viability standard helps eliminate weak candidates early in the process.

The precinct caucuses for both parties are the first step in electing delegates to county and district conventions where delegates to the state convention will be elected. At the state convention, delegates are elected to the national convention. So there are several stages at which the delegate strength of a candidate can change—but the national media attention is almost always on the first-in-the-nation precinct caucuses which, in reality, are the first inning of the Iowa ball game.

It is a system that a layman might find difficult to understand but which anyone running for president must not only understand but also master. In 2004, Democrat Howard Dean logged more hours and raised more money in Iowa than any of his rivals but finished third in the caucuses simply because not enough of his supporters showed up. By contrast, in 2008, Barack Obama, a relative political newcomer, serving just his first term in the U.S. Senate, used his skills from his previous work as a neighborhood organizer in Chicago to rally his troops and win the Iowa caucuses. Ten months later, he was elected president.

Money is an important factor but it does not always produce the desired results. Massachusetts Democratic senator John Kerry poured millions of his own fortune — or, more accurately, his wife's — into his 2004 caucus campaign and pulled off an upset victory. In 2008, former Massachusetts governor Mitt Romney, a Republican who was favored to win, also spent millions but finished second.

Presidential campaigns have become part of Iowa's way of life — a fifth season of the year, and by far the longest. Candidates from all over the country come so they can speak at the Keokuk Rotary Club and march in the Clear Lake Fourth of July parade. They address groups of 25 or 30 (and sometimes less) at the Fort Dodge Women's Club and the Marshalltown VFW and anyone who will listen to them in Council Bluffs and Dubuque and Cedar Rapids.

They flip pancakes at charity breakfasts, eat corn dogs at the Iowa State Fair, tour factories, pose for pictures on family farms, sign autographs and eat corn dogs in as many communities between the Mississippi and Missouri rivers as their schedules will permit, all leading up to the all-important Iowa caucuses. In 1988, Gephardt's mother rented a home in Des Moines so he could spend maximum time on the campaign trail. In 2007, Senator Christopher Dodd of Connecticut actually moved his family to Iowa and enrolled his child in school so he could campaign full-time.

In presidential politics, Iowa sets the table for the rest of the nation. Why? How did the Iowa caucuses, with all of their quirks, become the first testing ground for presidential hopefuls and how have they remained such a focal point for all of these years? This book takes a look at the unusual events that led to Iowa coming to the forefront and the role it has played in the rise and fall of two generations of American politicians.

At its roots was the need for national political reform that began when a group of disenfranchised blacks in Mississippi demanded the right to be represented at the 1964 Democratic National Convention. Their protests got the attention of President Lyndon Johnson, who quickly assembled a team to work out a compromise, hoping to avoid anything that would taint his renomination on the convention floor.

By 1968, there was an even louder cry to end the reign of party bosses and to bring more blacks, women and young people into the process. There was turmoil both inside and outside the convention hall in Chicago and Democrats realized vast changes had to be made.

When the reforms they made took hold, all roads led to Iowa and the evolution of what came to be known as grassroots politicking, with all the quirks that came with it.

Jimmy Carter was the trailblazer in 1975, coming to Iowa and virtually talking to anyone who would listen to him, even leaving notes on people's doors if they weren't home when he came door-knocking. Thirty-two years later, Barack Obama and Hillary Clinton consistently spoke to crowds of hundreds, sometimes thousands as they campaigned for the 2008 Democratic nomination.

In between, there was Indiana senator Richard Lugar, chairman of the Agriculture Committee, a position seemingly important to Iowans, walking into a dining room in central Iowa where he was the featured speaker, and having no one in the room recognize him.

There was Governor Howard Dean, spotting an undecided voter in a diner in 2004 on a snowy January day, putting his arm around him and saying with a big smile, "Can I shovel your walk for you?"

There was Pat Buchanan, eating Frosted Flakes for breakfast in a Holiday Inn dining room and going unnoticed by passers-by and people eating at tables around him. "I'm flying a little under the radar right now," he said sheepishly.

There were the throngs of people all going to a Bob Dole function in 1995 but remaining in their vehicles in a hotel parking lot for several minutes — because they were listening to a broadcast of a University of Iowa basketball game on their car radios — and the game had gone into overtime.[4]

To fully understand why candidates place so much importance on Iowa and the face-to-face opportunities they have with voters, one need only reflect on the conversation between an out-of-state telephone pollster and Mary Grandon, wife of Cerro Gordo County treasurer Michael Grandon, in the spring of 1983. The pollster was calling on behalf of Senator John Glenn of Ohio, who intended to be a candidate in the 1984 Iowa caucuses.

"Are you supporting Senator John Glenn for president?" the pollster asked.

"I don't know," said Mrs. Grandon in all candor. "I haven't met him yet."

The answer might have sounded flip to people in most other states but would make perfect sense to anyone living in Iowa. Little did Mrs. Grandon know then, that in a few months she would be hosting a social for the former astronaut in her own backyard.

That's how presidential politics works in Iowa.

ONE

1964

"There were two absurdities face to face."

Two great social conflicts in the second half of the 20th century — the civil rights movement and opposition to the war in Vietnam — had great influence on the emergence of the Iowa caucuses as a major factor in American presidential politics.

Reforms that started first in the Democratic Party resulted in Iowa becoming the first- in-the-nation presidential testing ground. Those reforms did not begin until 1972 but the first inkling that profound changes were imminent in the presidential selection process occurred eight years earlier, far from Iowa, at the Democratic National Convention in Atlantic City, New Jersey.

The convention began on August 24, 1964, a scant nine months after President John F. Kennedy was assassinated in Dallas on November 22, 1963. His successor, Lyndon B. Johnson, was a man who was almost the total opposite of Kennedy in personality and political style.

Kennedy was a product of a rich, powerful, eastern establishment family, a Harvard educated, Pulitzer Prize–winning author who was perceived as being young and dynamic. Johnson was a Texan who smoked and drank and swore and got things done politically not through diplomacy and fancy rhetoric but by backroom arm-twisting and influence-peddling — "a born wheeler-dealer, an artist at compromise, a master at acquiring power," as one history magazine described him.[1]

The unlikely pairing of Kennedy and Johnson on the same political ticket came about because the Kennedy forces knew they needed to carry Texas to win the election and Johnson could — and did — deliver Texas for them.

When Johnson took office as president, he inherited two issues that would be of growing concern to diverse segments of the American public. The U.S. had begun sending troops to the small Southeast Asian country of South Vietnam which was engaged in fighting with Communist-controlled North Vietnam.

It was hoped that American forces could help defeat the North Vietnamese and thereby stifle the potential spread of Communism throughout the region. American involvement in Vietnam would escalate during the Johnson administration and ultimately result in his declining to seek re-election in 1968.

At home, black Americans, particularly in the south, were demanding that they be afforded the same rights that all other Americans enjoyed, the "life, liberty and the pursuit of happiness" that was supposed to be the groundwork for achieving the American dream. But in the south, blacks were subjected to overt discrimination, being denied access to hotels, restaurants, schools, libraries and other public places solely on the basis of their skin color.

In many areas of the south, they were covertly being denied the right to vote by being subjected to requirements such as literacy tests made so difficult that even the most literate people of any race or ethnic group would have trouble achieving a passing score. They contained questions such as: "How many bubbles are there in a bar of soap?" and "How many people are on the payroll of the United States government?" The tests were not required of white people.[2]

As black Americans, led by leaders such as the Rev. Martin Luther King, Jr., became more assertive in seeking equality, they organized and began staging what were intended to be peaceful protests in the form of marches and rallies. Segregationists such as members of the Ku Klux Klan and other similar organizations were just as adamant about keeping their way of life the way it always had been.

They often had the support of powerful southern political leaders who were steadfastly against the passage of any laws that would provide equal rights to black citizens. The tension that existed between the black citizens seeking equality and the white citizens intent on defeating them often led to violence.

In the spring of 1963, blacks staged a protest in the streets of Birmingham, Alabama, that was broken up when Birmingham's police commissioner, Eugene "Bull" Connor, ordered fire hoses turned on them. Television cameras captured the scene as the blacks were knocked down and rendered defenseless by the sheer force of the water. Those who were able ran for their lives. Others were hauled off to jail.

In another highly-publicized incident, in June, Alabama governor George Wallace defied a federal court order and refused to allow two qualified black students to enroll at the University of Alabama. President Kennedy ordered the Alabama National Guard to go on campus to assure the peaceful enrollment of the two students.

On the evening of June 11, 1963, a few hours after the students were enrolled, Kennedy addressed the nation, urging equal treatment for all Americans. He asked, "Are we to say to the world and, much more importantly, to each other, that this is a land of the free, except for the Negroes, that we have no second-class citizens except Negroes, that we have no class or caste system, no ghettos, no master race except with respect to Negroes?"

He made reference to the most recent problems at the University of Alabama but urged the nation to realize it was much more than a racial problem on a college campus. He said:

> My fellow Americans, this is a problem which faces us all — in every city of the north as well as the south. Today there are Negroes unemployed, two or three times as many as compared to whites; inadequate education, moving into large cities unable to find work, young people in particular out of work, without hope, denied equal rights, denied the opportunity to eat at a restaurant or lunch counter or go to a theater, denied the right to a decent education, denied almost today the right to attend at state university even though qualified.
>
> It seems to me these are matters which concern us all, not merely presidents or congressmen or governors but every citizen of the United States.
>
> This is one country. It has become one country because all of us and all the people who came here had an equal chance to develop their talents. We cannot say to ten percent of the population that you can't have that right, that your children cannot have the chance to develop whatever talents they have, that the only way they are going to get their rights is to go to the streets and demonstrate. I think we owe them and we owe ourselves a better country than that.[3]

He followed up a few days later by asking Congress to pass sweeping civil rights legislation that would make equality the law of the land. After Kennedy was assassinated, Johnson, the born-and-bred southerner, urged Congress to pass the legislation as a fitting legacy to the fallen president who proposed it. In so doing, Johnson found himself at odds with many of his old Senate cronies such as Senator Richard Russell of Georgia and Senators James Eastland and John Stennis of Mississippi, all staunch segregationists.

There were emotional debates on the floors of both the House and Senate, particularly in the Senate where opponents offered more than 500 amendments in an effort to water down the legislation passed by the House. Senate debate lasted five months, including a 534-hour filibuster staged by southern senators.

It would take a vote of cloture — requiring a two-thirds majority (67 votes) — to end the filibuster and bring the legislation to a vote, which required only a simple majority for passage. The Senate was made up of 67 Democrats and 33 Republicans. Twenty-one southern senators were sure to vote against cloture. That meant 22 of the 33 Republicans would have to vote in favor of it.

Senator Everett McKinley Dirksen of Illinois, the minority leader, vowed to put any personal beliefs aside. "I trust I can disenthrall myself from all bias, from all prejudice, from all irrelevancies, from all immaterial matters," he said, "and see clearly and cleanly what the issue is and then render an independent judgment." He urged his colleagues to do the same.

On June 10, 1964, one day shy of one year from the time President Kennedy spoke to the nation urging fair treatment for Negro citizens, Dirksen spoke on the Senate floor, quoting Victor Hugo: "Stronger than all the armies is an idea whose time has come." The Senate voted 71–29 for cloture, ending the filibuster and then voted to approve the landmark legislation.[4]

On July 2, 1964, Johnson signed a Civil Rights Act that outlawed discrimination in hotels, restaurants, theaters and all other public accommodations engaged in interstate commerce and also prohibited discrimination in employment. It did not fully address voting rights.

By this time, the civil rights movement had attracted supporters from all over the country, many of them white and coming to the south to help in the efforts of blacks to achieve equality. Among them were Michael Schwerner, 24, and Andrew Goodman, 20, both from New York, who came to Mississippi and teamed up with James Chaney, 21, a black man who had joined one of the civil rights groups, the Congress of Racial Equality (CORE) in 1963.

On June 16, 1964, Ku Klux Klan members entered Mount Zion Methodist Church, a black church in Philadelphia, Mississippi, thinking they would find the three civil rights workers there. But Chaney, Goodman and Schwerner were in nearby Meridian, organizing a voter registration drive. The Klansmen beat up many of the members inside the church and then torched the building.

Five days later, on June 21, Chaney, Goodman and Schwerner drove to Philadelphia from Meridian to begin organizing a voter registration drive there. On their way back to Meridian, a deputy sheriff stopped their car, arrested them for suspicion of arson and put them in jail. Seven hours later, they were released, told to leave the county and never come back.

As the three men headed out of Philadelphia in the middle of the night, they vanished. News of their disappearance made national head-lines. The FBI was called in to investigate. On June 23, the burned wreck-age of their car was found — but there was no sign of the missing men. Their disappearance underscored for the nation how serious the racial problems were in the deep south and put tremendous pressure on federal officers to find the men and solve the case. It was while all of this was swirling that President Johnson signed the Civil Rights Act.

On August 4, the remains of the three civil rights workers were found buried in an earthen dam near Philadelphia. They had been shot to death, with Chaney, the black man, suffering multiple bullet wounds.

Twenty days later, as the Democratic National Convention began in Atlantic City, no one had been arrested in connection with the murders and racial unrest was becoming a part of the American fabric, not only in the south but in northern cities that had significant black populations.[5]

Meanwhile, Robert Moses, a 29-year-old black, Harvard-educated teacher from New York, was continuing his efforts to help southern blacks achieve equality. He had abandoned the relatively safe life of a school-teacher to join the civil rights movement in 1961. He became field secre-tary of the Student Non-Violent Coordinating Committee (SNCC), which was another of the civil rights organizations that had sprung up.

By 1964, he headed SNCC's Freedom Summer Project, an effort to end black people's political disenfranchisement in the deep south. Its goals were to expand black voter registration in Mississippi, to organize a legally constituted Freedom Democratic Party that would challenge the whites-only Mississippi Democratic Party, to establish freedom schools that would teach reading and math to black children, and to open community cen-ters where poor blacks could get both legal and medical help when needed.[6]

As white political bosses in Mississippi were conducting business as usual, blocking blacks from registering to vote or participating in any way in the political process, the Mississippi Freedom Democratic Party held political meetings of its own. They elected a slate of delegates to the Democratic National Convention, boarded a bus, and headed for Atlantic City to challenge the seating of the all-white Mississippi delegation.

It was with this backdrop that some of the most powerful men in American government began arriving in Atlantic City for the convention, men like Senator Hubert Humphrey of Minnesota, known as the "Happy Warrior" of the Democratic Party; Senator Henry "Scoop" Jackson of Washington, less flashy than Humphrey and not well known outside of the Pacific Northwest, but a respected man on Capitol Hill; Senator Richard Russell, the Georgia segregationist; Speaker of the House John McCormick of Massachusetts, who was next in the order of succession to be president; Senator Russell Long of Louisiana, son of the legendary governor and senator Huey Long who was shot to death in his state capitol building 28 years earlier; and Mayor Richard J. Daley, the roly-poly, ruddy-cheeked ruler of the Chicago political machine.

There was plenty of preliminary party business to take care of before the pageantry of the convention began — routine things like meetings of the Credentials Committee and the Rules Committee, boring but necessary functions of party business that few people paid any attention to outside the meeting rooms where the sessions were held.

That all changed on Saturday, August 21, 1964, when Fanny Lou Hamer, a poor black woman who was part of the Mississippi Freedom Party, spoke to the Credentials Committee, urging that her delegation be allowed to be seated at the convention instead of the hand-picked delegation that had excluded blacks from the process.

She did not speak with eloquence and her testimony sometimes rambled as she did her best to describe how blacks in the south were not only persecuted for trying to register to vote but were often harassed, beaten, had their homes set on fire and lived in constant fear.

Though sometimes her testimony was difficult to follow because she was trying to say so much in a short period of time, it was nonetheless spellbinding to those who watched in person and on television because it was coming from someone who had lived through it.

"Mr. Chairman and the Credentials Committee," she said, "my name is Fanny Lou Hamer and I live at 626 East Lafayette Street, Ruleville, Mississippi, Sunflower County, the home of Senator James O. Eastland and Senator (John) Stennis."

She then began to describe in vivid detail the mental and physical abuse that black citizens in Mississippi were subjected to as they tried to register to vote. Her testimony was televised nationally and much of the public, particularly in the north, was stunned by what they were hearing.

> It was the 31st of August in 1962 that 18 of us traveled 26 miles to the county courthouse in Indianola to try to register to vote to become first-class citizens. We was met in Indianola by Mississippi men, Highway Patrolmen, and they only allowed two of us in to take the literacy test at the time. After we had taken this test and started back to Ruleville, we was held up by the city police and the State Highway Patrolmen and (ordered) back to Indianola where the bus driver was charged that day with driving a bus the wrong color.
>
> After we paid the fine among us, we continued on to Ruleville and the Rev. Jeff Sunny [drove] me four miles in the rural area where I had worked as a timekeeper and a sharecropper for 18 years. I was met there by my children who told me that the plantation owner was angry because I had gone down to try to register.

Though her testimony was emotional, Mrs. Hamer's voice was steady, her demeanor stern as she pressed on.

"After they told me, my husband came and said that the plantation owner was raising cane because I had tried to register and before he quit talking, the plantation owner came and said, 'Fanny Lou — do you know — did Pap tell you what I said?' And I said, 'Yes, Sir.' He said, 'I mean that.' He said, 'If you don't go down and withdraw your registration, you will have to leave ... because we are not ready for that in Mississippi.'"

The Credentials Committee hearing was being televised. President Johnson, watching in Washington, hastily called a press conference, summoning news men and women to the White House, hoping to take the spotlight off the Mississippi woman who was capturing the attention of the nation and threatening what he hoped would be a convention that would be more like a coronation for him. While Mrs. Hamer was testifying in a committee room, workmen were hanging 40-foot banners, featuring the face of Lyndon Johnson, in the convention hall, a salute to the man, who among other things, signed the Civil Rights Act.

Her testimony continued as she told of how her efforts to register to vote nearly got her killed.

> On the 10th of September, 1962, 16 bullets was fired into the home of Mr. and Mrs. Robert Tucker for me. That same night, two girls were shot in Ruleville, Mississippi. Also, Mr. Joe McDonald's house was shot in.
>
> And on June the 9th, 1963, I had attended a voter registration workshop, was returning back to Mississippi. Ten of us was traveling by the

Continental Trailways bus. When we got to Winona, Mississippi, which is in Montgomery County, four of the people got off the bus to use the washroom and two of the people to use the restaurant....

During this time, I was on the bus. But when I looked through the window and saw they had rushed out, I got off of the bus to see what had happened, and one of the ladies said, "It was a State Highway Patrolman and a Chief of Police ordered us out."

I got back on the bus and one of the persons [who] had used the washroom got back on the bus too. As soon as I was seated on the bus, I saw when they began to get the four people in the highway patrolman's car. I stepped off the bus to see what was happening and somebody screamed from the car ... "get that one there" and when I went to get in the car, when the man told me I was under arrest, he kicked me.

I was carried to the county jail and put in the booking room. They left some of the people in the booking room and began to place us in cells. I was placed in a cell with a young woman called Miss Ivesta Simpson. After I was placed in the cell, I began to hear the sound of kicks and horrible screams and I could hear somebody say, "Can you say, yes, sir, nigger? Can you say yes, sir?"

And they would say other horrible names. She would say, "Yes, I can say, yes sir." "So say it." She says, "I don't know you well enough." They beat her, I don't know how long, and after a while she began to pray and asked God to have mercy on those people. And it wasn't too long before three white men came to my cell. One of these men was a state highway patrolman and he asked me where I was from and I told him Ruleville. He said, "We are going to check this."

And they left my cell and it wasn't too long before they came back. He said, "You are from Ruleville, all right and he used a curse word and he said, "We are going to make you wish you was dead." I was carried out of that cell into another cell where they had two Negro prisoners.

The state highway patrolman ordered the first Negro to take the blackjack. The first Negro prisoner ordered me, by orders from the state highway patrolman, to lay down on a bunk bed on my face and I laid on my face.

The first Negro began to beat and I was beat by the first Negro until he was exhausted and I was holding my hands behind me at that time on my left side because I suffered from polio when I was six years old. After the first Negro had beat until he was exhausted, the state highway patrolman ordered the second Negro to take the blackjack.

The second Negro began to beat and I began to work my feet and the state highway patrolman ordered the first Negro who had beat me to sit upon my feet to keep me from working my feet. I began to scream and one white man got up and began to beat my head and told me to hush. One white man, since my dress had worked up high, walked over and pulled my dress down and he pulled my dress back up.

All of this is on account of wanting to register, to become first-class citizens, and if the Freedom Democratic Party is not seated now, I question America. Is this America, the home of the free and the land of the brave where we have to sleep with our telephones off the hooks because our lives are threatened daily, because we want to live as decent human beings in America? Thank you.[7]

Historian Theodore White was at the hearing and heard Fannie Lou Hamer's presentation. "There were two absurdities face to face before the Credentials Committee," he wrote. "There was the all-white Mississippi delegation — legal but morally absurd. And there was the Mississippi Freedom Party delegation — impeccably moral but legally absurd because it had no lawful standing."[8]

President Johnson had a dilemma that he knew was coming. Eight days earlier, five southern governors, including Mississippi governor Paul B. Johnson, Jr., met to discuss the potential Mississippi convention problem and four days after that, Johnson met with advisers at the White House to try to come up with a compromise. Johnson was also putting pressure on Governor Johnson to find the killers of the three civil rights workers.

Paul Johnson was not swayed easily when it came to civil rights for blacks. He was a hardcore segregationist who, while serving as lieutenant governor two years earlier, had stood in front of a door at the University of Mississippi, physically blocking James Meredith, a young black student, from enrolling. When the civil rights workers were reported missing, Paul Johnson said publicly they were probably in Cuba — a not-so-subtle inference that they had Communist ties.

The president appointed Senator Hubert Humphrey of Minnesota to put together a compromise in Atlantic City with the two competing Mississippi delegations. It was an important test for Humphrey, a longtime civil rights advocate, because he was on Johnson's short list to be the vice presidential nominee.[9]

Humphrey, 53, was born in South Dakota and had ambitions to follow in his father's footsteps and become a druggist. He became a registered pharmacist but later got a master's degree in history and began teaching college classes in Minnesota, his adopted state. He was elected mayor of Minneapolis in 1945 and drew national attention three years later when he gave a stirring speech at the Democratic National Convention advocating a civil rights plank in the party platform. In November of that same year, he was elected to the U.S. Senate.

The compromise worked out by Humphrey and his hastily put–together negotiators was that all of the Mississippi regular delegates could be seated as long as they signed a loyalty oath to the Democratic Party; that two Mississippi Freedom Party delegates would be seated and the rest could remain there as honored guests; and that delegates to the 1968 convention be elected without regard to race, creed, color or national origin.[10]

In working out the compromise, Humphrey enlisted the help of one of his young protégés in Minnesota, Walter F. Mondale, the state's attorney general. A lot was riding on the outcome of their efforts. Johnson wanted a controversy-free convention. Humphrey wanted to be his vice president and possibly his successor some day. If Johnson picked Humphrey and they won, he would have to give up his Senate seat — and Mondale could be his successor.

So the compromise toward equal treatment for Negroes in Mississippi provided yet a third absurdity; two of the men most instrumental in bringing it about, Humphrey and Mondale, could see their own political careers advance in addition to achieving a morally acceptable solution to a big civil rights problem.[11]

"I was on the Credentials Committee. I had no other role other than being a member," said Mondale, reflecting on it more than 40 years later.

> But the Mississippi Freedom Party issue was too explosive to be handled at the committee level. Everybody could see that. So I was picked as one of six or seven people on the committee to work out the compromise.
> What we did is still controversial today, I know that. But it has proven the test of history. We made everybody take a loyalty oath to the Democratic Party and a lot of them didn't like us for that. We seated two members of the Freedom Party as delegates. Some thought they shouldn't have been seated at all. The Freedom Party thought more of them should have been seated. But the big thing was we put into effect what I call the Civil Rights Act of the Democratic Party because it opened up the process to blacks. The party had been hypocritical. We were saying one thing in Washington but ignoring what was happening in the south. We took the steps needed to change that.[12]

Johnson was nominated and selected Humphrey as his running mate. They won a landslide victory in the November elections, defeating Senator Barry Goldwater of Arizona and Congressman Bill Miller of New York, the Republican candidates. Humphrey resigned from the Senate to become vice president. Mondale was appointed to fill Humphrey's Senate seat. In the years to come, each of them would run for president and in between Mondale would be elected vice president.

Mondale says the administration of Lyndon Johnson and Hubert Humphrey is remembered by most historians for the escalation of American involvement in the war in Vietnam. What is not often noted, he says, is that Johnson and Humphrey were two of the greatest civil rights activists in American politics in the 20th century — Johnson the southerner who withstood the pressure of his segregationist friends, Humphrey the northerner who spearheaded the convention compromise.[13]

Fanny Lou Hamer's testimony before the Credentials Committee informed the nation of the often violent bigotry of the south. Though President Johnson had tried to stave off national publicity by calling a news conference during Mrs. Hamer's testimony, nightly newscasts covered her story.

Her testimony was a stepping stone to reforms that included not only passage of the Voting Rights Act of 1965, guaranteeing equal voting rights to all Americans, but also to reforms in delegate selection for national conventions that eight years later would put little Iowa, one of country's least consequential states in terms of presidential politics, into the national spotlight.[14]

Meanwhile, the war in Southeast Asia was escalating and that too would lead to dramatic changes in the political fabric of America.

CHAPTER TWO

1968

"To hell with what the people wanted."

Racial strife continued during the Johnson years but much of America's attention was focused on the continuing war in Vietnam, seemingly without an end, seemingly without a chance for victory and punctuated every night by bloody images shown on television screens throughout the country.

"Any understanding of the politics of 1968 and 1972 must begin with Vietnam," said Senator George McGovern, a Democrat from South Dakota. "That conflict divided the American people as it had not been divided since the Civil War."[1]

President Johnson, winner of a landslide victory in 1964 and up for re-election in 1968, recognized the emotional toll the war had on the American people and the political toll it had on the Democratic Party.

On March 31, Johnson addressed the nation about the war and ended by saying, "I have concluded that I should not permit the presidency to become involved in the partisan divisions that are developing in this political year. Accordingly, I shall not seek and I will not accept the nomination of my party for another term as your president."

That was the beginning of a year full of surprises, many of them tragic. Senator Eugene McCarthy of Minnesota, proclaiming his opposition to the Vietnam War, had already announced (on November 30, 1967) that he would challenge Johnson in Democratic primaries. On March, 12, 1968, McCarthy embarrassed the incumbent president by finishing a close second in the New Hampshire primary election. On March 18, Senator Robert F. Kennedy, brother of the slain president, announced his candidacy. Thirteen days later, Johnson made the startling announcement that he would not run.

On the Republican side, former Vice President Richard M. Nixon emerged as a candidate. Nixon had lost the presidential race to John Kennedy in 1960 and lost the California gubernatorial race to Pat Brown in 1962. After the California loss, Nixon announced his withdrawal from politics, saying to the press, "You won't have Nixon to kick around any more." Six years later he had a change of heart and won the Republican presidential nomination in 1968.[2]

Five days after Johnson's dramatic announcement, the Rev. Martin Luther King, Jr., the leading civil rights advocate in the country, was assassinated in Memphis, Tennessee, where he had gone to lend support to striking sanitation workers. Two months later, Senator Robert Kennedy, after achieving victory in the California primary, was shot to death in Los Angeles, just after giving a victory speech and telling his supporters, "It's on to Chicago."

When Democrats met for the national convention in Chicago in August, it was an atmosphere in which both the party and the nation were in turmoil. Anti-war protesters came from all over the country and demonstrated on the streets of Chicago, precipitating what came to be known as a police riot as Chicago police officers fended off protesters by beating them with nightsticks and dragging them to paddy wagons in full view of a national television audience.

Inside the convention hall, tempers flared. Two weeks before the convention, Senator McGovern announced his candidacy for the presidential nomination, hoping to pick up the support of delegates who had backed Kennedy. McCarthy had the following of many delegates inside and many protesters outside the arena. But the majority of the delegates backed Vice President Humphrey, who had been loyal to Johnson and received the fruits of that loyalty by getting the support of the Democratic power brokers who controlled their state delegations. In fact, Humphrey secured the presidential nomination without ever participating in any primary elections.

Just four years after the Mississippi uprising in Atlantic City, the feeling of disenfranchisement — of being left out of the political process — had become a pot boiling over and included far more than an isolated group of unhappy blacks. There was a rising tide of unrest among people of all colors and ethnic backgrounds, men and women, young and old who were tired of the politics-as-usual maneuvering of power brokers.

In Georgia, Lester Maddox, the segregationist governor, handpicked his state's delegation. In Illinois, Chicago mayor Richard J. Daley controlled that state's delegation. In Pennsylvania, the trio of Governor David

Lawrence, Pittsburgh mayor Joseph Barr and Philadelphia mayor James H.J. Tate called the shots.

Former vice president Walter Mondale said political machines — the term used to describe how the power brokers controlled state and local party politics — were a force that was a way of life in many big cities throughout the country. "In those machine states, man, some of those delegates were picked two years in advance," he said.[3]

Because of the control of the party bosses, primary elections and caucuses were for the most part beauty contests — there were just 16 in 1968 — that gave candidates some exposure but little political clout. Johnson won the earliest primary, in New Hampshire, with 49 percent of the vote, but McCarthy, the upstart anti-war junior senator from Minnesota, was a strong second with 42 percent. McCarthy's strong showing was an indication of President Johnson's drop in popularity, even in his own party, and hastened his decision not to run.

McCarthy went on to win primaries in Wisconsin, Illinois, Massachusetts, New Jersey, Oregon and Pennsylvania. Senator Kennedy won in Indiana, Nebraska, South Dakota and California.

The Pennsylvania primary stirred unrest among middle class Democrats just as the Mississippi delegate controversy had done four years earlier. McCarthy was the landslide winner with just under 72 percent of the vote. Yet Humphrey, who was not on the ballot, received most of the state's delegates because that's who Tate, the leading power broker, decided should be the candidate. Mayor Daley had the same thought in Illinois as did John M. Bailey, the political boss in Connecticut who was the Democratic national chairman from 1961 to 1968. The bosses wanted Humphrey so Humphrey was going to be the candidate. That's how the system worked.

Political activist David Mixner wrote, "The bosses picked the candidates and the delegates, defiantly saying to hell with what the people wanted."[4]

The result was that Humphrey won the nomination for a party so divided that Richard Nixon, the Republican candidate, who had written his own political obituary six years earlier after losing the governor's race in California, was elected president in November. Humphrey's nomination came from delegates who were 14 percent women, 5 percent black and 2 percent under the age of 30.[5]

"By and large, the majority of the delegates were the kind of men and women who had always come to American conventions — middle-aged, established in their parties, their unions, in civic responsibility, in high office," wrote historian Theodore White. The so-called unit rule, adopted many years earlier to give small states some political clout, had strangled its original purpose in the hands of the political opportunists. Small states like Connecticut had agreed to bind all of their convention delegates to vote as a unit, thereby maximizing their influence. "But a unit has to be controlled by a leader — thus unit rule, in the new dialogue, was synonymous with boss control."[6]

The unit rule made it impossible for candidates who got less than a majority of the votes at county conventions, caucuses or primary elections to receive any delegates at the national convention. In some states, party leaders acquired proxy votes by one means or another and therefore controlled enough votes to pick the candidate. In other states, filing fees or hospitality charges for attending a county or state convention could be as high as $500 per delegate, eliminating all but the most well-to-do from participating.[7]

Reform-minded Democrats — historian White called them insurgents — knew theirs would be a lost cause at a convention that was predisposed to nominate Humphrey, but, working within the system, took steps to make sure it would never happen again.

An ad hoc group was formed to study the nominating process. It included Eli Segal, Geoffrey Cowan and Anne Wexler, all McCarthy supporters; Congressman Don Fraser of Minnesota, a Humphrey backer; and Fred Dutton, who had been an aide to Senator Kennedy. Iowa governor Harold Hughes, a McCarthy supporter who was elected to the Senate in November, chaired the commission.

Almost lost amid the turmoil of the riots outside the Chicago convention hall and the bickering inside was the adoption by the Rules Committee of the Hughes Commission's report calling for massive changes in the delegate selection process which were to take effect for the 1972 national convention.

As expected, delegates nominated Humphrey and Senator Edmund Muskie of Maine as his running mate. In November, they lost the general election to the Republican tandem of Nixon and his vice presidential choice, Governor Spiro Agnew of Maryland.

In January 1969, Democrats formed a commission to study the delegate selection process. It was to hold hearings throughout the country and then recommend changes. Congressman Fraser, who would serve on the commission and later chair it, said the goal was to have a convention with "reasonable representation" of women, minorities and people with a range of ethnic backgrounds. George Meany, a hard-nosed Democrat and head of the AFL-CIO, a powerful labor union, scoffed at the idea, saying it gave undue status to "hippies, women's libbers, gays, kooks and draft dodgers."[8]

Senator Fred Harris of Oklahoma succeeded John Bailey as Democratic national chairman. It became his task to select members of the commission. The reformers wanted Hughes to chair it but he had supported McCarthy so he was unacceptable to the Humphrey backers. Harris picked McGovern, who had been a last-minute anti-war candidate for the nomination but who had vigorously supported Humphrey in the fall campaign.

In naming the rest of the commission, Harris said he made sure to pack it with reformers who would recommend changes to destroy the old party-boss system and open up the process to all factions of society. Warren Christopher, a commission member, said Harris's picks for the commission "ran the gamut from A to B."[9]

One of the people selected by Harris was Aaron Henry, state Democratic chairman of Mississippi, who, four years earlier had come to Atlantic City as a founding member of the Mississippi Freedom Democratic Party.

Commissioners in addition to Christopher and Henry were Congressman Don Fraser of Minnesota; Senators George McGovern of South Dakota, Harold Hughes of Iowa and Birch Bayh of Indiana; Governor Cal Rampton of Utah; former governor Leroy Collins of Florida; William Dodds, director of the Community Action Department of the United Auto Workers union; I.W. Abel, president of the United Auto Workers union; Adlai Stevenson III, state treasurer of Illinois; Katherine Peden, former secretary of commerce for the state of Kentucky; Oscar Mauzy and Albert Pena, state legislators from Texas; Will Davis, state Democratic chairman from Texas; Bert Bennett, former state Democratic chairman from North Carolina; Patti Knox, Democratic vice chairman from Michigan; John English, national committeeman from New York; George Mitchell, national committeeman from Maine; Carmen Warshaw, a Jewish businesswoman and national committeewoman from California; Louis E. Martin, former deputy chairman of the Minorities Division of the Democratic National Committee; Fred Dutton and Earl Graves, former aides to Senator Robert F. Kennedy; Austin Ramney and Samuel Beer, political science professors; Peter Garcia, former director of the Community Action program in San Francisco; David Mixner, co-director of the Vietnam Moratorium Committee; and John Hooker, a Democratic candidate for governor in Tennessee.[10]

One of the people on the research team was Ken Bode, who later became well known as a television journalist for NBC and later the host of the PBS program *Washington Week in Review*.

The commission held hearings all over the country but was not always warmly received, particularly by power brokers in various states. Texas governor Preston Smith said, "This is an absurd way of going about this." J. Marshall Brown, a national committeeman from Louisiana ordered the commission to stay out of his state. Governor Maddox and officials from five other southern states boycotted commission hearings in Louisiana.[11]

The commission reported its findings and guidelines in a report issued September 22, 1971. Through implementation of the guidelines, party bosses could no longer pick convention delegates and states could not rig the rules to prevent registered Democrats from participating in the process. To achieve maximum participation, the commission guided states to create systems of open primary elections or party caucuses to determine their delegates.

"Our commission guidelines ended domination of the presidential nomination by those who controlled state and local organizations of the Democratic Party. The guidelines opened up a pathway to the nomination for candidates outside the party establishment," said McGovern.[12]

He was convinced that through the new process, political operatives could no longer control delegate votes through secret meetings, unit rules and other ploys far in advance of the conventions. More blacks, Hispanics, women and young people would be engaged in the process.

As the new system took hold, 22 primaries were held in 1972, compared to 16 in 1968. That number increased to 30 in 1976 and steadily increased to 39 in 2008 (plus 17 caucuses), including the District of Columbia and some American territories outside of the United States.

Bailey, the Connecticut political boss who had been head of the Democratic National Committee for eight years prior to Harris taking over, thumbed his nose at the changes, still wishing that he and his cronies could pick the candidates rather than the Democratic public at large. "I go with the bird that can fly, not with the pigeon that can't get off the ground," he scoffed.[13]

Commission member David Mixner saw it differently. He said, "The people were finally allowed into their party."

Some of the results of the new guidelines were expected. One that wasn't expected was how they inadvertently thrust the little state of Iowa into the national spotlight for decades to come.

CHAPTER THREE

1972

"We had a slow mimeograph machine but we weren't stupid."

Iowa's caucuses had been held in relative obscurity for 125 years from the time Iowa became a state in 1846. Political parties conducted their business in caucuses and conventions, out of the national limelight and frequently out of sight of many of the registered voters of their respective parties. While Iowa did not have power brokers that had any influence outside of Iowa such as a Governor Lawrence of Pennsylvania or Mayor Daley in Chicago, it was commonplace for party operatives to hold secret caucuses and quickly elect a slate of delegates to the county convention.[1]

Sometimes, when the process did open up, the only difference was that the power brokers did in public what they typically did behind closed doors, such as in 1960 when Governor Herschel Loveless told the state delegation it would be supporting John F. Kennedy at the national convention.[2]

In 1907, the Iowa General Assembly passed legislation that created a statewide primary election system for local and state offices but did not include nomination of presidential candidates. A few years later, the law was changed to allow for a presidential preference primary. It was held in 1916 and was a complete bust. None of the major presidential candidates participated, voter turnout was less than 33 percent and it cost the state $122,000. In the next session of the state legislature, the presidential primary was scrapped and the state returned to the convention and caucus system. The laws have been tweaked several times since then. The most important factors are that precinct caucuses, district conventions and the state convention must be held as necessary preliminaries to electing delegates to the national convention.[3]

It was with this framework of state law that the Iowa Democratic Party tackled the reforms initiated by the McGovern-Fraser Commission, which later became just the Fraser Commission when McGovern announced his candidacy for president in 1971. The recommendation was for each state to open up its process to be inclusive for everyone who wanted to participate and for the delegations to have fair representation of blacks, women, young people and citizens of various ethnic backgrounds.

Clif Larsen, who had been elected state Democratic chairman in 1971, was responsible for putting a team together to overhaul the Iowa caucus system. He enlisted the help of Bob Fulton, a longtime Democratic politician. Fulton had served as lieutenant governor, and as governor for two weeks in 1969 after Governor Harold Hughes was elected to the Senate and before the new governor, Robert Ray, took over. Richard Seagrave, an Iowa State University professor, later to be interim university president, was part of the team as was Clark Rasmussen, former state party chairman, and Blanche Koenig, a longtime party activist. Richard Bender, who worked for the Iowa Democratic Party, was a staff member for the team.

Bender said the national Democratic Party had guidelines for the states but no rules they had to follow. "I don't think we gave much thought to the McGovern Commission and I know we weren't thinking about presidential elections. That's why what has occurred as a result of all of this is so surprising," he said.

"At the 1968 state convention, anti-war forces had a substantial number of people there (including Bender)." He continues, "But we were told we would get three delegates. It was that simple. Rasmussen, the party chairman, was the provider of the message but the message came from Harold Hughes. That's the way things worked."

Another incident occurred at the Polk County (Des Moines) convention where there were two competing forces for delegate strength. "One won by three votes so his people got to run the whole slate. This created a lot of umbrage," he said.

"We wanted to create a system of proportional representation and we didn't want any tiny factions. We thought that would be too divisive. That's how we came up with the 15 percent viability," he said. Anyone getting 15 percent support would move on to the next level with a proportional share of delegate strength.

"We thought the proportional representation, where people would be aligned to a candidate, would get rid of the slate system where party bosses told you what to do," said Bender.[4]

They established apportionment formulas which assigned delegates to precincts based on voting performance — percentage of registered voters actually voting — in the last presidential and gubernatorial elections.

They also added a new layer to the process. A district convention was added after the precinct caucuses and county convention and before the state convention.

Larsen said, "We were a very small party then, very broke, not very vigorous and not very strong. But I was determined, because of what happened in 1968, that every delegate at every stage of the process, would have in his hands a copy of the rules, of the platform proposals and of everything else that counted."[5]

The state convention in 1972 was to be held on May 20 — because that's the date that was available for the convention hall. Bender, who was putting all the paperwork together for the caucuses and conventions, said he would need at least 30 days and maybe more between the precinct caucuses, the district conventions and the state convention to fulfill Larsen's goal of having copies of the rules, the platform and other pertinent information into the hands of everyone attending every event.

One of the problems was that the state Democratic Party was using an antiquated mimeograph machine to make copies of all the materials — and the mimeograph machine was slow. In order to get everything accomplished by the May 20 state convention, Bender and Larsen had to back up the calendar from May 20 to determine when the district conventions could be held and then back up the calendar some more to pick a date for the precinct caucuses. And they determined that the caucuses would be held on January 24 rather than in March or April when they were usually held.[6]

So Iowa's hallowed place in presidential politics was born not out of political savvy or as a public relations boon but because of a lot of paperwork and old, slow office equipment. Its caucuses were now the first-in-the-nation testing ground for presidential candidates, a position it has held for nearly 40 years.

"We kind of knew we would be first and we thought that would be nifty. But we didn't do it to be first," said Bender. "Then again, no one had ever paid any attention to us before. We never dreamed the amount of attention we would get."[7]

Larsen said, "We knew we were going to be first or one of the first when we thought about it. As I always say, we had a slow mimeograph machine, but we weren't stupid. We knew were going to be early in the process, but when the national press showed up, we were totally amazed."[8]

Bender said the group putting together the changes knew their reforms would be a tough sell with the state central committee.

"We knew not everyone was going to like them. Harold Hughes didn't like them because he wanted to run for president some day and he wanted a 'favorite son' status in Iowa where he would get unanimous support. Eighty percent would be embarrassing to him. So when it came time to present the changes to the central committee, Larsen said, 'I won't present it. Let the kid do it,'" said Bender. So Bender was assigned the task of presenting the changes, which were approved by a narrow margin.

The next step was to give the new process a test run. "We went down to Osceola in south central Iowa to the county convention and held a mock caucus," said Bender. "And we discovered they couldn't do the math on the proportional representation. We had to make some adjustments, We had to make some charts. There were lots of nitty-gritty things that needed doing or redoing. If we hadn't, there would have been chaos."[9]

Nationally, Senator McGovern, whose commission rewrote the rules of engagement, was the first to take advantage of them, announcing his candidacy for president in 1971, more than a year before the election and several months before the Iowa caucuses. The early favorite for the nomination was Senator Edmund Muskie of Maine, who had been Humphrey's running mate in 1968 and had the backing of party bosses. Iowa would be the first test of whether the power brokers had any influence in the new system.

McGovern enlisted the help of a rising young Democratic activist, Gary Hart of Colorado, to be his campaign manager. Lacking the funds to mount a huge advertising campaign, Hart sent a team of volunteers to Iowa to put together a statewide organization.

"The grassroots, McCarthy-style campaign stressed McGovern's lack of ties to special interests and emphasized his desire to win the support of the average citizen of Iowa and the nation."[10]

One of his Iowa strategists, Rick Stearns, said one of the differences between McCarthy's and McGovern's quest for volunteers was that McCarthy's was based on volunteers flocking to him whereas McGovern's people actively and systematically sought out volunteers.

They started with a computerized list of the names of 125 Iowa Democrats. "Selecting one at random in Des Moines — Chris Froisheiser — a 25-year-old insurance agent — we called him, gave him a list of 14 other Des Moines names and asked him to organize a meeting on the following nights," said Stearns.

Thirteen of the 14 showed up in the basement of Froisheiser's apartment complex. One was a former Polk County precinct committeeman who had once been a candidate for county Democratic chairman. He was the most experienced of the bunch so he was named temporary state chairman.

Stearns and another campaign staffer, Gene Pokorny, set out to do the same thing in other parts of the state with their only ammunition being the computerized list of names, whittled down to 111 after the meeting in Des Moines.

Pokorny went north and Stearns went south, setting up meetings similar to the one in Froisheiser's basement. Two days later, they met in Iowa City to compare notes. "By that time, we had a statewide organization, albeit skeletal, but with at least one contact in each major county or city," he said. A month later, they held another organizational meeting in Des Moines. This time, 175 volunteers showed up. It was their job to spread the word about George McGovern — a method that fit their situation perfectly — cheap advertising and devoid of any influence peddling.[11]

Muskie had an organization in Iowa but his campaign benefited most from his presumed position as the front-runner, his longstanding name recognition and his reputation as a party leader. Humphrey, always interested in becoming president, got a late start in Iowa and, knowing that he couldn't win, tried to convince caucusgoers to be uncommitted.

One of the goals of opening up the nominating process had already gotten results as many other potential candidates emerged. They included McCarthy, who had sought the nomination in 1968; Hughes, the Iowan who helped put forth the reforms; and Senator Edward Kennedy of Massachusetts, younger brother of the president and the presidential candidate who had both been assassinated.

Others included Senator Henry "Scoop" Jackson of Washington, Senator Birch Bayh of Indiana, Senator Vance Hartke of Indiana, Governor Terry Sanford of North Carolina, Congresswoman Shirley Chisholm of New York, Congressman Wilbur Mills of Arkansas, Mayor Sam Yorty of Los Angeles and Mayor John Lindsay of New York.

Jackson was elected to the U.S. House in 1941 and served six terms before being elected to the Senate in 1952. He was part of the old guard in the Senate. Critics said his speeches were so boring that "he could douse the flame of a fireside chat." Similarly, his presidential campaign never caught fire.[12]

Bayh, 44, a three-term senator and one of the architects on the

McGovern-Fraser Commission, was a liberal who was in a plane crash in 1964 that killed two people and seriously injured Senator Kennedy. Bayh and his wife sustained minor injuries. He withdrew as a presidential candidate when it was learned his wife had contracted terminal cancer.

Hartke, 57, Indiana's senior senator, was mayor of Evansville when he was elected to the Senate in 1958 and was re-elected in 1964 and 1970. He was known in the Senate for his opposition to the Vietnam War but was not as well known nationally as several of the other candidates and his campaign was short-lived.

Sanford, 55, was an FBI agent early in his career but turned his attention to education and politics and was elected governor of North Carolina in 1961. He served one term and returned to private life and became president of Duke University in 1969. He still had a strong interest in politics, however, and in 1972, when George Wallace, the Alabama segregationist, was seeking the Democratic nomination, Sanford decided to get into the race to offer a southern alternative to Wallace.

Congresswoman Shirley Chisholm, 48, of New York was the first black woman elected to Congress and the first to seek the presidential nomination of a major political party. She was an activist with a particular interest in child care when she won a seat in the New York State Assembly in 1964. In 1968, she ran for Congress and won on a slogan of "Shirley Chisholm — Unbought and Unbossed."

In Congress, she quickly gained a reputation as a champion of women's rights, equality for minorities and advocacy of programs for children. She was a co-founder of the National Organization for Women (NOW). On January 25, 1972, she announced her candidacy for the Democratic presidential nomination, saying, "I am not the candidate of black America although I am black and proud. I am not the candidate of the women's movement although I am a woman and equally proud of that. I am not the candidate of any political bosses or special interests. I am the candidate of the people."[13]

Congressman Wilbur Mills, chairman of the House Ways and Means Committee, Los Angeles mayor Sam Yorty and New York mayor John Lindsay also explored candidacies.

On January 12, McGovern spoke in Des Moines and reminded Iowa Democrats that he and their senator, Harold Hughes, were instrumental after the 1968 convention in opening up the process so it could be "an open, honest and fair process ... and Iowa comes very close to the ideal."[14]

On January 18, six days before the caucuses, the McGovern forces took a huge political hit. Hughes, the Iowa senator who had toyed with seeking the nomination, endorsed Muskie. It took the McGovern forces by surprise because Hughes had been a McGovern ally who chaired the ad hoc reform committee in 1968 and served on the McGovern Commission which created the reforms.

Long after the 1972 campaign was over, Hart, the young McGovern campaign manager, was still bitter. "Someday men will follow their convictions or admit they have none; someday men will consistently support their beliefs or admit they are false; Someday men will do what is right. But this was not the day and Harold Hughes was not the man," he said.[15]

The Hughes endorsement was one of many endorsements from what Hart later called "an honor roll" of liberal senators — Frank Church of Idaho, Thomas Eagleton and Stuart Symington of Missouri, Philip Hart of Michigan, Tom McIntyre of New Hampshire, Adlai Stevenson of Illinois, John Tunney of California and Harrison Williams of New Jersey.

Muskie's strategy was to create the image of a man whose support was so broad that he couldn't lose, that he was unstoppable, that his nomination was inevitable. Hart said the McGovern forces didn't think the Muskie plan would work — "partly because we had no choice and partly because we thought we had entered a political period when the people at large were not about to be told by their political leaders whom to support or for whom to vote."[16]

The two ways that the Muskie endorsements hurt the most, according to Hart, were in the effect they had on the morale of the McGovern volunteers and, more importantly, on fund-raising.

Iowans awoke on the morning of January 24 to find blizzard conditions developing throughout the state. By nightfall, roads were icy, the wind was howling and temperatures were at zero or below from Davenport and Dubuque on the eastern edge of the state to Council Bluffs and Sioux City to the far west. The wind chill factor was — 56 in some areas. It was under these conditions that organizers for the various presidential candidates had to convince people to leave the warmth of their homes and head to the local school, library or church basement to participate in their precinct caucuses.

Weather conditions were so bad that Larsen postponed caucuses in 20 counties in northwest Iowa, opting to have them conducted within the next few days when the ice and snow melted. Hart and other McGovern backers urged him not to do it.

"Our theory was a conventional one: Committed supporters turn out in adverse conditions and we had the committed supporters," said Hart. But Larsen stuck to his decision. He did not want people risking their lives to get to a caucus.[17]

As statewide returns started coming in, party officials set up two tables at the headquarters in Des Moines to tally the results. There were a smattering of reporters on hand, including staffers from the two wire services, The Associated Press and United Press International; the three television networks, ABC, CBS and NBC; three major East Coast newspapers, the *New York Times, Washington Post* and *Baltimore Sun;* and the *Des Moines Register.*

Reflecting on the scene 36 years later, Bender put it this way: "The total press that came to headquarters in 1972 was probably a dozen reporters. Now, we probably have that number from Japan."[18]

The results reported that night were the start of the incredible impact the media would have in what would become the importance of the Iowa caucuses on the landscape of presidential politics.

The media had the same basic question in Iowa on the night of January 24 that it has on any election night anywhere — who won and who lost? What could be so complicated about that? The answer is: the caucus system devised by Bender, Rasmussen, Fulton, Seagrave and Koenig. There were no votes cast like there are in most elections. Rather, there were preferences shown and percentages taken. And instead of every candidate being counted, only those who had support of at least 15 percent of those in attendance at the precinct caucus were eligible.

So a candidate could be eligible in one caucus but not in another, depending on the amount of people who showed up on his behalf. Not only that. The precinct caucuses were just the first stage in the process. By the time of the state convention, all of the percentages from January 24 would surely have changed. Yet another factor was that because of the snowstorm, results were incomplete. Caucuses in 20 counties had not even been held.

None of that mattered to a media and, for that matter, a nation that wanted to know who won in Iowa. State party officials tried to accommodate them. Using figures from sample precincts throughout the state, they tried to project what each candidate's delegate strength would be at the national convention — an almost impossible task to do accurately. They also came up with a concept of delegate equivalents which was based on giving certain weights of delegate strength, another risky venture in terms of accuracy. The results:

Uncommitted	35.8%
Muskie	35.5%
McGovern	22.2%
Humphrey	1.6%
McCarthy	1.4%
Chisholm	1.3%
Jackson	1.1%
Others	0.7%

Despite the obvious flaws, these results were reported as facts on radio, television and in newspapers. Among the candidates, Muskie was the clear winner even though there was a higher percentage of uncommitted delegates — further evidence that the outcomes would certainly change as the process continued all the way through the state convention. Hart, the young campaign manager for McGovern, saw an opportunity to advance his candidate's cause even though almost 80 percent of the delegate equivalents favored someone else.

On the morning of January 25, Hart held a press conference in which he assessed what had happened the night before. "I claimed an unqualified moral victory for McGovern, stating that we had far exceeded our expected turnout, that we had drawn within 10 percent of Muskie with all his political weight and advantages and that, together with the uncommitted, there were an overwhelming majority of Iowa Democrats who preferred some other candidate to Senator Muskie."[19]

He exaggerated on coming within 10 percentage points of Muskie but that was of little matter since the results were so bogus anyway. But he managed to put a spin on the results that campaign managers have used successfully for decades since then.

The spin has had a lasting effect on American presidential politics. It has this premise: a losing candidate wins if he exceeds expectations and a winning candidate loses if he fails to meet expectations.

And who determines the expectations? Often, it is the media, based on polling and other factors. "The reporting of Iowa caucus results is a part of the game focus of presidential campaigns: essentially meaningless caucus outcomes are reported to satisfy the media's need for results or hard news. Further ... they also interpret the outcomes for the American public in terms of expectations that the media themselves often had helped to create."[20]

And so it was that R.W. "Johnny" Apple, writing in the *New York*

Times on January 26, reported that Senator Muskie's win was "clouded by the unexpected strong showing of Senator George McGovern" and that the size of his triumph "was not big enough to add much to the bandwagon psychology he has been building."

Apple was considered by his peers as being one of the sharpest political reporters of his day. It was not unusual for other reporters to meander around him when he was filing a story to get a hint of what his take was on whatever had happened. So when Apple started banging out a story about McGovern's "unexpected strong showing," many other reporters followed his lead (pun intended.)[21]

A veteran reporter who didn't need to look over Johnny Apple's shoulder or anyone else's was Bill Lawrence of ABC News. On January 25, Lawrence reported on ABC television that "the Muskie bandwagon slid off an icy road in Iowa last night."

Hart's reaction: "We sweated blood for that one sentence."[22]

McGovern, buoyed by the media perception of his good showing in Iowa, finished first in the next presidential test, the New Hampshire primary and went on to win the presidential nomination. In November, he was buried in the landslide re-election victory of President Richard Nixon.

Though the McGovern experience set the example of grassroots politics that has been emulated by an entire generation of future presidential hopefuls in Iowa, there are some ironies that are worthy of mention.

For one thing, McGovern campaigned in Iowa only three days prior to the caucuses. In his autobiography, he gives no mention whatsoever to the Iowa caucuses. And Theodore H. White, author of the detailed chronicle of the entire campaign, similarly does not make a single mention of the Iowa caucuses in his book *The Making of the President 1972*.

Twenty-eight years later, Hart looked back on the Iowa experience and said, "A number of people in the McGovern campaign saw Iowa as a chance to show McGovern as a viable candidate. We saw an opportunity. As it turned out, we were right."[23]

The Republicans held their caucuses on April 4. President Nixon had token opposition from Congressman John Ashbrook of Ohio, a conservative who had been in Congress since 1960, had supported Barry Goldwater's presidential run in 1964 and Nixon's in 1968. By 1971, Ashbrook broke ranks with Nixon, citing Nixon's "presentation of liberal policies in the verbal trappings of conservatism." Nixon got near unanimous support in the caucuses and Ashbrook withdrew his candidacy a week later.[24]

The GOP sessions got little attention from the press. Four years later,

Republicans wanted to bask in the national limelight and thus voted to hold their caucuses on the same day as Republicans, thereby sharing the distinction of being first in the nation.

Politicians in the rest of the nation would eventually take notice as well. "The 1972 caucuses marked the beginning of a dramatic change in American electoral politics. As the impact of the Iowa caucuses continued to grow in succeeding years, other states would move their primary elections and caucuses to earlier in the presidential nominating season."[25]

One closing note on 1972: Though McGovern was soundly defeated in the presidential election that year, the reforms he spearheaded in the nominating process had taken hold. Here is a comparison of the delegate makeup in 1968 and 1972.

	Women	*Blacks*	*Under 30*
1968	14%	5%	2%
1972	36%	14%	23%

The work of his commission had taken hold and would be the framework for the presidential nominating process for generations to come, though they didn't have an impact on his own bid for the presidency.

As for Iowa with its quirky system that so many scoff at yet today, Bender is unapologetic about the process he helped invent nearly 40 years ago. "I conceptualized it and I explained it to the state central committee," he said. "The rules are just about the same today as they were in 1972 — so no one can claim they were hurt by a change in the rules over the years. You can't pull one over on people."[26]

CHAPTER FOUR

1976

*"It's not exactly the precise figures that will be important, it's
whether or not the media and the politicians agree that this man
won and this man lost."*

President Nixon's second term in office was marked by two major
scandals, one leading to his resignation as president, the other having a
direct bearing on the man who would succeed him.

Nixon's vice president, Spiro Agnew, was governor of Maryland when
Nixon tabbed him as his running mate in 1968. Agnew is remembered for
his brashness in defending administration policies and in chastising the
press, referring to them in one memorable press conference as "nattering
nabobs of negativism."[1] His political world came crashing down when a
federal investigation resulted in his being charged with accepting bribes
and falsifying federal tax returns dating back to when he was governor of
Maryland. He pleaded nolo contendere — no contest — to the tax charges
and resigned as vice president on October 10, 1973.

Two days later, Nixon nominated Congressman Gerald Ford of
Michigan to be the new vice president. Ford had been in the House of
Representatives since 1948 and had been minority leader since 1965. After
confirmation hearings in the House and Senate, he took office as vice president on December 6, 1973.

A political firestorm was brewing in Washington at the time. In June
of 1972, a band of thugs broke into the Democratic National Headquarters in the Watergate office complex in Washington, D.C. The investigation into the break-in continued for months, spurred first by reports in
the *Washington Post* and later by media from all over the country. Many
of Nixon's aides were jailed for their part in either helping to plan the
break-in or in obstructing justice in their efforts to cover it up.

Tapes of conversations in the Oval Office were subpoenaed; many of them implicated Nixon in the cover-up. On August 9, 1974, Nixon resigned from the presidency rather than face impeachment hearings for allegedly obstructing justice. Ford, who ten months earlier had been a congressman with ambitions of someday becoming Speaker of the House, became the only man in American history to be both vice president and president and not being elected to either position.

On September 8, one day short of a month after he took office, Ford granted a pardon to Nixon even though the former president had not been formally charged with any crime. The president explained the nation had to move on past the Watergate scandal and that wouldn't happen if Nixon was put on trial.

Usually, incumbent presidents face little or no opposition from their own party when they seek re-election. But Ford's accidental presidency and his pardon of Nixon made him politically vulnerable. Governor Ronald Reagan of California, torchbearer of the party's conservatives, decided to challenge Ford for the Republican nomination.

Meanwhile, James Earl "Jimmy" Carter, Jr., a peanut farmer who rose through the political ranks to become governor of Georgia, also decided to make a run for the presidency and, learning something from the McGovern campaign, targeted Iowa as fertile ground not only for votes but for publicity. One was as important as the other for a relatively unknown candidate.

And Carter was unknown outside of his home state. In 1975, he appeared as a guest on the popular CBS television quiz show *What's My Line?* People from all walks of life would come on and answer "yes" and "no" questions from a panel of celebrities whose job it was to guess the occupation of the guest. Nobody recognized Carter when he appeared and nobody guessed his occupation.[2]

While Democrats began jockeying for position, the Iowa Republican Party decided to move up its caucus date to coincide with the Democrats. They saw what happened with the Democrats in 1972 and wanted their fair share of publicity too. In what caucus historian Hugh Winebrenner called "a marriage of convenience," Republicans and Democrats agreed to hold their precinct caucuses on January 19, 1976.

Carter, a graduate of the U.S. Naval Academy, was active in local politics in his hometown of Plains, Georgia, and eventually was elected to the state legislature. He was elected governor in 1971. On December 12, 1974, nearly two years before the next presidential election, Carter announced he was running for president. He and his strategists had taken note of how the McGovern candidacy had taken off four years earlier after what the media perceived was his good showing in the Iowa caucuses. Carter's plan was to start early, come to Iowa often and establish himself as a bona fide candidate well ahead of any challengers.[3]

Carter had always looked on the presidency with "reverence and awe" and thought of those who held the office as extraordinary people. That all changed, he said, when he had the opportunity to meet President Nixon and other high government officials when he was governor of Georgia and came to think of them as human beings with similar interests and passions as his own.

From his boyhood days in Plains and his days at the Naval Academy, Carter was an academic type of person who had a wide range of interests and read constantly, sometimes two to three books a week. As part of his research for making a presidential run, he read biographies of past presidents and even studied the platforms of as many losing candidates as he could find, hoping to avoid the same mistakes they did.

Carter knew it was a disadvantage, from the standpoint of publicity, not to be a Washington insider — "a former Georgia governor, age 50, politically unemployed," as he put it. "On the other hand, there are 535 members of Congress reaching for every microphone and struggling for every headline. I reasoned I likely would be the only presidential candidate that day in Sioux City."[4]

The early days of the campaign were humbling. Carter made his first trip to Iowa in February 1975 — almost a year before the caucuses were to be held. On February 26, he was the guest speaker in the little town of LeMars, population 9,000, on the western edge of Iowa, where a dinner was held honoring a woman named Marie Jahn. She was stepping down after serving nearly 40 years as the Plymouth County recorder. (In Iowa, county recorders are responsible for the filing of everything from property deeds to marriage licenses). Carter's honorarium for his appearance: a movie pass and coupons for a free pizza and a car wash.

Harold Brady, host of the event, said later they wanted somebody of national prominence who was relatively inexpensive. Carter seemed to be a natural fit, at least in terms of being inexpensive. It wasn't big-time politics, to be sure, but it was a start.[5]

The next day, Carter was the host at a reception at a hotel in downtown Des Moines. He arrived with Jody Powell, one of his top aides. As Carter recalled years later, "There were Jody and myself and the man and woman who arranged the reception — and I think there were three other people." There was enough food on hand to serve several hundred people. "I stood around embarrassed."[6]

David Yepsen, who spent 30 years as a political reporter and columnist for the *Des Moines Register*, was a young reporter then, and he was assigned to cover the Carter event, which was to include a press conference. "I was the only one there," he recalled years later. "I sat down and ate grapes with Jimmy Carter."[7]

Tom Whitney, who succeeded Clif Larsen as state party chairman, hastily made arrangements for Carter to go to the Polk County Courthouse where some local Democrats had been rounded up to shake hands with the candidate.

That first trip to Iowa, with its pizza-dinner honorarium, empty ballroom and courthouse glad-handing did have one substantial benefit. The *Des Moines Register* took note in its news columns of the arrival of the first presidential candidate.[8]

Carter later described the early days of his campaign as lonely. "Often just Jody and I would fly into the state in a small, private plane. When I began my campaign, I didn't have a built-in organization. There were no television cameras, no tape recorders, no radio reporters. I was a lonely, unknown candidate. I came here [Iowa] looking for a TV camera. I never found it."

What he did find, he said, were many people who took an interest in him. Instead of hotel ballrooms, Carter said he started going to one living room after another, and to labor halls and even to livestock confinements. The pattern was the same, said Carter. He would talk for 10 minutes and then answer questions for 45 minutes. "That personal give- and-take was the decisive factor in getting me known," he said.[9]

Marilyn Davis of State Center, Iowa, got a call one afternoon from a local Democrat who needed a favor. "He said, 'There's this governor coming from Georgia who's running for president. We need someone to drive him around — and we know you've got a new car.' That's how I got connected with Jimmy Carter," said Davis, who is now Marilyn Garst and living in Coon Rapids, Iowa. "I had no idea who he was. I mentioned him to a neighbor who found a picture of him in some magazine and showed it to me."

State Center is so named because it is near the geographic center of Iowa. A community of 9,000 that promotes itself as "the rose capital of Iowa," it is on U.S. Highway 30, 20 minutes from Marshalltown, 30 minutes from Ames, the home of Iowa State University, and 45 minutes from the state capital city of Des Moines. Garst remembered:

> We picked him up at the little airport in Marshalltown and took him to Ames where he was to speak. There weren't any crowds in those days, just groups of people that he would shake hands with and give a little talk. He'd always start out the same way. He'd say, "My name is Jimmy Carter. I'm a peanut farmer from Georgia and I'm going to be president of the United States." And then he'd talk about his ideas.
>
> He was the nicest person but he had the strongest Georgia accent; you had trouble understanding him. He always said, "I'm going to get rid of this." I think he practiced getting rid of it by talking into a tape recorder. He didn't have much money either. We would take him different places and bring him sandwiches.
>
> I would have never met Jimmy Carter except for two things. One is that we had the new car. The other is that the Iowa State football team was playing an away game that Saturday. If they had been playing at home, I would have told them I couldn't do it."[10]

Once again following up on a strategy the McGovern people had adopted four years earlier, Carter began putting together a statewide organ-

Jimmy Carter (left) shares a moment with two supporters during a campaign stop in Mason City in March 1975. Carter's early ventures into Iowa established a strategy that candidates in future decades have tried to follow (courtesy *Mason City Globe Gazette*).

ization made up mostly of ordinary working people who were willing to work for him — volunteer work, that is. What Carter did in 1975 and 1976 epitomized grassroots campaigning and has been practiced by dozens of people with presidential aspirations ever since.

Carter's statewide committee included Charles Hammer, a physicist and anti-war activist; Soapy Owens, retired chief of the United Auto Workers; Jim Schaben, a conservative who had been the Democratic nominee for governor in 1964; Jim Maloney, auditor of Polk County, part of the oldline courthouse crowd; and Fred McLain, a farmer from rural Ames who had met Carter only once but was impressed when he came home one day and discovered that the candidate had pinned a handwritten note to his front door.[11]

Other potential candidates started making their way to Iowa, including Senator Henry "Scoop" Jackson of Washington, Senator Birch Bayh of Indiana, Senator Fred Harris of Oklahoma, Congressman Morris "Mo" Udall of Utah and Duke University president Terry Sanford.

Jackson and Bayh were making return visits to Iowa, having tested their potential candidacies four years earlier. Jackson bowed out then because his poll numbers never came close to double digits. Bayh had withdrawn because of his wife's illness, which proved to be fatal.

Harris, 46, was a liberal who was the Democratic national chairman and had appointed the commission that came up with all of the reforms in the delegate selection process. His political career began when he was elected to the Oklahoma legislature in 1956 at the age of 26. He ran for governor in 1962 and lost. In 1964, he was elected to fill the unexpired U.S. Senate term of Robert Kerr, who died in office. Harris was elected to a full term in 1966 and chose not to run for re-election in 1972 when he explored the possibility of running for president. This time around, Harris tried to make himself known through a couple of unique tactics. He traveled in a recreational vehicle and, to save expenses, stayed in private homes. Those who housed him received a card from him entitling them to a one-night stay in the White House, should he be elected president.

Udall, 54, the son of an Arizona Supreme Court justice, was a tall, lanky lawyer who played pro basketball for the old Denver Nuggets franchise in 1948–49. He started a law practice with his brother Stewart in 1949. Stewart was later elected to Congress. In 1961, when Stewart Udall was named secretary of the interior in the Kennedy administration, Mo ran for his House seat and won. He was in his eighth term when he announced his candidacy for president.

Udall was known for his sharp, often self-deprecating wit. While campaigning in Iowa, one of the staples of his stump speech had to do with the sagging economy. "The difference between a pigeon and an Iowa farmer," he said, "is that a pigeon can still make a deposit on a tractor." Coming out of a Democratic caucus meeting in Washington, Udall remarked, "I have learned the difference between a cactus and a caucus. On a cactus, the pricks are on the outside."

As the number of candidates increased, Whitney, the state party chairman who, months earlier, had rescued Carter from the empty hotel ballroom and found some Democrats he could shake hands with at the courthouse, saw an opportunity for some media exposure for the party. On September 22, 1975, he held a statewide straw poll in which Democrats were to vote for their presidential choice. Carter came in first with 9.9 percent. Sargent Shriver, McGovern's running mate in 1972, was second with 8.7 percent. Bayh came in third with 8.1 percent, followed by Hubert Humphrey, 7.2 percent; Jackson, 6.5 percent; Udall, 6.1 percent; and Harris, 5.7 percent. Though no candidate got even 10 percent of the vote — and 45 percent of voters were uncommitted — and though the results were nonbinding and virtually meaningless, they did provide the press with a winner and provided the Iowa Democratic Party with a windfall of publicity.

On October 25, the party held its annual Jefferson-Jackson Day Dinner in Ames. This is an event historian Winebrenner describes as a pep rally in which Democrats from throughout the state gather to eat, drink, hear speeches from the party faithful and, most important, contribute money to be used to help finance the operations of the party and future political campaigns. In 1975, something new was added. Presidential candidates were given the opportunity to speak. Carter, Bayh, Harris, Jackson, Shriver, Udall and Sanford all took a turn at the podium. McGovern, the party's standard bearer in 1972, was the keynote speaker.

The event was, in effect, a mini-convention with volunteers manning booths set up in support of the various candidates and boisterous floor demonstrations after many of the speeches. A significant aspect of the evening was a straw poll conducted by the *Des Moines Register* to get an idea of a candidate's strength three months before the caucuses. Nearly 1,100 Democrats participated. The results:

Carter	256
Humphrey	135
Bayh	112

Shriver	93
Udall	77
Harris	61
Jackson	56
Sanford	7
Wallace	6
Bentsen	2
Schapp	2
Write-ins	47
Undecided	240
Total	*1,094*

Though Carter was the clear winner, there were nearly as many unde-cided voters as those who favored him. Humphrey, the old political war-rior who wasn't even there, was favored over Bayh, Shriver, Harris, Udall and Jackson, who had been actively campaigning in the state.[12]

Not only the *Des Moines Register*, but the *New York Times* and *Washington Post* also carried stories on the results of what Udall later called "that silly poll in Iowa." Carter had not only received a lion's share of public-ity for his eight months of campaigning in Iowa, but he was receiving good national publicity as well, something that would help him long after the Iowa caucuses had been held.

On caucus night, January 19, 1976, the scene was far different in Des Moines than it had been four years earlier. Instead of a couple of tables set up in the basement of Democratic headquarters, the setting now was the Des Moines Hilton Hotel where close to 200 radio, television and newspaper reporters gathered to find out the results. The enterprising Whitney sold tickets to the event for $10 each, for anyone who wanted to come in and watch the media and the politicians.

The Democrats used the same system devised by Clif Larsen and Richard Bender four years earlier where there were no ballots and some candidates were eliminated if they did not meet the 15 percent viability standard. Once again, the totals represented state delegate equivalents that could and probably would change at the forthcoming district and state conventions. But the media and the public were interested in winners and losers and, at the end of the night, the results were:

Uncommitted	37.2%
Carter	27.6%
Bayh	13.2%

Harris	9.9%
Udall	6.0%
Shriver	3.3%
Jackson	1.1%
Others	1.8%

The peanut farmer and former governor of Georgia, unknown in most of the country a year ago, was no longer unknown. Though he finished more than 10 percentage points behind "uncommitted," his victory was trumpeted in media throughout the country and on the day after the caucuses, Carter was a guest on the three major networks' morning news programs — *Today* on NBC, *Morning News* on CBS and *AM America* on ABC. He was a hot topic in the next editions of *Time, Newsweek* and *U.S. News & World Report*.

In short, as a national political figure, he had arrived, and the Iowa precinct caucuses delivered him. On the night of the caucuses, Roger Mudd reported on CBS television, "It's not exactly the precise figures that will be important, it's whether or not the media and the politicians agree that this man won and this man lost." The next night, Mudd reported, "Jimmy Carter was the clear winner."

In 1976, Carter built on the campaign strategy of McGovern and Hart in 1972 by focusing on Iowa, hopefully making it a springboard for a successful national campaign. But whereas McGovern spent only two days campaigning in Iowa, leaving most of the groundwork to his staff and volunteers, Carter campaigned in the state on 17 days — about once every six weeks from the time of his first stop in LeMars in February of 1975.

"The great strength of the Iowa caucuses is that it allows good but unknown people to compete," said Walter Mondale, a senator from Minnesota whom Carter picked as his running mate. "That's how Carter won. He got there early, he knocked on doors; people got to know him and they liked him. He worked hard in Iowa and it's still the only place in a national campaign where a Carter phenomenon can take place."[13]

Meanwhile, President Ford, far from being a political unknown, faced an unusual task for an incumbent president — the prospect of a serious challenge from a member of his own party, Governor Reagan of California. Reagan was popular in the conservative wing of the Republican Party, which included a growing number of people unhappy with Ford for a number of reasons.

His pardon of Nixon compromised his image of honesty and forthrightness because it smacked of a deal being made in exchange for Nixon's resignation. Then there was his appointment of New York governor Nelson Rockefeller as vice president. Rockefeller was to the liberal wing of the party what Reagan was to the conservatives with one big difference. Conservatives were growing in number; liberals within the party were shrinking.

In June 1975, less than a year after Ford took office as president, a group of conservative Republican senators led by James Buckley of New York, Jesse Helms of North Carolina and James McClure of Idaho proposed that the 1976 Republican National Convention in Kansas City be an open convention since neither the current president nor vice president had been elected to their respective offices. Their idea was to decide the choices for president and vice president at the convention without any preconceived notion that the incumbents would automatically be renominated.

The Ford campaign strategy was twofold; the president would hit the campaign trail vigorously, speaking all over the country while his operatives worked behind the scenes to (1) convince Rockefeller to withdraw as a candidate for vice president or (2) persuade Reagan, in the interest of party unity, not to challenge Ford for the nomination.[14]

On July 8, Ford announced that he would seek election to a full term as president in 1976. He criss-crossed the country espousing his Whip Inflation Now program that included everything from a theme song written by Meredith Willson to "WIN" buttons that people could wear on their lapels. He purposely scheduled several events in California, Reagan's home state, and ran into some unexpected difficulties there that were far beyond the scope of partisan politics.

On September 5, in Sacramento, as he was leaving one event and walking toward the nearby state capitol for another function, Lynette Fromme, a 26-year-old woman who was among thousands of spectators on the street, drew a gun and pointed it at the president. She was disarmed by a Secret Service agent before she could fire a shot. Fromme was a follower of Charles Manson, a notorious mass murderer of that era. Ford vowed that he would not curtail his plans to meet and greet the American public because of the assassination attempt.

Sixteen days later, on September 22, as Ford was leaving a speaking engagement at a San Francisco hotel, Sara Jane Moore, a 45-year-old radical who was part of the crowd waiting for the president outside the hotel, drew a gun and fired a shot at him. The shot missed. She was wrestled to the ground and arrested. Again, Ford vowed to continue campaigning.

In November, Rockefeller, saying he was tired of all the infighting, announced he would not be a candidate for vice president in 1976. That solved one part of the Ford problem. The other part not only remained but was magnified on November 20 when Governor Reagan formally announced his candidacy. Columnist James Reston of the *New York Times* wrote, "The astonishing thing is that this amusing but frivolous Reagan fantasy is taken so seriously by the news media and particularly by the President. It makes a lot of news but it doesn't make much sense."[15]

As the Iowa caucuses drew near, state Republicans looked forward to holding their caucuses on the same day as the Democrats so they could share the national limelight that news coverage of the caucuses would surely bring. The Republican candidates, in stark contrast to the Democrats, hardly paid attention to Iowa. President Ford, who was traveling all over the country, flew over Iowa many times but never landed in the state. Governor Reagan made one appearance, when a plane taking him from New Hampshire to California, refueled in Des Moines two days before the caucuses.

The state Republican Party, wanting to feed into the expected media frenzy, arranged for a straw poll at 62 precincts around the state. They hired a firm to conduct the poll and did not announce in advance which precincts were selected.

The concept was to provide a glimpse of the voter appeal of the candidates but had nothing to do with delegate strength of either candidate. It did provide numbers, however, and in the game of politics, where the press wanted to report winners and losers, the straw poll would fulfill the mission.

Ford came out the winner with 264 votes to 248 for Reagan. Nine votes were cast for other candidates and 62 were undecided. The Republican Party had provided the media with what they thought would generate big publicity but it didn't work out that way. The next day, the *New York Times* devoted 123 lines to the Democratic caucuses and 26 to the Republicans. On January 21, two days after the caucuses, the newspaper gave 357 lines to the Democrats, 26 to the Republicans. Robert Ray, Iowa's Republican governor, summed up the impact of the GOP foray into the land of national publicity: "I don't think our caucuses hold quite the same meaning as the Democrats," he said.

Nonetheless, with Ford capturing just 16 more votes than Reagan in what was essentially a meaningless poll, the results did fit the mindset established by Gary Hart four years earlier: The winner did not meet expectations and the loser exceeded them.

"The media interpretation that Reagan was a viable challenger was based on a 16-vote plurality among 583 Iowa Republicans. Such a poll may be very slim evidence for that judgment but it again illustrates the media quest for reportable news about the progress of the campaign."[16]

Carter and Ford went on to become their party's nominees and Carter ascended to the presidency by defeating Ford in the November elections. History will forever link his rise to become the leader of the free world to the lonely winter days he spent in Iowa, receiving free car washes and pizzas as honorariums and chatting with anyone he could find who would shake his hand.

It is a style that has been emulated by dozens of candidates for more than 30 years as if that was the sure path to reaching the White House. Yet, until Barack Obama won in 2008, Carter was the only Democratic candidate to lead all other candidates in the Iowa caucuses who went on to win the presidency.

But the Carter legacy remains. It is the reason veteran political warriors as well as rising young upstarts make the pilgrimage to Iowa with their aspirations high. As author Alexandra Pelosi puts it: "Their goal is to 'pull a Jimmy Carter' which means they will come out of nowhere to win."[17]

CHAPTER FIVE

1980

"The action begins in Iowa. It's where everything starts for every-body."[1]

By 1980, Iowa had established itself as the launching pad for presidential politics. Thanks in part to the national media's appetite for results, as faulty and inconclusive as they might be, coupled with the state political parties each recognizing the opportunity for virtually unlimited free publicity by catering to the media, the caucuses were treated like a Super Bowl rather than the first game of a long season.

Eight years earlier, a dozen or so reporters hovered around the basement of Democratic headquarters in Des Moines while caucus results were compiled by party honchos sitting around a couple of tables. By contrast, in 1980, NBC had a full contingent of correspondents, producers and technicians in Des Moines, "practically taking over the Fort Des Moines Hotel," ABC had more than 100 of its people at the Savery Hotel and CBS had found space for its people by renting the entire Des Moines Civic Center.[2]

The objects of their attention were two fascinating political battles. On the Democratic side, President Jimmy Carter faced a serious challenge from within the ranks of his own party in the person of Senator Edward "Ted" Kennedy of Massachusetts. He was the last icon in a generation of Kennedy men who sought the presidency and whose brothers President John F. Kennedy and Senator Robert F. Kennedy had each been assassinated. On the Republican side, former governor Ronald Reagan, who himself had challenged an incumbent president four years earlier, was once again a candidate. But this time, six other Republicans, all sensing the political vulnerability of President Carter, had joined in the hunt.

George Herbert Walker Bush, 55, the son of former U.S. senator

Prescott Bush, was a political insider who had served in government as a two-term member of the U.S. House, ambassador to the United Nations, U.S. envoy to China, and director of the Central Intelligence Agency. Bush, who was the youngest Navy pilot during World War II, also served for a time as chairman of the Republican National Committee. He was a loyal Republican stalwart who had served in the Nixon administration but was not soiled by the Watergate scandal.

Senator Howard Baker, 54, of Tennessee, had been in the Senate since 1966 and was elected minority leader in 1977. The son-in-law of the famous former Illinois senator Everett Dirksen, Baker gained national recognition as vice chairman of the Senate Watergate Committee investigating President Nixon's involvement in the scandal. The committee hearings were televised and millions of Americans watched Baker as he repeatedly asked witnesses: "What did the president know and when did he know it?" When the answers started coming, they led to Nixon's fall from grace and Howard Baker became a well-known political figure.

Former Texas governor John B. Connally, 62, was a maverick who served as President Kennedy's secretary of the Navy until he was elected governor of Texas in 1962. Though still a Democrat, President Nixon appointed him as his secretary of the treasury in 1971. Connally became increasingly disenchanted with liberal Democratic policies and formally switched parties in time to become a candidate for the 1980 Republican presidential nomination.

Connally was best known to many Americans as the man sitting in front of John F. Kennedy in the motorcade in Dallas when Kennedy was assassinated on November 22, 1963. Connally was wounded in the attack.

Senator Robert Dole of Kansas, President Ford's running mate in 1976, was a combat infantry officer in Italy during World War II who was wounded so severely that he was hospitalized for 39 months and sustained a permanent injury to his arm. Dole was elected to five terms in the U.S. House before being elected to the Senate in 1968. He was known for both his wit and his grit, often lacing his speeches with humor and biting sarcasm.

Congressman John B. Anderson of Illinois was a 10-term member of the U.S. House who campaigned as a centrist opposed to Reagan's highly conservative views. Anderson would subsequently drop out of the Republican race and run as a third-party candidate (National Unity Party) in the November elections.

Congressman Philip Crane, 48, a conservative from Illinois,

announced his candidacy on August 2, 1978, more than two years before the presidential election. Crane was first elected to the House in 1969 to fill the unexpired term of Donald Rumsfeld, who had resigned to take a position in the Nixon administration. Crane said he decided to become a candidate because he did not think Reagan would run again but he stayed in the race long after Reagan announced.

Carter's administration was marked by a series of setbacks that off-set accomplishments such as his overseeing a Middle East peace agreement between Egypt and Israel that came to be known as the Camp David Accords. At home, inflation was up and the economy was sluggish. Abroad, two developments, and the Carter administration's reaction to them, hurt him politically. One was the Soviet Union's invasion of Afghanistan in 1979. As a form of protesting the Russian aggression, Carter announced that the United States would boycott the Olympic Games scheduled for Moscow in 1980. Many Americans opposed the action because it kept America off of the world stage and penalized young athletes who would not be allowed to compete in what, for many of them, would be a once-in-a-lifetime experience.

The other world event that impacted the Carter administration was much more serious and far-reaching. On November 4, 1979, a band of Iranian militants stormed the American Embassy in Tehran and took nearly 70 Americans hostage. The ordeal lasted 444 days and included one botched rescue attempt when two American helicopters collided.

The hostage crisis came to become a symbol of public concern and frustration. *Nightline*, a popular ABC late-night television news program, offered daily reminders of the crisis by opening each show with an announcer giving that day's date followed by the number of days Americans had been held in captivity.

With all of this as political ammunition, in the fall of 1979, groups of senators, congressmen and labor leaders began lobbying Kennedy to challenge Carter for the Democratic nomination in 1980. People like Senator McGovern, the party's nominee in 1972, and Senator Bayh, Senator Jackson and Congressman Udall, all of whom had sought the nomination in 1976, now feared their chances for re-election in the Senate and House were in jeopardy if Carter led the Democratic ticket. So they made the pilgrimage to Kennedy's office in the Russell Senate Office Building.

The senator from Massachusetts, 47 years old, had the Kennedy name going for him, an almost priestly name among liberal Democrats. He was a dynamic speaker and it was no secret that he was unhappy with the

Carter administration. But there were some obvious obstacles. Kennedy's marriage was on shaky ground, a personal matter for most people but one that becomes public for public figures and particularly for people seeking the presidency.

Mark Manoff, a reporter for the *Philadelphia Daily News* who covered both the Republican and Democratic caucuses, said Joan Kennedy accompanied her husband on some of his campaign trips and both the candidate and his wife looked uncomfortable. "She looked like she was chained to him," said Manoff.[3]

Another Kennedy nemesis was the haunting shadow of Chappaquiddick — a tragedy that occurred ten years earlier, in July 1969, when Kennedy drove a car off of a bridge while taking a young woman home from a party. The woman, Mary Jo Kopechne, drowned. Kennedy made his way out of the water but did not report the accident until several hours later, an action that he later described as "incomprehensible and inexcusable."

Senator Ted Kennedy emerges from an airplane as a throng of newsmen waits at a campaign stop in 1979. Kennedy waged what one reporter called "an airport campaign," holding news conferences at one airport after another in Iowa in his unsuccessful bid to unseat President Carter (courtesy *Mason City Globe Gazette*).

Despite the baggage he carried from his personal life, the political circumstances of the times carried the day. On November 7, 1979, after much deliberation, Kennedy announced his candidacy.[4]

He may have hoped for a forgiving or perhaps forgetful public but the past is always fair game for both the press and political opponents. CBS television aired a documentary on Senator Kennedy on November 4, three days before Kennedy's candidacy announcement. It was scheduled to be broadcast later in the month but the network moved it up when it learned Kennedy was about to enter the race. In it, correspondent Roger Mudd questioned Kennedy about Chappaquiddick while images of his overturned Oldsmobile and the bridge were shown on the screen. Mudd concluded the segment saying, "It is now obvious that Kennedy and his advisers plan to volunteer nothing more on Chappaquiddick or make any attempt to clear away any of the lingering contradictions."

Some Republicans didn't hesitate to remind voters about Kennedy's indiscretions. John Connally, when questioned about his own past, told a reporter, "I never drowned anybody."[5]

Kennedy also stammered and seemed ill-prepared to answer when Mudd asked him why he wanted to be president. The senator usually did well in front of cameras, just as his brothers did, but Mudd's questions, though he must have anticipated them, seemed to catch him off guard.

In his campaign, Kennedy tried to fashion himself as a New Deal Democrat, harkening back to the days of Franklin Delano Roosevelt, one of the heroes of the Democratic Party. Kennedy's statement during the campaign, "The only thing that paralyzes us today is the myth that we cannot move forward," was strikingly similar to Roosevelt's famous line, "The only thing we have to fear is fear itself."[6]

Connally campaigned with a bruskness and a swagger. At Waverly, Iowa, on January 18, three days before the caucuses, he made a stop at Bill Deal's livestock auction wearing a pinstripe suit and cowboy boots and he didn't pull any punches with the farmers in the crowd who may have been expecting some support and encouragement for their toils in the fields. They didn't get it.

"None of you have made the sacrifices for the dairy industry that I have," said Connally. "I got indicted for it, if you want to know something. You think I don't know about milk producers and milk prices — you're crazy."[7]

Reagan was clearly the front-runner in Iowa. He had done well in the caucuses of 1976, still had an organization in place from that campaign, and many Iowa voters were aware of his Iowa roots. Before he went to California to become an actor and, later, a politician, he was a sports announcer on WHO in Des Moines, a radio station heard statewide, in which, among other things, he broadcast play-by-play accounts of Chicago Cubs baseball games based on teletype accounts that came into the radio station.

Bush was the most frequent visitor to Iowa, often sleeping in the back of his campaign bus as it rambled across the state. He clearly was emulating the campaign strategy of Carter in 1976, hitting as many towns as he could, shaking as many hands as possible and hoping those he came in contact with would remember his message.

Roy Reed wrote in the *New York Times*, "I have covered a lot of political candidates in the past 25 years but I have never known one — not even Hubert Humphrey — who ran with more zeal and determination."[8]

Bush tried to draw a distinction between him and Reagan by describing some of Reagan's theories on the economy as "voodoo economics" — a phrase that was widely and repeatedly quoted in the media.

Baker, recognizing Reagan's front-runner status and Bush's workaholic efforts in Iowa, tried to keep pace. But at one point, he staked a claim on what he apparently hoped the public and the national press might consider a victory for him, saying, "The real race is for third place."[9]

Reagan accepted the status of front-runner, awarded to him early on by the media, and adopted an Iowa strategy of avoiding events that would give his opponents publicity that they needed but he didn't. So Reagan didn't take part in candidate forums or other such events and let his campaign staff and county organizers do his bidding while he concentrated on other states. He made a total of four appearances in Iowa.

Bush was in Iowa 31 days in the year before the caucuses and developed a staff of 18 full-time and 80 part-time workers who, among other things, looked for Republicans who were most likely to attend the caucuses and tried to woo them to support Bush. Baker and Connally relied on big advertising campaigns but, like Crane and Dole, had organizations that were better suited for primaries than caucuses. Anderson focused hardly any attention on Iowa.[10]

Dole's stature was a paradox. Though he had been President Ford's running mate in 1976, he was in some ways, as the *Washington Post* noted, the least experienced of the Republican presidential field. He sprinkled his campaign with one-liners and, like Baker, he was well aware of who was the front-runner in the pack. He told the public things like, "If you want a younger Ronald Reagan, I'm your man." As it turned out, the public didn't buy it.

Historian Hugh Winebrenner noted a revealing aspect of the GOP campaigns. In a statewide Iowa poll, conducted by the *Des Moines Register* in August 1979, Reagan was the leader, as expected, with Bush getting just 1 percent support. But in two straw polls conducted by the Republican Party, Bush was the clear winner. Winebrenner pointed out that straw polls conducted by the party are more likely to include potential caucusgoers than a poll that includes virtually everyone.

The most significant of these occurred in Ames on October 13 at a dinner much like the Democrats' Jefferson-Jackson Day shindig. More than 3,000 Republicans came. They ate, drank, donated money, heard speeches from presidential candidates and took part in a straw poll. Most of the major candidates attended. Reagan did not. The results:

Bush	36%
Dole	15%
Connally	15%
Reagan	11%
Others/Undecided	23%

Bush was not the only decisive winner. The Iowa Republican Party was able to pay off its 1978 campaign debt and have some money left over because of the $50-a-plate dinner that was part of the evening's festivities. Organizers didn't realize it at the time, but they had started something with their straw poll that in future years would take on a life of its own.

The straw poll was destined to draw attention similar to that given the caucuses, even though the straw poll results were non-binding and were presumed to have no impact on the campaigns except by how they were perceived by the press and the public. It was exactly those perceptions that were to create an impact on future campaigns. But in 1979, the thought was that the event was just a good old-fashioned political rally and fund raiser.

On January 5, two weeks before the caucuses, the *Des Moines Register* sponsored a debate between the Republican candidates and planned one for January 7 featuring President Carter and Senator Kennedy. The Democratic debate was cancelled when Carter declined to participate, citing pressing matters in Washington, primarily the Iran hostage crisis. Following his ongoing strategy, Reagan opted out of the Republican debate.[11]

The Iowa Republican Party made the decision in 1980 to provide the media with more complete caucus results than it had four years ago when it relied on results from a sampling of precincts. This year, it conducted what amounted to a statewide straw poll of caucusgoers. The poll had no bearing on delegate selection but it fed the media frenzy for a winner. Straw polls were conducted at most every precinct. The results were:

Bush	33,530	31.6%
Reagan	31,348	29.5%
Baker	16,216	15.3%
Connally	9,861	9.3%
Anderson	4,585	4.3%
Undecided	1,800	1.7%
Dole	1,576	1.5%

Reagan, who had taken the Muskie approach of relying on front-runner status, money and endorsements to pull him through, was "Bush-whacked" by someone who employed the Carter 1976 tactic of being in Iowa early and often.

Anderson, the independent, got only a little over 4 percent of the vote but the fact that he was even a player in Iowa was proof that the reforms started by the Democrats eight years earlier and emulated four years later by the Republicans were working. Anderson had been in the House of Representatives for 19 years but was not a favorite of conservatives in his own party. He had survived a tough primary fight the previous year and saw his candidacy for president as a way of validating his political credentials within the Republican Party. But he was an unknown nationally who wouldn't have had a chance to even participate in the old system where party bosses controlled who ran and who didn't.

"That a man like John Anderson would even consider running is testimony to the revolution that has occurred in the last 20 years. The revolution has come in two forms: changes in the way parties choose their candidates and changes in the way voters choose their presidents."[12]

On the Democratic side, Senator Kennedy came to Iowa often and various members of the famous family also appeared throughout the state on his behalf. On numerous occasions, Kennedy said the Iowa caucuses were the first "true test" of his candidacy. President Carter, engulfed in trying to find a solution to the Iranian hostage crisis, did not come to Iowa at all but had a solid organization in place as a result of his 1976 campaign. Many Iowans were surprised during the latest campaign to have their

Senator Ted Kennedy fields reporters' questions after an appearance at the Holiday Motor Lodge in Clear Lake in January of 1980 (courtesy *Mason City Globe Gazette*).

telephones ring and discover the caller was the president of the United States.

A late entry into the race, and, as it turned out, a lame entry, was California governor Jerry Brown, who announced his candidacy, made a half-dozen trips to Iowa and then withdrew before the caucuses took place.

The caucuses were now a full-fledged media event. Hundreds of reporters came to Des Moines. All three major networks broadcast their nightly news programs from Des Moines and one of them, CBS, conducted entrance polls. Exit polls, in which voters were interviewed as they left their polling places, had become a part of the normal election coverage and worked well in states where there were primary elections.

But with caucuses, where voters gave up their bowling night or poker game to spend a couple of hours supporting the candidate of their choice, CBS staked out nearly 100 precinct caucuses and talked to caucusgoers as they arrived. On the basis of those entrance polls, shortly before 9 P.M., the network projected Carter to be the decisive winner — with good reason. The results were:

Carter	59.1%
Kennedy	31.2%
Uncommitted	9.6%

Carter clearly benefited from the popularity he achieved in the state in 1976 and also from a public that was reluctant to abandon an incumbent president in the middle of a crisis. Kennedy fell victim to his own words, for if Iowa was the first "true test" of his chance to be president, he had failed it.[13]

Manoff, the Philadelphia reporter who came to Iowa and covered both the Republican and Democratic caucuses, summed up the candidates' strategies this way: Kennedy made stops at airports, Bush made stops at radio stations, Connally made stops at fraternity parties and Carter campaigned from the Rose Garden.

"Kennedy didn't do much retail politicking," said Manoff. "He had the Kennedy name going for him and he expected to pummel Carter in Iowa and go on from there. Reagan didn't campaign hardly at all in Iowa while Bush made stops at every little radio station across the state. Connally tried to get the younger vote and even attended a fraternity party at Iowa State University," he said.

"This was back in the days when big money didn't mean too much. You had to make your case with Iowans or you didn't get their support."[14]

Vice President Mondale played a key role as a surrogate for the president. He recalled,

> It was the year of the big shoot-out with Kennedy. Carter was in Washington, tied down with the hostage crisis, so I carried the brunt of it in Iowa. Others came and campaigned, of course, Rosalyn [Carter's wife] and other members of his family and staff, but I had the biggest load.
>
> We knew if we lost Iowa, we were cooked. Kennedy would have had the momentum. It was one of the most exciting times in my political life. I told Iowans I was in their state more than their county commissioners. I really liked it — talking to people on their farms and in their living rooms. It reminded me of politics when I was a young man just starting out.
>
> In Iowa, the crowd will always tell you something without saying a word. You can just feel it. I came to Iowa in 1968 to campaign for Hubert Humphrey when the Vietnam War was on and the public didn't like it. And you could feel it. They didn't have to say anything. When I came in 1980, just the opposite occurred. We were warmly received, and you could feel that, too.[15]

Vice President Walter Mondale dons a newspaper carrier's bag during a 1980 visit to the *Mason City Globe Gazette* newspaper office. As a child, Mondale was a *Globe Gazette* paper boy (courtesy *Mason City Globe Gazette*).

Reagan went on to win the Republican nomination and defeated Carter in the November election — the second straight election in which an incumbent president was toppled. His victory, in part, came from what he learned the hard way in Iowa.

"For Reagan, victory began in Iowa in the lessons learned from an unexpected and unnecessary defeat: a candidate must be himself, must do the things that work for him, must follow his own best instincts even against the advice of those who understand the political process better than he does."[16]

One of Reagan's best friends was Nevada senator Paul Laxalt. They were political confidantes and men who enjoyed each other's company. Not long before the Iowa caucuses, they had watched the Super Bowl together in which the Pittsburgh Steelers beat the Los Angeles Rams. "The Steelers wouldn't have won if Terry Bradshaw had sat on his ass for three quarters," Laxalt told Reagan after the caucuses. "You were sitting on your ass in Iowa."[17]

Roger Ailes, a conservative activist and ardent Reagan supporter, said Reagan came up short in Iowa because too many people knew him as an "affable ex-actor and ex-governor" who didn't show enough range of emotions in his limited appearances in Iowa to get anyone excited about him.[18]

Ronald Reagan makes one of his few appearances in Iowa, speaking to a gathering at Mason City Municipal Airport on January 19, 1980. After losing the Iowa caucuses to George Bush, a Reagan adviser chided him for "sitting on his ass" in Iowa (courtesy *Mason City Globe Gazette*).

As a campaigner, Reagan, the old actor, always did better when every-thing was scripted. His campaign manager, John Sears, realized this, and it became abundantly clear shortly after he announced his candidacy when he bumbled his way through some interviews with local reporters. Sears rearranged his schedule, relegating him mostly to airport terminals and speaker's rostrums, and avoiding debates with other candidates such as the big one sponsored by the *Des Moines Register*.

Another campaign staffer, Ed Rollins, summed it up this way: "Just like in the movies, (Reagan) was content to take direction and he did it very well. He knew what his job was and he went out and did it superbly every day. He was always confident the boys over at the campaign knew what they were doing."[19]

But the low-key, carefully scripted strategy with few public appear-ances backfired in Iowa. "Sears overdid this regal, front-runner status," and Reagan lost. Not long after that, Sears was replaced as campaign manager by William Casey.[20]

Reagan, who was usually careful not to criticize those in his inner circle, said afterwards that Sears made him uncomfortable. "He never looked me in the eye. He looked me in the tie," said Reagan.

Lyn Nofziger, another Reagan adviser, summed up the mistake of the Iowa caucus campaign this way: "If you're going to follow a Rose Garden strategy, you better be already in the Rose Garden."[21]

One thing was accomplished by keeping Reagan behind a speaker's podium. He often used note cards but didn't want his audience to see them because he didn't think that would fit his image as the "Great Com-municator." So he kept the note cards in his bottom left suit coat pocket. When he got up to give a speech, he would stand behind the lectern, wave to the crowd with high right hand and remove the cards from his pocket with his left hand and place them on the lectern, out of sight of the audi-ence.[22]

The Iowa caucuses in 1980 solidified what reformers envisioned when they made the changes to get the public more involved in the political process. Bush's presence in Iowa — and Reagan's absence — were examples of how the system would work for a generation to come. Reputation alone would not carry the day.

Bush attributed his victory to the "old Mo" — short for "momen-tum" — which made his advisers cringe because they thought it made him sound too preppy — too much like a Yale-ee, an image his handlers were trying to eradicate.

One of his top advisers, James Baker, who would later serve in many capacities in his administration, said the Bush campaign still had a big problem to try to solve. The people now know "George Who," said Baker. "But we did not answer the question of George Why."[23]

The grassroots politics of going from barber shop to union hall, from living rooms to county fairs, of signing autographs and posing for pictures, was now etched into the landscape of how to win in Iowa.

And how a candidate did in Iowa, and how the outcome was portrayed in the media, was another lesson relearned. Bush exceeded expectations. Reagan and Kennedy did not. For Bush's campaign, it was a boost. For Reagan's, it was a wake-up call. For Kennedy's, it was an omen.

Republicans had discovered a new weapon in their publicity and fund-raising armament in 1980 that would serve them well for the next generation; the straw poll at Ames would become a fixture of the pre-caucus summer in any year in which a Republican was not in the White House or when an incumbent Republican president did not seek re-election.

A footnote to 1980: historian Theodore H. White described a scene at the 1980 Democratic convention that showed how the reforms of 1972, the ones that helped propel Iowa into a national political force, had transformed the party. Kennedy, denied the presidential nomination, had just spoken to the convention and was given a thunderous ovation.

Excited Kennedy backers cheered wildly and jumped around and hugged each other in a manner not unlike they would have done if he had just received the nomination. Their demonstration on the floor of the convention hall lasted several minutes.

White, observing all of this from a vantage point he'd staked out for himself on the convention floor, described how the aisles were so crammed with delegates that it was difficult for anyone to inch their way forward.

One who tried was Senator Warren Magnuson of Washington, who was 75 years old, a veteran political warrior who had been in the Senate since 1944. He had somehow separated himself from his state delegation and now was trying to meander his way back to it.

White wrote, "Old Senator Warren Magnuson of Washington, tottering, seemed to be caught in the jam and I tried to clear a way for him by pushing through the crowd."

Then it occurred to White who he was pushing aside to make way for the elderly senator. "I realized how different it had all become. I was pushing women; it was women who were dominating the floor."[24]

CHAPTER SIX

1984

"I know Abraham Lincoln didn't start like this."

After the 1980 elections, the Democrats were in the mood to reform once again. The reforms that had taken hold in 1972 opened up the nominating process to more women, minorities and young people. But it had also produced elections in which one of their candidates, George McGovern, lost 49 out of 50 states, and another, Jimmy Carter, rose from virtual obscurity to win the presidency, but, in the opinion of voters, didn't handle it very well and was soundly defeated in his bid for re-election by Ronald Reagan. When the top of a party ticket is struggling, officeholders further down the line get nervous about their own political survival.

The party bosses, who once controlled the process, and who had picked winners such as John F. Kennedy in 1960, wanted some of that power returned to them. They were stung not only by the poor showing of Carter in the November election but by how Senator Kennedy, who had immense popularity at the national convention, was prevented from competing for the nomination on the convention floor because a majority of delegates were already bound, by party rules, to Carter.

The solution was to change the rules to make sure that scenario did not happen again. A commission was formed, headed by North Carolina governor James Hunt, to come up with some reforms.

Congressman Gillis Long of Louisiana was a beneficiary of the Long political machine that started with his uncles, Huey Long and his brother Earl, who each had been governor, and continued with Huey's son, Russell, who currently was a powerful United States senator. Gillis Long testified before the Hunt Commission about the importance of control —

in effect, pleading for a return to a form of the party boss system of nominating candidates.

He said, "We in the House, as the last vestige of Democratic control at the national level, believe we have a special responsibility to develop innovative approaches that respond to our party's constituencies."[1]

Weeks later, Hunt spoke at Harvard University and amplified on the same theme. He said, "We must give our constituencies more flexibility to respond to changing circumstances in cases where the voters' mandate is less than clear."[2]

The commission's solution was the creation of superdelegates — unelected, unfledged delegates who could go to the national convention and vote for whomever they chose.

As writer Ari Berman put it: "It returned power to the elected officials and party regulars. They (superdelegates) included all Democratic members of Congress and every governor. Roughly half of them were Democratic National Committee officials elected by state parties."[3]

The new rules called for several hundred of the delegates to be superdelegates. In other words, to some degree at least, the party bosses were back in business. Historian Rhodes Cook said superdelegates were to serve several purposes. They were to "re-engage Democratic leaders across the country in the presidential nominating process, add an element of 'peer review' that had been missing from the process since the 1970s and create a firewall to blunt any party outsider that built up a head of steam in the primaries."[4]

An irony to the new rules is that while they were established in part because of what happened to Kennedy at the convention in 1980, they were opposed by many Kennedy supporters who thought he might make another run in 1984 and feared that other Democrats, such as former vice president Walter Mondale, might benefit more from superdelegate support. As it turned out, Kennedy didn't run and Mondale did benefit from superdelegate support.

Their importance went well beyond the presidential nominating process. "If the convention's platform committee is adopting something that would be really detrimental in the general election, the party leaders can take steps to prevent that from happening," said Elaine Karmack, a teacher at Harvard University's Kennedy School of Government . In other words, it was another example of the firewall referred to by Cook.[5]

U.S. senator Tom Harkin of Iowa, who was to seek the Democratic nomination for president in 1992, said his view of why superdelegates were created was not a power play as much as it was another means of keeping the process open. "The reason they did it in the first place is that if we, as office-holders, ran to be delegates and won, we'd cut other deserving people out of the process. So the thought was to make us automatic delegates and give others the chance to be elected," he said.[6]

The Hunt Commission also set up changes that compressed the length of the primary and caucus seasons while keeping the Iowa caucuses and the New Hampshire primary number one and number two. That was important to candidates such as Senator Alan Cranston of California, Senator John Glenn of Ohio and Governor Reuben Askew of Florida who, following the example of Carter in 1976 and George Bush in 1980, campaigned early and often in Iowa.

As one newsmagazine proclaimed in its May 24, 1982 edition, "Believe it or not, the 1984 presidential race is already on in Iowa."[7]

Kennedy was still the straw that stirred the drink in Democratic politics. So when Kennedy announced, on December 1, 1982, that he would not run for president in 1984, it opened the gates for other Democrats to formally announce what they had been thinking about and working towards for a long time. The candidate lineup filled up quickly.

On February 2, 1983, Senator Alan Cranston of California announced. Cranston, 69, had been in the Senate since 1969 and had been Democratic whip for the past six years. Cranston had the distinction of having once been sued by Adolf Hitler. A journalist in his younger days, he noticed that the American edition of Hitler's *Mein Kampf* had excluded many of the German dictator's inflammatory and anti–Semitic comments. So Cranston published an unabridged version and added some annotations of his own. Hitler's publisher sued for copyright infringement and won.

Cranston favored a worldwide nuclear freeze and campaigned heavily on that theme. He spent more time in Iowa than any other Democratic candidate and had the misfortune of looking like a man who was nearing the age of 70. He was bald and gaunt and the age difference between him and his opponents in Iowa was easy for voters to recognize. To compensate, Cranston dyed the white fringe above his ears as well as his eyebrows a color that was closer to orange than brown.[8]

David Yepsen, political writer for the *Des Moines Register*, said Cranston was a distinguished senator who expressed himself well when he went toe to toe with other candidates and took unfair ribbing in the media for dying his hair. "Hell, they all dye their hair," said Yepsen.

Next to enter the race, on February 17, 1983, was Senator Gary Hart,

47, of Colorado, the lawyer who ran McGovern's failed 1972 presidential campaign — a campaign that might not have ever developed had Hart not used the media to spin McGovern's strong showing in the Iowa caucuses that year. Hart was a graduate of Yale Law School and Yale Divinity School. He was a lawyer for the U.S. Department of Justice for two years, was elected to the Senate in 1974 and was re-elected in 1980. Hart was an eloquent speaker and knew how to put together an organization in caucus states.

He also knew the value of meeting voters face to face — and how to do it on a limited budget. In laying the groundwork for his presidential campaign, Hart came to Iowa in 1982 to campaign for Lynn Cutler, a woman striving to become Iowa's first female in Congress (unsuccessfully, as it turned out). He met Steve Lynch, an accountant at the Sara Lee food plant in New Hampton, a small northern Iowa community. The two men immediately hit it off. When Hart returned to Iowa the following year, he and Lynch hooked up again.

"I knew his campaign manager. That's how we got connected again," said Lynch.

> The campaign didn't have a lot of money at the time. I had a van. In those days, not everybody had a van. But we could get him and me and his aides and a local TV guy and a newspaper reporter in my van and go from place to place. Sometimes, we'd go places and there would only be five or six people there. It didn't matter. Gary was a great one for punch lines. He'd say, "Did Abe Lincoln start like this?"
>
> One time in late January or early February, I was driving on I-80 [the main east-west interstate highway across Iowa] and there was a terrible snowstorm. I was trying to follow the lead car but I could hardly see in front of me, it was snowing so hard. We had to go practically at a crawl. One of his managers kept telling me to be careful, that I was crossing the center line or that I was on the shoulder of the road and I don't know how she could tell — because I couldn't see anything.
>
> As it turned out, the lead car had turned off at an exit but I hadn't seen it. We just kept going at a snail's pace in that blinding snow. We went for three hours like that when Gary nudged me and said, "Getting bad out, isn't it." We all just burst into laughter.
>
> We got to a motel in Dubuque [on the eastern edge of the state] and decided to go into the lounge to get something to eat and drink. They had the strangest act there. A woman came out in some sort of costume and sang. Then she would leave and come back in another costume and sing some more and she kept doing this. Finally, she came out dressed like a leopard. Gary leaned over to me and said, "I know Abe Lincoln didn't start like this."[9]

Four days after Hart announced, on February 21, 1983, former vice president Walter F. Mondale, 55, made it official that he too was a candidate. Mondale, who 20 years earlier, when he was attorney general of Minnesota and a Hubert Humphrey protégé, helped broker the deal with the Mississippi Freedom Democrats, was clearly the front- runner in Iowa. He was elected to the Senate in 1968 as Humphrey's replacement and served as Jimmy Carter's vice president from 1977 to 1981. He obviously was the most experienced of all the candidates in national and international affairs and had the advantage of being the favorite of party bosses who, with the reforms of the Hunt Commission, had more say and more sway in the nominating process than they had experienced in the past 12 years.

In addition to all of this, he was from a neighboring state. In fact, as a youngster he grew up in southern Minnesota and was a delivery boy for the *Mason City Globe Gazette*, a daily newspaper in northern Iowa that had some subscribers in Minnesota.

But as Muskie learned in 1972, as President Ford did in 1976 and Ronald Reagan in 1980, being the front-runner in Iowa brings with it high expectations and the capacity to fall further than any of the other candidates.

"Rotten luck, Mondale, we've made you the front-runner," wrote Russell Baker in the *New York Times Magazine*. "Without a front-runner, we'd have nobody to suffer surprising setbacks in the early stage of the campaign and without setbacks, we'd be stuck with a very dull story."[10]

On February 23, 1983, two days after Mondale's formal entry, Reuben Askew, former governor of Florida, entered the race. Askew had once been considered a rising star in the Democratic Party and was the keynote speaker at the Democratic National Convention in Miami in 1972. Askew, 55, was elected governor of Florida in 1970 and re-elected in 1974. Florida law prohibited him from running for a third term. President Jimmy Carter appointed him as a U.S. trade representative, a position he held throughout the Carter administration.

Askew went into the campaign with some disadvantages. Democrats were not eager to nominate a southern governor so soon after Carter. Also, he lacked experience in national and international politics compared to some other Democrats in the race.

Grassroots campaigning, the mother's milk of Iowa presidential politics ever since Jimmy Carter shook every hand he could find and left handwritten notes on the doors of potential supporters in 1975, had some built-in drawbacks. Candidates are so closely scrutinized that it doesn't take long for their ill-spoken words or gaffes to become part of their legacy, such as Connally telling Iowa farmers "I never drowned anybody" in 1980. Many years after the 1984 campaign, those who were there recalled vividly a television interview Askew did with KIMT-TV in Mason City. While he was being interviewed, one of the bright klieg lights above him blew out. Askew flinched and ducked as if someone had taken a shot at him.[11]

In April, Senator John Glenn of Ohio and Senator Ernest "Fritz" Hollings of South Carolina joined the fray. Glenn, 62, gained national fame more than 20 years earlier in the U.S. space program. On February 20, 1962, Glenn piloted the *Friendship 7* spacecraft and became the first American to orbit the earth, a distinction that made him instantly recognized throughout the country but dogged him during his presidential campaign. Glenn had trouble shaking the astronaut image, even though he had served in the Senate since 1974.

It didn't help that *The Right Stuff,* a movie about Glenn and other astronauts, came out in 1983. Glenn admitted that constant press references to his campaign "taking off" or "going into orbit" or worse, "not getting off the ground" or "fizzling" hurt his image as a statesman worthy of presidential consideration. A newspaper cartoon depicted two images of Glenn — one in a business suit, one in a spacesuit. In the caption, the Glenn in the business suit says to Glenn the astronaut, "Get out of here."

Glenn was personable but not dynamic. His speeches were filled more with facts and figures than with vision and, for a man with such a celebrity status, he was not one to light a fire under any voters with his personality. He participated in the annual Fourth of July parade in Clear Lake, Iowa, a community of about 8,000 close to the Minnesota border. Afterwards, in the grand style of Iowa pre-caucus politics, he attended a luncheon at the home of Michael Grandon, the local county treasurer, and his wife, Mary.

Bill Schickel, the TV reporter who witnessed the klieg light blowout with Askew, attended the event at the Grandon home. He talked with Glenn and asked him how he responded to people who said that he lacked charisma. "Lack charisma?" said Glenn in mock disbelief. "I have charisma." He then vigorously moved his feet for a few seconds as if doing a soft-shoe dance, then stopped and began talking politics again.[12]

Hollings, 61, had been in the Senate eight years longer than Glenn and seemed to resent the public's adulation for Glenn as an astronaut and what Hollings perceived to be Glenn's lack of political experience. Known for his mint julep accent and his quick, often biting wit, Hollings often

Posing for pictures is part of the process for anyone running for president. Here, Ohio senator John Glenn poses with Genevieve Grandon (left) and her daughter-in-law, Mary Grandon. Mary Grandon and her husband hosted a luncheon for Glenn at their Clear Lake home on July 4, 1983 (courtesy Michael and Mary Grandon).

referred to Glenn condescendingly as *Sky King* (a fictional television character from the 1950s) and once chastised him in a debate, accusing him of still being "all confused in that 'capsoool' of yours."[13]

In September 1983, McGovern, now 62 years old, decided to make a third run for the presidency, running against, among others, five former Senate colleagues in Cranston, Mondale, Hollings, Glenn and Hart, the man who had run his 1972 campaign, as well as Askew, the former Florida governor who had been the keynoter at the 1972 convention that nominated McGovern.

The last entry into the Democratic sweepstakes was the Rev. Jesse Jackson, 42, a civil rights leader from Chicago who became the second black person to actively campaign for a presidential nomination (Congresswoman Shirley Chisholm had been the first in 1972). Jackson had been a protégé of the Rev. Martin Luther King and was with King in Memphis when King was assassinated in 1968. Under King's direction, Jackson started Operation Breadbasket, a civil rights initiative that promoted selective buying — a means of boycotting white businesses that did not hire blacks or purchase goods and services from black people. Later, he formed another activist group called Operation PUSH which later became the Rainbow Coalition.

The 1983 pre-caucus season was one in which forums became the event-du-jour for political candidates. Many of the forums had specific themes. On August 13, an Open Forum on Arms Control was held in Des Moines, sponsored by a peace organization and attended by Mondale, Hart, Cranston and Glenn. It was a forum tailor-made for Cranston, the most ardent nuclear freeze candidate. But it gave all of the candidates a chance to criticize President Reagan's arms control policies.

On October 8, the annual Jefferson-Jackson Day dinner in Des Moines drew seven candidates (Jackson had not yet entered the race) and 6,000 Democrats who ate dinner and listened to speeches. Another forum, on January 10, 1984, also in Des Moines, focused on civil rights. Cranston, Glenn, Hart and McGovern attended. The next forum in Ames on January 21, had agriculture as its topic and drew Askew, Cranston, Hart, Hollings and McGovern.

The fifth and final forum was a debate sponsored by the *Des Moines Register* on February 11, nine days before the caucuses, which were being held later than usual this year but were still the first-in-the-nation test of presidential potential. All eight presidential candidates participated. More than 200 media representatives were there. CNN broadcast the debate live and C-SPAN and Iowa Public Television taped it and did delayed telecasts of it.

Historian Winebrenner noted, "It is evident from the amount of campaign activity in the state that the compressed and front-loaded primary schedule did not minimize the importance of the Iowa caucuses. If anything the candidates emphasized the caucuses more in 1980."[14]

Dinners brought in money, forums brought in television cameras, but grassroots campaigning — in barnyards and factories, in dining rooms and courthouse squares, at shopping malls and county fairs — still brought in the votes, or so the candidates believed. In the year prior to the 1984 caucuses, Hart, traveling by van from one rural town to another, spent 60 days in Iowa; Cranston, with his orange-tinged hair, spent 55; Askew was in the state for 47; McGovern 37; Mondale 34; Glenn 33; Hollings 14; and Jackson 1.

The caucus results:

Mondale	48.9%
Hart	16.5%
McGovern	10.3%
Uncommitted	9.4%
Cranston	7.4%
Glenn	3.5%
Askew	2.5%
Jackson	1.5%
Hollings	0.0%

Mondale, who benefited not only from being a former vice president but also from being from a neighboring state, was expected to win but not by a 33-percent margin. He exceeded expectations. So did Hart by finishing second even if it was a distant second. And from his experience in running McGovern's campaign 12 years earlier, Hart knew how to capitalize on doing better than expected. Never mind that nearly 85 percent of caucusgoers, or more precisely, delegate equivalents, chose someone else. Hart trumpeted his good showing and parlayed it into a victory in New Hampshire eight days later. Hart articulated what the perception of a good showing in Iowa can do for a candidate. "You can get awful famous in this country in seven days," he said.[15]

As for those who didn't meet expectations in Iowa, the Ted Kennedy syndrome from 1980 reappeared, and candidates disappeared. Cranston dropped out of the race on February 29, one day after finishing poorly in the New Hampshire primary. Hollings and Askew both withdrew on March 2. McGovern got out on March 13 and Glenn was gone on March 16. The death knell for all of them had sounded on the night of February 20 in Iowa because not enough Democrats had given up their bowling night or bridge club or they just didn't care enough to give up 90 minutes of their lives to come to the caucuses and support them.

McGovern's situation was particularly interesting. In 1972, he benefited from finishing second to Ed Muskie and, with the help of campaign manager Hart, parlayed that better than expected finish in Iowa all the way to the Democratic nomination.

Now, 12 years later, Hart, in taking second place, bested McGovern by only 1,500 votes. Yet, Hart got a media bounce going into New Hampshire, just as McGovern had in 1972 — and McGovern, though coming ever so close to exceeding expectations, folded his tent not long after that.[16]

Glenn said afterwards he made a tactical mistake by focusing too much attention on his national campaign and adapting that strategy to Iowa, a strategy that didn't work. "Rather than concentrate on the traditional early battlegrounds of a contested nomination, I started focusing on building a nationwide organization aimed at the 'sensible center,'" Glenn wrote in his autobiography.

He said his aim was to appeal to both Republicans and Democrats, which would help him develop a solid political base for the general election. In doing so, he said, "I failed to excite passion among the core constituencies most likely to vote in Democratic caucuses and primaries.[17]

Four-term Iowa Governor Terry Branstad (center), who later managed Lamar Alexander's presidential campaign in Iowa, talks politics with the author (left) and Dick Gross, publisher of the *Council Bluffs Daily Nonpareil,* at a political gathering in Council Bluffs on October 19, 1984 (photograph from author's personal collection).

One other compelling set of statistics. Glenn spent $759,000 in Iowa, Cranston $727,000, Mondale $678,000 and Hart $454,000.

On the Republican side, President Reagan, with no caucus opposition, came to Iowa once — on caucus day, February 20. His staff spent $194,000 in the state.[18]

Iowa was reaping millions of dollars because of its first-in-the-nation status and the importance that politicians and the media put on it. It started with a slow mimeograph machine in 1972 but owed its enduring legacy to Carter four years later.

"When it came to running for president, no Democrat after Carter's 1976 election would fail to be guided in his own contemplation of a candidacy, or usually in his implementation, by how Carter had used Iowa as a springboard to the White House."[19]

One footnote to the 1984 campaign: The perception of Hart exceeding expectations by finishing second in the Iowa caucuses, albeit with 16 percent support, created in effect a two-man race for the nomination (with Mondale), strengthened by the fact Hart won the New Hampshire primary eight days later. Hart mounted a formidable challenge to the front-running former vice president to the extent that each appeared to be going to the national convention with considerable delegate strength.

Many observers thought that for the first time since John Kennedy challenged Estes Kefauver for the Democratic vice presidential nomination in 1956, there might be a floor fight to woo uncommitted delegates. That did not happen, however, because the superdelegates, that category of entrenched officeholders and party chiefs created by the Hunt Commission, came on strongly for their man Mondale.

The party bosses made sure the candidate of their choice received the nomination. In November, President Reagan was re-elected in a landslide. Thus, Republicans had won three out of four presidential elections since the Democrats enacted the reforms of 1972 that opened up the nominating process to be more inclusive. Not even the introduction of superdelegates 12 years later could help them buck the trend.

CHAPTER SEVEN

1988

"Oh, that's that guy Dumbrowski. He's running for president."

The start of the presidential campaign in 1988 was an economic bonanza for Iowa which found itself in the middle of a farm credit crisis that led to dozens of foreclosures and, in some cases, bank closings. It was also the first campaign in 20 years in which the incumbent president was not running, allowing for a wide open field of candidates from both parties to make their way to Iowa.

Their staffs came with them and eventually, journalists from all over the country arrived, all of whom stayed in Iowa motels, gassed up at Iowa service stations, ate their meals in Iowa restaurants and fed the state's economy by patronizing all manner of retail outlets. For almost two years, politics was a hot commodity.

Early on, each party sported eight candidates, all of whom braved cold winters and hot, muggy summers for the chance to convince Iowans, one at a time if that's what it took, that they had the experience and the know-how to be president.

First, the Republican candidates.

Vice President George Bush, 64, had been a good soldier in the Republican army for many years, serving as a congressman, national party chairman, U.N. ambassador, director of the Central Intelligence Agency and as Reagan's vice president for eight years. Bush was not only a veteran campaigner but a veteran of Iowa campaigns, having defeated Reagan in the 1980 precinct caucuses and, as vice president, having campaigned for re-election in 1984.

With his knowledge and experience, Bush entered the 1988 GOP sweepstakes as the front-runner and surely knew the history of that distinction via the experiences of Muskie as the man to beat in 1972 and his own victory over Reagan eight years earlier.

Senator Bob Dole, 63, of Kansas was also well-known and had previous Iowa caucus experience, finishing well down in the field in 1980. He also had experience as a national campaigner from his days as President Ford's running mate in 1976. He had the respect of many fellow Republicans and served as the minority whip in the Senate. Like Mondale, he touted himself as a neighbor and someone who understood Iowans' problems.

A surprise entrant was Marion G. "Pat" Robertson, 57, an ultra-conservative television evangelist who founded the Christian Broadcast Network in 1960. Robertson was no stranger to politics. His father, H. Willis Robertson, served in the U.S. House of Representatives for 34 years.

Robertson had a built-in following because of his television programs and vast experience in fund-raising through his nationally-televised program, *The 700 Club*. He often expressed his political views on his program but he had never run for public office and was counting on the conservative Christian right wing of the Republican Party to support him. His political message centered on the ideals of political and social morality more than specific policies and programs.

Congressman Jack Kemp, 52, of New York, had been in the House of Representatives for 16 years and was a political conservative who had helped steer Ronald Reagan's tax cuts successfully through the House. He considered himself the heir apparent to Reagan in terms of carrying on conservative principles. Kemp was a former professional football player, having been an All-Pro quarterback for the San Diego Chargers and Buffalo Bills during a 13-year career.

A fifth Republican candidate had a well-known name in business circles but not in national politics. Pierre du Pont IV, 52, of Delaware, had served three terms in the U.S. House and two terms as governor. Delaware law prevented him from seeking a third term. He went by "Pete," which served him better in Iowa than "Pierre" but, as someone who, at least by pedigree, was a poster boy for the eastern establishment elite, had some built-in obstacles to gaining popularity in Iowa.[1]

On the national front, he was considered a maverick because some of his unconventional ideas. Du Pont was one of the first politicians to espouse the idea of giving Americans the option of investing in their own private savings accounts as an alternative to Social Security, a concept that became part of the standard Republican litany 20 years later.

After having served his two terms as governor, du Pont toyed with the idea of running for the U.S. Senate but entered the presidential race instead. Had he run for the Senate, his Democratic opponent would have been the incumbent, Joseph Biden, Jr., who was now one of the Democrats seeking the Democratic presidential nomination.

Donald Rumsfeld, 55, who had served as secretary of defense and White House chief of staff in the Ford administration, toyed with the idea of running. Rumsfeld was also a four-term congressman and a former U.S. ambassador to NATO.

Another Washington veteran, Senator Paul Laxalt, 65, of Nevada, who, eight years earlier, had told Ronald Reagan "you were sitting on your ass" after Reagan finished second in the Iowa caucuses, also explored a candidacy. Laxalt had served as Nevada's lieutenant governor, then was governor for four years and had been in the Senate for 16 years. Two lesser candidates, Ben Fernandez, a businessman and GOP fundraiser from California, and Kay Heslop, who gained notoriety by walking a pig across the state, also were in the hunt for a short time.[2]

A late entry for Republicans was General Alexander Haig, former NATO commander and former chief of staff for President Richard Nixon who was part of the inner circle during Nixon's turbulent last days in office, and who served for a time as President Reagan's secretary of state.

It was Haig who seemingly ignored the Constitution shortly after Reagan was shot in March 1981 when he declared on national television, "I'm in control here." Haig made a campaign stop in a northern Iowa nook called Greene, an apt name for his candidacy, and soon after that he decided to skip the Iowa caucuses.

The field of Democrats was headed by Gary Hart, now 51, the senator from Colorado who ran the McGovern campaign in 1972 and made a strong bid for the Democratic nomination in 1984. Because of his experience, the media tagged Hart as the front-runner, a label he knew only too well could be the kiss of death.

Congressman Richard Gephardt, 46, of Missouri was a young, well known member of the House. He hoped to capitalize on his Midwest background and his familiarity with farm problems, such as those that Iowans were experiencing, to gain support from caucusgoers. But he also made a trip to Georgia to confer with the man who set the standard for campaigning in Iowa, former president Jimmy Carter, and his wife, Rosalyn.

He made his first visit to Iowa on March 25, 1985 — almost three years before the next caucuses and barely two months after Reagan took the oath of office to start his second term in the White House. Gephardt was so intent on becoming an Iowan for political purposes that his mother rented an apartment in Des Moines so the Gephardt family could live in Iowa while he campaigned.[3]

The Rev. Jesse Jackson, 46, who had entered the 1984 race, was by now an internationally known civil rights leader and activist of black causes and had earned the right to be taken seriously in Democratic politics. He was a flamboyant speaker, particularly compared to the other candidates.

Massachusetts governor Michael Dukakis, 53, was not well known outside of the eastern seaboard but he came to Iowa touting his "Massachusetts Miracle"— a balanced budget — and his interest and knowledge in economic development.

His name recognition problem was never more evident than the day he visited a small Iowa town and was getting a walking tour of the downtown area. As he and his entourage walked toward a fairly new shopping

Mason City Community Development Director Jon Ewing (gesturing) talks about downtown redevelopment with presidential candidate Michael Dukakis (front) on May 8, 1987. Across the street, a man watching from a park bench told his companion, "That's that guy Dumbrowski. He's running for president" (courtesy *Mason City Globe Gazette*).

mall, two old men watched attentively from a park bench across the street. "What's going on?" one said to the other. The companion pointed and said, "Oh, that's that guy Dumbrowski. He's running for president."[4]

Dukakis was a man given to facts and figures rather than charm to win over audiences and his campaign was marked by periodic foot in mouth disease, such as the time he told Iowa farmers they needed to diversify and try growing "apples, blueberries, flowers and Belgian endive." He was talking to farmers just trying to survive, many of whom didn't know what he was talking about and suspected he didn't either.[5]

Former Arizona governor Bruce Babbitt, 49, was the most unorthodox of the Democratic candidates. He literally entered the race on a bicycle, participating in a week- long, border to border bike ride, an annual event sponsored by the *Des Moines Register* called RAGBRAI, an acronym for Register's Annual Great Bicycle Ride Across Iowa. The trip is grueling, covering about 500 miles, but is filled with camaraderie among participants and draws bicyclists from around the nation. It was Babbitt's way of seeing the Iowa countryside and meeting and talking with people from all walks of life, all within one week.

Senator Paul Simon of Illinois, 59, was a professorial type with thick horn-rimmed glasses, a bow tie that was his signature piece of apparel, and a smooth, mellow voice that made him sound more like a midnight radio announcer than a politician. Simon was a newspaper editor in Troy, a small, southern Illinois community, when he got involved in politics, running first for the state legislature and eventually becoming lieutenant governor before being elected to the Senate.

As a presidential candidate in Iowa, he hoped to capitalize on being from a neighboring state but did not have the charisma or the name recognition of Gephardt, who was also running as a neighbor. Simon came to Iowa to visit in September 1986 but said he was supporting Arkansas senator Dale Bumpers for president. When Bumpers announced, in February 1987, that he would not be a candidate, Simon jumped into the race.

Senator Joseph Biden, 45, of Delaware was known in the Senate as a verbose, often witty, sometimes eloquent advocate of liberal causes but who was not afraid to ruffle the feathers of fellow Democrats if he did not see eye to eye with them. Like Dukakis, Biden hoped for a respectable showing in Iowa, followed by a win in New Hampshire, much closer to his home territory, eight days later. He too came to Iowa in 1985 and gave a rousing speech at the annual Jefferson-Jackson Day dinner that made Democrats who were not familiar with him sit up and take notice.

Senator Albert Gore, Jr., 39, was the son of a longtime Tennessee senator who years earlier had contemplated a run for the presidency. Gore came to Iowa early in 1987, built an organization and made numerous public appearances. By November, he pulled up stakes, deciding to bypass Iowa and concentrate on states holding primaries on Super Tuesday, March 8, about a month after the Iowa caucuses and so named because 21 states and territories were holding caucuses or primaries on that date.

Hart was so well known, compared to the others, and was considered such a favorite by the media, that the other candidates came to be known in some circles as "the seven dwarfs" and were characterized as such in a *Des Moines Register* cartoon.[6]

But in the grind of the campaign, the field was to narrow because of some unusual and totally unpredictable sets of circumstances. Hart announced his candidacy on April 13, 1987, in Denver, saying, "All of us must try to hold ourselves to the very highest standards of integrity and ethics, and soundness of judgment." But rumors were rampant that Hart was a womanizer. His marriage to his wife, Lee, had been a rocky one and had included two separations, and Hart was known to have an attitude of "boys will be boys" while on the road.[7]

Hart scoffed at the reports of his womanizing and, in a *New York Times* story published on May 3, challenged reporters to "put a tail on me" if they didn't believe him and that they would be bored if they did. The *Miami Herald* had been looking into the womanizing allegations for several weeks and, acting on a tip, had reporters stake out Hart's townhouse in Washington, D.C. There they saw an attractive young woman, later identified as Donna Rice, a model, enter the townhouse with Hart. Later that same night, the reporters questioned Hart about it. He said it was an innocent relationship with no romance involved. The *Herald* ran the story about Hart's guest at the townhouse on May 3, coincidentally the same day as the *New York Times* story in which he challenged the press to follow him.

It became a national story that included a published photo of Rice sitting on Hart's lap while they relaxed on a boat named *Monkey Business*. The publicity suffocated his candidacy. After several days of trying to get his campaign back on track, Hart formally dropped out of the race on May 8, blaming an aggressive press for the problems that led to his downfall. Jack Germond and Jules Witcover, two reporters covering Hart's campaign and his departure said many in the media were reminded of Richard Nixon's "you won't have Nixon to kick around anymore" speech when he conceded the California governor's election to Pat Brown in 1962.[8]

Just as Hart's "boys will be boys" tendencies landed him in political trouble, Joe Biden's style of long-winded speech-making, filled with what he hoped would be good quotes and sound bites, ultimately did him in.

On August 23, 1987, Biden gave a rousing speech at the Iowa State Fair. In closing, he did what he often did. He paraphrased lines from a commercial made by Neil Kinnock, a British Labor Party leader who tried unsuccessfully to unseat Prime Minister Margaret Thatcher. In it, Kinnock asked his audience: Why was he the first Kinnock in a thousand generations to go to a university? Why was that also true of his wife? Was it because his ancestors were weak or dumb or lacked talent? "Of course not," he said. "It was because there was no platform on which they could stand."

Biden asked his audience in Des Moines that day why he, Joe Biden, was the first in "a thousand generations" of Bidens to get a college degree? Was it because his ancestors were weak or dumb or lacked talent? No, he said. "It's because they didn't have a platform on which they could stand."

Biden's advisers who were there that day noticed right away that he had failed to attribute his remarks to Kinnock and breathed easier when no one in the press was aware that his thoughts were not original. Biden used the Kinnock material several times in the next few weeks, always crediting Kinnock. For that matter, he had used the Kinnock lines prior to the Iowa State Fair speech and had given proper credit.

But on September 12, the *New York Times* and the *Des Moines Register* both had stories intimating that Biden had plagiarized Kinnock's comments in his Des Moines speech of August 23. Reporters began to dig and discovered that earlier in the year, Biden had given a speech in California in which he used lines from a Robert F. Kennedy speech without attributing them. Further research showed that while Biden was a law student at Syracuse University more than 20 years earlier, he had been given a failing grade and had to repeat a class because he apparently had used material from a law review article in a paper he wrote and passed it off as his own work. On September 23, Biden dropped out of the presidential race.[9]

The Democratic field was further narrowed when Gore, the young senator from Tennessee, decided to pull up stakes from his Iowa campaign to concentrate on the Super Tuesday sweepstakes of states later on. He was lagging far behind in the polls and he left no doubt about his feelings toward Iowa when he spoke at the annual Jackson- Jefferson Day Dinner in Des Moines. "I won't do what the pundits say it takes to win in Iowa," he said, "flatter you with promises, change my tune, back down on my convictions.... If that's what it takes to win the Iowa caucuses, I won't do it."

Gore hoped that his speech damning the Iowa caucuses would be seen as a courageous stand to take and would boost his standing in other states. He knew he wasn't going to do well in Iowa anyway — it was Gephardt territory — but he thought his biting remarks, made at the popular Jefferson-Jackson Day dinner, might bring him some national attention.

But by the time he delivered his speech, full of "righteous indignation," as one observer called it, it was after 11 p.m., he was the last of six candidates to speak, and many of those in attendance had already started heading for home. Of those who remained, hardly anyone was listening.[10]

With Hart, Biden and Gore gone (although Gore was never much of a factor), Gephardt, the young congressman from neighboring Missouri, took on a new role. "We went from insurgent to front runner," he said.[11]

On the Republican side, Vice President Bush had a little more trouble than he might have anticipated on the campaign trail. Bush, a realist

Congressman Richard Gephardt of Missouri was the leading Democrat in the 1988 caucuses and was one of the favorites in the caucuses of 2004 but finished fourth and dropped out of the race (courtesy Andrew Hampton).

whose presidential ambitions were formed almost a decade earlier, had hitched his wagon to the political express of Ronald Reagan. In 1979 and 1980, while campaigning against Reagan, he had mocked Reagan's economic proposals, calling them "voodoo economics." He then accepted Reagan's invitation to be his running mate and heartily and loyally endorsed the popular president's programs for the next eight years, eyeing a White House bid for himself.

But Reagan ran into some tough political times in his second term and his loyal vice president sometimes had difficulty standing quite as close to the president as he once did. The biggest controversy in Reagan's second term was the discovery that he had approved a deal in which the U.S. supplied arms to Iran in exchange for U.S. hostages — a deal Reagan had said repeatedly he would never make. Bush had to either defend the president or plead ignorance — that he did not know what was going on. To admit that would be to admit he wasn't in the inner circle, not a good position for a vice president touting his experience to be in.

The issue came to a head on January 25, 1988, on the *CBS Evening News* in which Dan Rather, the anchorman, had a live interview with Vice President Bush. Bush had been told that CBS was doing profiles on the candidates and that this would be one of them. But Bush had been warned by his aides to watch out for an ambush, that Rather would grill him on "what did you know and when did you know it?" with respect to the arms for hostages deal.

They were right. Rather hit Bush with one question after another on the arms deal until Bush snapped, "I don't think it's fair to judge a whole career, it's not fair to judge my whole career by a rehash on Iran." He asked Rather, "How would you like it if I judged your career by those seven minutes when you walked off the set in New York?" He was referring to an incident four months earlier when Rather left the set of the *CBS Evening News* because he was upset that a tennis match ran so long that the newscast would be late getting on the air. While Rather vented off camera, there was seven minutes of dead air time — a cardinal sin for any broadcaster.

Roger Ailes, the Republican insider who eight years earlier had worried about Ronald Reagan's lack of "a range of emotions" when he was under fire, was working for Bush now and had briefed him on the Rather walkout. Perhaps recalling how Reagan's calm spirit hurt him in Iowa, Ailes told Bush to use Rather's walkout against him if the interview got too rough.

Rather appeared to be stunned by the vice president's candor. He asked a couple of more questions, then cut the interview off abruptly. Bush, thinking his microphone was off, said, "The bastard didn't lay a hand on me." Then, comparing Rather to a female correspondent at CBS, he added, "That guy makes Lesley Stahl look like a pussy." Another Bush aide hurriedly unhooked his microphone and explained later that Bush meant a "pussycat."

The public reaction to the Rather-Bush exchange was favorable to Bush for two main reasons. One was that the public did not hold the media in high esteem and thought Rather was disrespectful to the vice president. The second reason was more important to Bush and his people: he had acted tough, like a leader should, and not wimpy, which is how many people looked on him as vice president because he was such a yes man for Reagan.[12]

Kemp ran as a Reaganite, the man most qualified to carry the conservative torch being handed off by the president, more qualified in fact than Reagan's own vice president. His problem was that Reagan wasn't as popular in Iowa as he was in other parts of the country. The state was in the midst of an agriculture crisis in which banks were foreclosing on farms and, in some cases, banks were closing down because of bad agriculture loans. A bad economy is never good for a sitting president so in 1987, the Reagan legacy wasn't doing Bush or Kemp any favors in Iowa.

Dole, however, could speak the language of farmers and came from Kansas, not as agricultural as Iowa but certainly more of a farm state than New York or Texas. Dole had two other things going for him. He was from the Middle West — and he got the endorsement of Iowa's popular United States senator, Charles Grassley, an old farmer himself, who said of Dole, "He's one of us."

Just as the Democrats have their annual Jefferson-Jackson Day Dinner to fire up the troops, the Republicans had turned their Iowa Straw Poll in Ames into a major fund-raiser for the party.

First held in 1979, its setting is the Hilton Coliseum, the home of the Iowa State University Cyclone basketball team and the year-round venue for concerts and a wide variety of other crowd-gathering activities. But in late summer of every year prior to Iowa caucuses, whenever the Republican presidential nomination will be up for grabs the following year, the Straw Poll provides a unique, non-binding way of sorting out the candidates.

It has been described aptly as part carnival, part convention in which

Senator Robert Dole ponders a question from an interested citizen after a
speech at Handicap Village, a complex benefiting special needs individuals,
in Clear Lake on January 14, 1988. Dole was the leading Republican in the
caucuses of both 1980 and 1988 (courtesy *Mason City Globe Gazette*).

Republicans from across the state buy a ticket to come to Ames to eat,
drink, be merry — and of course vote for the candidate of their choice after
listening to the politicians preach and pander to them.

The results of the Straw Poll have no official standing but they provide those who do well with great national publicity — with not-so-good
publicity for those who fare poorly. The big winner each time is the Iowa
Republican Party which uses the proceeds to help fund state and local
GOP candidates.

In 1987, Republicans dubbed the Straw Poll as the "Cavalcade of
Stars." Candidates realized in order to do well, they needed to get their
supporters to Ames, much like they would need to get their people to the
caucuses six months later and to the polls on election day. The easy answer
was to purchase thousands of tickets and give them away to anyone willing to come to Ames to support them.

To make that an easier decision, they also arranged free transportation. Busloads of supporters for many of the candidates converged on

Ames from all over the state, armed with a free ticket which, in effect, was a vote for the candidate of their choice. The price was right.

Each of the participating candidates had tents set up outside the coliseum to help promote them. To sweeten the deal even more, some candidates hired well-known professional entertainers and athletes to make an appearance on their behalf.

It turned out to be the setting for the political surprise of the year. "It was readily apparent to those entering Hilton Coliseum for the evening program that Pat Robertson's 'invisible army' had taken form. The center of the hall was packed with Robertson supporters dressed in white campaign T-shirts and hats and sitting in a sea of Robertson balloons and campaign signs."[13]

After hearing speeches from Robertson, Bush, Dole, Kemp, du Pont and Heslop, the 5,700 in attendance, all of whom paid $25 to the Iowa Republican Party (or the candidate of their choice picked up the tab), participated in the Straw Poll. The results were:

Robertson	1,293
Dole	958
Bush	864
Kemp	520
du Pont	160
Heslop	13
Haig	12
Fernandez	8
Others	15
Total	*3,843*

The poll, non-binding as it was, nonetheless, had big political ramifications. More than 200 news media representatives were on hand and they sent out a message that Bush, who had the treacherous front-runner label on him, had been thumped, that Dole had been upended and that Robertson "shocked" his rivals, according to the *Washington Post*.[14]

The 1988 pre-caucus season provided another benchmark in Iowa presidential politics. While candidates continued the Jimmy Carter style of door-to-door, backyard barbecue, grassroots politics, they also started to pour money into radio and television advertising. Gephardt ran what even his opponents, including Dukakis' campaign manager, Susan Estrich, considered the most effective television commercial. It featured a Hyundai automobile, manufactured in Korea. Gephardt, a free trade advocate, asserted that if a Chrysler K-car were sold in Korea, the taxes and tariffs would increase the price to $48,000 and questioned how many Hyundais would be sold in the United States if the same tariffs were applied.[15]

The campaign advertising added to the economic bonanza that presidential politics had created in Iowa. By the time the caucuses rolled around, estimated campaign spending was about $8 million in just short of a year's time. Among Republicans, Dole, Bush, Kemp and du Pont had each spent more than $600,000. Dole's total was $793,228, according to Federal Election Commission reports. By contrast, the Robertson campaign spent $78,165. Three Democrats — Dukakis, Gephardt and Simon — each spent more than $750,000 with Simon topping the list at $791,257.

Retail, face-to-face, meet-and-greet politics was still a dominant force. In the year prior to the caucuses, Gephardt spent 148 days in Iowa — close to every other day. Babbitt was in the state 118 days and Simon 91. Among Republicans, du Pont was in the state on 92 days, Kemp 79, Dole 68 and Bush 43.

Unofficial estimates show the total for all candidates was 999 days from January 20, 1987, to February 8, 1988, according to data collected by caucus historian Hugh Winebrenner. That meant there was an average of about three candidates per day in Iowa every day for about a year.

The national news media, buoyed by past experience, now considered the Iowa caucus season as a major news event. CNN and C-SPAN set up bureaus in Des Moines several months before the February 8 caucuses and CBS, NBC and ABC followed suit. By the night of the caucuses, some estimates had 3,000 newspaper, magazine, radio and television reporters and their crews in the state.

The results of the Democratic caucuses:

Gephardt	31.3%
Simon	26.7%
Dukakis	22.2%
Jackson	8.8%
Babbitt	6.1%
Uncommitted	4.5%
Hart	0.3%
Others	0.1%
Gore	0.0%

The Iowa Democratic Party reported that 125,000 Democrats took part, less than 25 percent of registered Democratic voters in Iowa. While

Gephardt, benefiting from the early meltdowns of Senators Hart, Biden and Gore, had achieved what appeared to be a clear victory, he suffered from the front-runner label that the press had put on him. So he did what he was expected to do — and that is not an exciting news event.

The news was in how well Simon and Dukakis had done in finishing second and third. The *New York Times* reported the next day that there had been no breakthrough and that no one emerged as the front-runner — and that was, in effect, a demotion for Gephardt.[16]

The Republican results:

Dole	40,661	37.4%
Robertson	26 761	24.6%
Bush	20,194	18.6%
Kemp	12,088	11.1%
du Pont	7,999	7.3%
No preference	739	0.7%
Haig	364	0.3%
Totals	*108,806*	*100%*

Dole met expectations. Bush's showing was described as "feeble" by the *New York Times* and "humiliating" by the *Los Angeles Times*. R.W. "Johnny" Apple, writing in the *New York Times*, reported that Bush had been disarmed, losing "his finest piece of political armor — the idea that he was Ronald Reagan's logical and legitimate, if unannointed successor."[17]

Robertson, the television evangelist with no previous political experience, clearly stole the limelight from the others by coming in second and finishing ahead of the vice president with a campaign championed by the religious right and a distaste for Bush, the man they helped elevate to stardom in Iowa eight years earlier.

Robertson's popularity with Iowa caucusgoers was noteworthy also because the national press following his campaign generally regarded him as good copy more than as a good candidate. He had a tendency in the heat of the moment to exaggerate the seriousness of a situation or make outlandish claims that he could not back up. For example, on occasion, he promised to fire 100,000 federal employees who had been hired by the president (for which there was no basis in fact). Another time, he implied that the Bush administration had leaked details about a sex scandal involving Jimmy Swaggart, another TV evangelist, in order to smear all TV evangelists. Still another time, he stated that Russia had missiles in Cuba, which was not true. Asked about these departures from the truth, Robertson said, "My mistakes went up geometrically in relation to my jet lag and fatigue."[18]

Nonetheless, he managed to get more support than the incumbent vice president of his own party. Bush now faced an uphill climb similar to what Reagan had to do after faltering in Iowa.

The 1988 caucuses showed that Gephardt, from Missouri, and Dole, from Kansas, both benefited by portraying themselves as good neighbors ("one of us," as Senator Grassley had referred to Dole).

It also showed that finishing in the top tier of candidates was a boost for Dukakis and Simon while being an also-ran was the exit sign for Haig, who withdrew four days after the caucuses; and for Babbitt and du Pont, who each withdrew nine days after the caucuses (and after poor showings in the New Hampshire primary) and for Kemp not long after that.

Gephardt got the win he had to have in Iowa if his candidacy was to have any chance of taking off. But he didn't get the bounce in the press that was usually accorded to a candidate who actually lived up to expectation in Iowa. He was the unfortunate victim of an unprecedented circumstance — being overshadowed by a loser in the other party's caucus.

Veteran political junkie Terry McAuliffe worked on the Gephardt campaign. (In years to come, he would be the party's national chairman and later yet, a co-chair for Hillary Clinton's campaign.) Summing up Gephardt's fate after winning the Iowa caucuses, McAuliffe said, "Sure enough, Dick won. But in a stroke of bad luck, the news coverage was all about the Republicans since Vice President George Bush had shocked everyone by coming in third place behind Bob Dole and Pat Robertson."[19]

Like Reagan had done eight years earlier, Bush regrouped and went on to win the Republican nomination. Gephardt couldn't muster much support in the east, where Dukakis had a stronghold, and the Massachusetts governor, despite a penchant for gaffes, secured the Democratic nomination.

It marked the first time since the reforms of 1972 that third-place finishers in the Iowa caucuses for both the Republicans and the Democrats eventually were their parties' nominees.

When it was all over with in Iowa, Michael Deupree, a columnist for the *Cedar Rapids Gazette*, looked back on the two years of campaigning with what might be described as sarcastic nostalgia.

He noted that Iowans would no longer hear Dukakis talk to them about the "Massachusetts Miracle" or Bruce Babbitt talk about how honest he was or Bob Dole talk about how Midwestern he was. They would no longer have to listen to Vice President Bush tell all the reasons why he couldn't tell anything or Pat Robertson talk about why he wouldn't inject religion into the campaign even though, by just bringing the subject up, he already had.

Furthermore, Iowans would no longer have to listen to Gary Hart talk about the importance of character (as long as no one questioned him about his) and Paul Simon talk about how much he cares and Al Gore rant that he no longer cares, at least in Iowa.[20]

Another long campaign season had ended.

CHAPTER EIGHT

1992

"Bob Kerrey and I ... were both steamed."

The 1992 Iowa caucuses, and the political scramble prior to them, lacked the pizzazz of previous years for two reasons. President George Bush, who defeated Michael Dukakis in the 1988 presidential election, enjoyed enormous popularity in 1991 when he exercised his powers as commander in chief and ordered American troops to the Persian Gulf after Iraq had invaded Kuwait.

In a matter of days, U.S. forces had overpowered those of Iraqi dictator Saddam Hussein, and Bush was basking in the glow of military victory. As the incumbent president, he was not likely to face serious opposition from within his own party anyway, but the military success pretty well assured there would be no need for Iowans to caucus for a presidential preference on February 12, 1992. They already had their man.[1]

On the Democratic side, Senator Tom Harkin of Iowa decided to run as a "favorite son" candidate in Iowa. Harkin, 52, was a graduate of Iowa State University and served as a Navy jet pilot on active duty from 1962 to 1967 and flew in the Naval Reserves after that.

In 1969, he went to Washington as an aide to Senator Neal Smith. While in Washington, he earned a degree from the American University School of Law. In 1972, Harkin ran for Congress and lost to the incumbent Republican Bill Scherle. He ran again in 1974 and won and was re-elected four times. In 1984, Harkin won a Senate race against the Republican incumbent, Roger Jepsen. He was re-elected in 1990.

Harkin's major accomplishment in the Senate was authoring and securing the passage of the Americans With Disabilities Act, which required that buildings provide access to persons with disabilities and that employers provide equal opportunities for jobs and job advancement.

Harkin had an engaging personality and was outspoken on issues important to him, but he was not well known outside of his home state. He and his supporters were counting on a big win in Iowa to give him a boost in the New Hampshire primary eight days later.

One major impact of Harkin's candidacy was that it cooled the motivation of many other potential candidates to challenge him on his home turf.

Some did, however. Former senator Paul Tsongas, 51, of Massachusetts, was the first to announce his candidacy in what was to be a much shortened campaign season compared to other caucus years. Tsongas declared his candidacy on April 30, 1991, a little more than nine months before caucus night and five months before Harkin announced.

As a young man, Tsongas had been a Peace Corps volunteer, first in Ethiopia from 1962 to 1964 and then in the West Indies in 1967 and 1968. He was in local and state politics and was elected to the U.S. House in 1978 and served two terms. He was elected to the U.S. Senate in 1984 and served one term. Tsongas battled cancer for several years and underwent a bone marrow transplant. By 1991, he considered himself a cancer survivor.

"I have been referred to as a pro-business liberal," he said in a television interview. "I have always been referred to that way. That's what I am." But he said on social and environmental issues, he was a "realist" and that might separate him from other Democrats.[2]

The second Democrat in the field was Virginia governor L. Douglas Wilder, 60, the first elected black governor in American history. Wilder, the grandson of slaves, was elected to the Virginia State Senate in 1969, becoming the state's first African American legislator since Reconstruction. He was elected lieutenant governor in 1986 and governor in 1990. Wilder announced his candidacy on September 13. Harkin followed with his announcement two days later.

Senator Bob Kerrey, 48, of Nebraska, a decorated war veteran who lost a leg due to Vietnam War injuries, joined the presidential field on September 30. Kerrey was awarded the Congressional Medal of Honor for "conspicuous gallantry and intrepidity at the risk of his life" while serving as a member of the Navy SEAL special forces unit in Vietnam. He was elected Nebraska governor in 1983 and served one term. He was elected to the Senate in 1987.

A bachelor governor, his friendships included that of actress Debra Winger, who on occasion was his overnight guest in the governor's mansion. Kerrey's candor added a freshness to the political campaign because he frequently said things that, in the vernacular of the times, were considered politically incorrect.

In a debate with a conservative opponent in his Senate race, Kerrey was described as being someone who would follow the traditional Democratic values. When called on for a response, Kerrey said simply, "So what?"[3]

Three days after Kerrey's announcement, Governor Bill Clinton, 45, of Arkansas got in the race. Clinton, a graduate of Yale Law School and a Rhodes Scholar to Oxford, ran for Congress and lost in 1974. He was elected Arkansas attorney general in 1976 and won the governorship in 1978. He was defeated in his bid for re-election in 1982 but ran again in 1986 and won.

One of the nation's first glimpses of Clinton came during the 1988 Democratic National Convention when he placed Governor Michael Dukakis' name in nomination. Clinton's speech was so long that when he said, "in conclusion," the convention hall erupted in applause.

The potentially embarrassing moment landed him an appearance on *The Tonight Show with Johnny Carson* in which he poked fun at himself and drew even more national exposure. Clinton had a history of being able to turn potentially-damaging incidents to his advantage and the appearance with Carson was evidence of that. He transformed himself from a babbling speaker who didn't know when to shut up to a man who was able to laugh at himself after an embarrassing moment and move on.

But Clinton's political liability was, like Gary Hart before him, his reputation as a womanizer, a trait that would eventually haunt him and come close to derailing his campaign.

Former California governor Jerry Brown, 53, a political maverick, announced his candidacy on October 21. Brown, the son of another former California governor, Pat Brown, began his political career in 1970 when he was elected California's secretary of state. He was elected governor in 1974 and re-elected in 1978. In 1984, he ran for the U.S. Senate and was defeated by Pete Wilson.

He then went to India and worked with Mother Teresa in helping care for poor and needy people before returning to California. He became head of the state Democratic Party but resigned because he became disgusted with the big money aspects of state politics. In his presidential campaign, he refused to take donations of more than $100 and used an 800 number to do his fund-raising.[4]

Harkin's entry into the race on September 15 changed the complexion of the campaign in several respects. Nationally, there would not be the media interest that previous caucus seasons had enjoyed. Economically, the state of Iowa would not benefit, as it had in the past, from the hordes of political operatives and media personnel who stayed in motels, ate in restaurants, drank in bars, filled up at gas stations and added to the retail business climate throughout the state.

Politically, the state went dry as well. Kerrey and Clinton both said it would be pointless to campaign in Iowa so they focused their efforts on New Hampshire as their starting block. Tsongas, who had campaigned in Iowa for five months before Harkin announced his candidacy, closed his Iowa operations in December. All the candidates appeared at the annual Jefferson-Jackson Day dinner on November 23, but, unlike previous years, there was no hoopla, the event got scant media attention and there was no straw poll. Wilder withdrew from the race on January 8, 1992.

Even though Harkin had the Iowa caucus results sewed up, he was irritated by media coverage prior to the caucuses. In early January, before the caucuses, *Time* magazine featured Clinton as its cover story with a headline that said, "Bill Clinton: Is He For Real?"

Then, on January 26, the television program *60 Minutes* featured an interview with Clinton and his wife, Hillary, in which Clinton denied having a sexual relationship with Gennifer Flowers, an Arkansas woman who claimed in a tabloid that she and Clinton had been having an affair for 12 years. A nationwide audience watched as the Clintons admitted to having some rocky times in their marriage but they had survived them and they loved each other. Clinton had received free publicity on one of the nation's most-watched television shows and in the most widely read newsmagazine two weeks before the caucuses.

"Bob Kerrey and I, boy I tell you, we were both steamed," said Harkin. "And Kerrey and I both said, 'by God, they have rigged this game.'" Harkin said he had raised more money, was on the ballot in more states and had more pledged support than Clinton. And Kerrey, he said, had been a governor and a senator, had been a Medal of Honor winner and had raised more money than Clinton. Yet Clinton appeared to be the fair-haired boy with the media.[5]

The caucus results were predictable.

Harkin	76.5%
Uncommitted	11.9%
Tsongas	4.1%
Clinton	2.8%
Kerrey	2.5%
Brown	1.6%
Others	0.6%
Total	*100%*

Harkin's overwhelming support in Iowa met the expectations of the media which meant it was no big deal. It had become well established in the Iowa caucuses over the years that big news occurred when a candidate exceeded expectations, such as George McGovern in 1972, George Bush in 1980 and Pat Robertson in 1988 or failed to meet them such as Ted Kennedy or Ronald Reagan in 1980 or Bush in 1988. Harkin's expected victory hardly made a ripple in the national press.

Clinton went on to win the Democratic nomination and the presidency and thus is the only Democratic candidate since the reforms of 1972 to finish below third place in the Iowa caucuses and go on to become president.

The Republican caucuses were also low key because of Bush's uncontested candidacy in Iowa. For the same reason, there was no Straw Poll in Ames. There was a fear among political leaders in the state that the lack of drama and excitement might carry over and have an impact on future caucuses — or threaten Iowa's status as being the first-in-the nation testing ground for presidential candidates which had proven to be such an economic boon to the state for 20 years. Their fears proved to be unfounded when, within weeks of the 1992 presidential election, hopefuls for 1996 began making journeys into the state.

CHAPTER NINE

1996

"There are four ingredients to running for president: Money, message, Iowa and New Hampshire."[1]

On April, 14, 1993, less than three months after Bill Clinton was inaugurated as the nation's 40th president, Phil Gramm, a conservative Democrat-turned-Republican senator from Texas, made his first visit to Iowa in his quest to defeat Clinton in 1996. Three days later, Senator Robert Dole of Kansas arrived. Two weeks later, Lamar Alexander, former governor of Tennessee and Bush's secretary of education, paid a visit.

They wouldn't officially announce their candidacies until much later because an unofficial protocol had developed over the years. A candidate would come into the state, talk to potential supporters and, more importantly, potential organizers. The candidate might take the opportunity to speak to the Cedar Rapids Kiwanis Club or the Dubuque Rotary Club because appearances like that were sure to get at least local press coverage.

If the candidate thought there was enough interest, he would form an exploratory committee — meaning he was thinking about running for president. That was newsworthy on a national level. As visits to various Iowa communities increased, so did the local, and now, national press coverage. Then the word would go out to the media that the candidate was going to announce his candidacy. More press coverage. Then, finally, the announcement would come, usually back in the candidate's hometown, in the gym of his or her old high school or in front of the drugstore where he got his first job — anywhere that would give the hometown roots atmosphere — or at the state capitol building where he cut his political teeth. Everything, including the site of the announcement, was carefully orchestrated for maximum attention.

The formal announcement would come in the morning, giving the candidate time to fly to Iowa and perhaps to New Hampshire to make similar announcements on the same day. Examples of the time sequence: Gramm's first visit to Iowa was on April 14, 1993; he announced his candidacy on February 24, 1995. Dole's first visit was on April 17, 1993; he opened his campaign office in Des Moines on May 1, 1994. Alexander's first visit was May 8, 1993; he announced his candidacy on February 28, 1995.

Gramm, Dole and Alexander were the earliest but they soon had company. Pat Buchanan, the former Nixon speechwriter and now a television commentator, who made a run against Bush in 1992, visited the state on June 24, 1994 and entered the race on March 20, 1995. Senator Arlen Specter, a liberal senator from Pennsylvania first visited on April 2, 1994, and announced his candidacy on March 30, 1995.

Others who eventually joined the fray were Indiana senator Richard Lugar, who took the unusual step of hiring a public relations firm to run his campaign; Maurice "Morry" Taylor, an Illinois multi-millionaire businessman who believed the country should be run like a business; Alan Keyes, an African American conservative radio commentator; Robert Dornan, a conservative congressman from California; Governor Pete Wilson of California; and Malcolm "Steve" Forbes, Jr., a millionaire magazine publisher.

Whatever else could and would be said about the 1996 Iowa caucuses, one thing was clear. The relative blandness of the 1992 caucuses had not carried over to 1996. The legacy of Jimmy Carter was alive and well in the nooks and crannies and hamlets all across Iowa where men who wanted to be president stood on street corners or at factory entrances or on the edge of cornfields to shake hands and offer a simple message: "I'm Phil Gramm (or Bob Dole or Lamar Alexander or whoever), and I'm running for president." The basics hadn't changed in 24 years.

Dole, now 72, was well known in Iowa for his work in the Senate and from his campaigning in previous caucuses. His political resume was enhanced in 1994 when, as a result of midterm elections, he was elevated to the rank of Senate majority leader. He still had a sharp tongue and a quick wit and was remembered also as a World War II veteran who suffered permanent war injuries. Dole again hoped to capitalize on his appreciation of the problems of Iowans because he was from a neighboring state, Kansas.

Alexander, 55, had ties to Washington dating back to 1967 but he portrayed himself as a Washington outsider, often showing up at campaign events wearing a red and black checkered flannel shirt (as if to say "I'm one of you") and would sit down and play "God Bless America" on the piano if one was nearby. As a young lawyer, he became a legislative assistant to Senator Howard Baker in 1967, then ran for governor of Tennessee in 1974 and lost. Four years later, wearing the checkerboard flannel shirt, he walked across the state, shaking hands, chatting with voters and generating a lot of publicity for himself. He won. He served two terms as governor and then became president of the University of Tennessee in 1988. In 1991 he returned to Washington when President Bush picked him as his secretary of education. The theme of his campaign, and a not-too-subtle swipe at Dole, Lugar, Gramm and Specter, was embodied in a 1996 stump speech when he said, "I don't know why you'd send a senator down the street to balance the budget when they've run up a $5 trillion debt in Washington, D.C."[2]

Gramm, 53, was a native of Georgia and had earned a doctorate degree from the University of Georgia before traveling to Texas where he was a professor of economics for 12 years at Texas A&M University. He was elected to the U.S. House as a Democrat and served three terms. On January 5, 1983, he resigned from the House and announced that he was switching to the Republican Party. He then ran as a Republican for the House seat he had vacated and won a special election on February 12, 1983. He was elected to the Senate in 1984 and re-elected in 1990.

Gramm's campaigns were financed by wealthy Texans such as oilman T. Boone Pickens, but on the campaign trail, Gramm always portrayed himself as looking out for the common man. One of his trademark themes was a reference to Dickie Flatts, a printer in the small Texas town of Mexia. Gramm told his audiences that before he voted on any spending bill, he would ask himself how it was going to affect his friend, Dickie Flatts, back in Texas.[3]

Buchanan, 56, believed his run for the nomination in 1992 had given him traction to make another run, even though he had entered the race four years ago after the Iowa caucuses. Buchanan was an outspoken conservative who had been co-host of the popular television program *Crossfire*, in which liberals and conservatives argued with one another on camera. The program gave Buchanan a platform and, more important, a national audience. Name recognition, particularly in Republican circles, was not a problem.

Lugar, 63, a Rhodes Scholar after graduating from Denison University, Granville, Ohio, was elected to the Indianapolis School Board in

1963. He was elected mayor of Indianapolis in 1967 and 1971. His U.S. Senate career began in 1976 and, with the Republican majority taking over in 1974, Lugar became chairman of the Senate Foreign Relations Committee. His areas of expertise were in foreign relations and in scientific research. His knowledge and intellect on these subjects gained him bipartisan respect on Capitol Hill but were ones in which most Iowans had no particular passion.

Keyes, the African American radio commentator, at one time worked as an aide at the United Nations. He was a dynamic speaker whose talks resembled sermons. He stressed the importance of family values and was critical of what he considered the hypocrisy of welfare reform that many Republicans advocated. Keyes contended that if all single- parent mothers went to work, some children would be left with no parents at home with them. He also did not hesitate to take eloquent verbal shots at the Clinton administration. A staple in his campaign speeches was, "Our politics has become a competition to see who can be the biggest liar and we only need to look at the White House to see who won."

Specter, Dornan, Wilson and Taylor were minor players. Specter, 65, was one of the Senate's most liberal Republicans who had been an assistant district attorney in Philadelphia, an assistant attorney general in Pennsylvania and who had served as a counsel on the Warren Commission that investigated the assassination of President John F. Kennedy. He had been in the Senate since 1980.

Dornan, also 65, was a former actor and was a flamboyant member of the U.S. House who was vocal about being pro-life and anti-gay. He used his brief presidential bid as a platform to criticize President Clinton. In a forum in Des Moines on January 13, 1996, Dornan called Clinton a "criminal and pathological liar."

Wilson, also 65, was a former mayor of San Diego and former U.S. senator. Illness forced him to curtail his campaign before it had a chance to attract much attention. He had throat surgery shortly after he announced his candidacy which made it difficult for him to talk. He withdrew from the race about a month after he entered it.

Taylor, chairman and chief executive officer of Titan International, a wheel and tire manufacturer, spent millions of his own money, espousing a pro-business, small government philosophy. He was active on the campaign trail in Iowa but his candidacy was seen in the eyes of the press and the voters as a millionaire's ego trip. He finished poorly in the Iowa caucuses and dropped out a month later.

Forbes, 48, was a multi-millionaire publisher of *Forbes* magazine, and his candidacy was, from the beginning, much more than an ego trip. Forbes was the last Republican to announce his candidacy, on September 22, 1995, and offered serious competition to the others because of his populist views on topics such as the federal income tax system which he thought should be radically simplified. Forbes added a new dimension to Iowa caucus politics — unlimited personal funds to flood the airwaves with advertising — yet he also participated actively and enthusiastically in grassroots, retail, "nice to meet you" politics.

Forbes was a forceful speaker who struck a responsive chord with voters with his unabashed criticism of the Internal Revenue Service and his call for a flat tax in which rich and poor alike would pay the same 17 percent tax — and a tax return could be done on a postcard. Forbes had a trademark line in his speeches that would light up a crowd. Speaking of the tax code, he would say, "You can't tame this beast. The only thing you can do is kill it, drive a stake through its heart."[4]

A fairly new development in the Iowa caucus cycle was the creation of events throughout the state in which several candidates would show up to meet and greet and speak. They did not replace the one-on-one living room chats and backyard picnics that were the throwback to the Carter years. But they had two advantages — they gave exposure to lesser known candidates, a Morry Taylor, for example, because prospective voters who might attend to see a Bob Dole or a Steve Forbes would get a chance to see Taylor as well. And for the candidates, it gave them a chance to speak to undecideds or those who hadn't given much thought to a caucus that was two years away. From the standpoint of the Iowa Republican Party, these events were a way to raise money to support their candidates, a lesson Democrats had learned long ago.

For all of these reasons, the Iowa GOP held what it called a Star Spangled Preview on June 24, 1994, nearly a year and a half before the caucuses and eight months before anyone had officially announced his candidacy. C-SPAN provided live television coverage to the program in which Iowa governor Terry Branstad, the master of ceremonies, introduced seven speakers — Alexander, Buchanan, Gramm, Specter, Dick Cheney (President Ford's old chief of staff), Pennsylvania governor Thomas Kean, and Lynn Martin, a Republican stalwart who had been President Bush's secretary of labor.

It was a long evening that included about 90 minutes of speeches and, even at this early stage, a straw poll. The results were:

Dole	356	Howard Baker	8
Alexander	205	Robert Dornan	6
Gramm	200	Arlen Specter	6
Kemp	156	John Engler	5
Cheney	130	Newt Gingrich	5
Quayle	81	Tommy Thompson	3
Buchanan	69	Thomas Kean	2
William Bennett	59	Christine Whitman	2
Lynn Martin	20	Pete du Pont	1
Colin Powell	19	Pete Wilson	1
James Baker	9	None of the above	8

The poll did not contain any surprises or revelations. Dole, Alexander and Gramm had been the earliest candidates to visit the state and had conducted Carter-style campaigns — particularly Gramm and Alexander, who did not have the name recognition that Dole enjoyed. In the months ahead, Alexander tried to counter that by investing in television advertising to help get his name in front of voters. Bruce Babbitt had tried that in 1988 and considered it a waste of money because Iowans as a whole didn't pay that much attention to presidential politics that far ahead of a general election. (Forbes was not a factor because at this early stage he had never indicated he was interested in running. When he did enter, his advertising blitz came much closer to the caucus date.)

The Iowa Republican Party continued to stage events to showcase the candidates but, more importantly, to raise money for the party. All events were an exhibition season leading up to what had now become known as the Iowa Straw Poll in Ames or Caucus Kickoff '96, as it was being called this year. The 1987 Cavalcade of Stars straw poll had elevated evangelist Pat Robertson's standing among the candidates. Alexander, Buchanan and Gramm all hoped for similar fortune in 1995, acknowledging that Dole was the front-runner.

The event was held August 19 with 10 candidates on hand to greet supporters and to give speeches; each was given 12 minutes to make his case. Candidates in attendance were Alexander, Buchanan, Dole, Dornan, Gramm, Keyes, Lugar, Specter, Taylor and Wilson.

As in 1987, a carnival atmosphere prevailed with candidates each having tents outside the Hilton Coliseum where supporters gathered and partied. Once again, busloads of political groupies poured into Ames, each holding a $25 ticket, in many cases paid for by a candidate. There was a new wrinkle this year. Out-of-state residents were allowed to take part in the festivities, including voting in the Straw Poll. To many observers, this tainted the outcome of the Iowa Straw Poll, but state party officials didn't mind. It was money in their coffers and they didn't care where it came from.[5]

The speeches were predictable. Dole stressed his experience, his expertise in Washington and his ability to get things done in a bipartisan way. Keyes provided fiery oratory on the decline of the American family and of the moral decay of the country. Dornan took potshots at the Clinton administration. Specter tried to promote his liberal agenda, including his pro-choice views, and was met with a chorus of boos. Gramm and Buchanan made passionate appeals to the conservatives in the crowd.

Though, as always, the Straw Poll results were non-binding, they did carry some significance in terms of momentum for the candidates and national exposure — both good and bad — that they wouldn't have gotten otherwise. This year, county election officials donated 50 voting machines to upgrade the process.

By the time all the speeches were done and the voting was completed, more than four hours had elapsed. Some of the crowd, who had traveled a long way, were heading out to their cars and buses to head home. Iowa Republican Party chairman Brian Kennedy announced what turned out to be remarkable results. Out of nearly 11,000 votes cast, Dole and Gramm were deadlocked at the top. Each had received 2,582 votes. The complete results:

Dole	2,582	24.4%
Gramm	2,582	24.4%
Buchanan	1,922	18.1%
Alexander	1,156	10.9%
Keyes	804	7.6%
Taylor	803	7.6%
Lugar	466	4.4%
Wilson	129	1.2%
Dornan	87	0.8%
Specter	67	0.6%
Total	*10,958*	*100%*

Dole's inability to dominate and Gramm's strong showing were the headlines the next day because one candidate failed to meet expectations while another one exceeded them.

Two developments occurred between the August 19, 1995, Straw Poll and the February 12, 1996, caucuses that changed the campaigns. One was speculation that Colin Powell, an immensely popular black Army general, might enter the race. He had just authored a best-selling autobiography and embarked on a well-publicized book tour that kept his name in front of the public for months. Powell ended the speculation by announcing on November 8 that he would not be a candidate.

The other development had a more lasting impact. That occurred on September 22, 1995, a month after the Iowa Straw Poll, when publisher Forbes, with his multi-million- dollar personal fortune and his pledge to drive a stake through the heart of the Internal Revenue Service, entered the race.

Forbes, described by one reporter as someone who probably had cuff links on his pajamas, took part in the retail politics that was so much a part of the Iowa game plan — but he had a lot of catching up to do — and he did it through television advertising to an extent that had never been seen before in pre-caucus campaigning.

Other candidates challenged Forbes with television and radio advertising of their own. In addition, the so-called ground war escalated. Between January 1 and February 12 (caucus night), nine candidates (Wilson and Specter had dropped out) spent 141 days in Iowa with Dole and Forbes leading the pack with 14 days each.

The media war also escalated. Forbes spent $440,000 on television advertising with two major Iowa television stations, paying for all of it out of his own pocket. The Dole campaign spent about $265,000, Alexander $240,000 and Lugar about $213,000. Major questions for the media and the public, going into caucus night, included: Could the caucuses be bought? Was the Carter-style retail politics a thing of the past?[6]

Yet another new development had emerged this year. Louisiana Republicans had decided to hold their primary caucuses on February 6, six days ahead of the Iowa caucuses and two weeks ahead of the New Hampshire primary. Most presidential candidates, wary of upsetting Iowa Republicans who were proud of their "we're first" tradition, signed pledges not to participate in the Louisiana caucuses.

Gramm, Buchanan and Keyes declined to sign the pledge, hoping a strong showing in Louisiana would give them a head start on the others. In fact, Gramm, from neighboring Texas, expected to win all 21 delegates and said so publicly. But the results were that Buchanan won 13, Gramm captured eight and Keyes had none. A disappointed Gramm again set his expectations high, saying he would now have to finish at least third in Iowa. It did not happen.

The results from caucus night were:

Dole	25,378	26.3%
Buchanan	22,512	23.3%
Alexander	17,003	17.6%
Forbes	9,816	10.2%
Gramm	9,001	9.3%
Keyes	7,179	7.4%
Lugar	3,576	3.7%
Taylor	1,380	1.4%
No preference	428	0.0%
Dornan	131	0.0%
Others	47	0.0%
Totals	*96,451*	*100%*

In the expectations race, Dole won but did not meet expectations; eight years earlier, he had won with 37 percent of the vote. Buchanan and Alexander had exceeded expectations and had earned the unofficial right to move on to New Hampshire. Since the reforms of 1972, no Republican finishing below third in Iowa had ever secured the nomination. Dole, Buchanan and Alexander had earned the three tickets out of Iowa.

Forbes' fourth place finish was disappointing to him, but he had entered the fray late and had done better than some who been campaigning longer than he had. Forbes was a man with money and a mission and was committed to continuing the fight.

Dole claimed victory and aimed his election night comments at Forbes, saying, "We withstood a barrage of millions and millions of dollars and still came out on top." The big loser was Gramm, who first arrived in Iowa on April 14, 1993, and who devoted nearly three years to a campaign that more than 90 percent of Iowa caucusgoers had rejected. His fifth place standing, coupled with his public predictions prior to the Louisiana and Iowa caucuses put his candidacy on life support. He dropped out of the race on February 14, two days after the caucuses.

"When you run fifth in Iowa, an important state, you would have to be brain-dead not to take a look at where you are and what you're doing," he said.[7]

An elated Buchanan boarded a plane and told the people of New Hampshire to keep a light on for him. As for Iowa, he said, "We did well with religious conservatives. I'm a religious conservative too, and we're nice people."[8]

Lugar, commenting on the campaign experience years later, had two reflections on his experiences in Iowa. He said he knew now that anyone running for president had to make it almost a fulltime effort. When he ran, he was a member of the Senate Agriculture Committee and was managing the farm bill through the Senate. It limited his time in Iowa to just weekends. "I thought managing the farm bill would be of importance to Iowans. As it turned out, it was just marginally important," he said.

The other reflection was his son David's observation about the rigors of retail politicking in Iowa. "He would complain that in three hours (of campaigning), he only saw about 20 people."[9]

Democrats held caucuses in 1996 to take care of routine party business but President Clinton was unchallenged. He campaigned in Iowa, however, and even flew in on Air Force One on the weekend prior to the caucuses and gave rousing speeches to big crowds in Mason City and Iowa City. His appearances had no impact on Democrats but took some of the media attention off Republicans as the major TV networks, all hunkered in Des Moines, had to scramble and dispatch crews to follow the president.

Dole went on to win the nomination and Jack Kemp became his running mate. President Clinton and Vice President Al Gore easily won re-election in November.

CHAPTER TEN

2000

"Every senator would like to run for president but most of them don't have the guts to do it."[1]

On November 1, 1996, five days before Americans re-elected Bill Clinton to a second term as president, Steve Forbes jetted from one small airport to another in Iowa. Asked if these were his first campaign appearances for the 2000 elections, Forbes smiled and said, "No, I'm here to support all Iowa Republican legislative candidates in the upcoming elections."

Such is the graciousness of out-of-state politicians with high ambitions. About a year and a half later, Lamar Alexander was spotted talking with people in a high school gym in rural Iowa. He too downplayed why a former governor and cabinet member would be spending a Saturday morning chatting with farmers 800 miles from his home in Tennessee. "I'm going around the state with Governor Branstad in support of Republican candidates," he said. It came as no surprise that a year later, both Forbes and Alexander were once again seeking the Republican presidential nomination — and Terry Branstad, Iowa's four-term governor, was Alexander's campaign manager in the state.

Retail politics had been the hallmark of presidential campaigning in Iowa ever since Jimmy Carter left his first handwritten note on the door of a prospective backer in 1975. It was still a force in the 2000 pre-caucus campaign cycle, but much had changed in 25 years. The caucus and primary season had been condensed with a majority of them being over by the end of February or early March. Candidates no longer had weeks between primary elections or caucuses to raise money to keep their campaigns alive. Instead of gearing up toward a California primary win in June, as McGovern had done in 1972, candidates now had to focus on Super

Tuesday three or four months earlier. That meant raising money early — and in order to do that, it was essential to win or to do well in Iowa.

As Senator Orrin Hatch of Utah, a late Republican entry into the 2000 campaign told a reporter, "I can win without the national media. I can't win without Iowa."[2]

Another factor that had changed since the Carter days was the increasing presence of the media, not only on caucus night, but throughout the pre-caucus cycle, and the growing influence of expensive, glitzy media advertising, another reason why fund-raising early was so important.

Candidates in the 2000 Iowa caucuses still did the same kinds of folksy, hands-on activities to attract voters that Carter and McGovern and George Bush did a generation earlier, the kinds of things that were sort of the "American Gothic" of Iowa politics. And there was still the need for each of them to reach the ultimate goal on caucus night which was not necessarily to win but to exceed expectations.

On the eve of the 2000 caucuses, Todd Dorman and Kathie O'Bradovich, writers for Lee Enterprises, which owns several daily newspapers in Iowa, put it this way: "During the past year, otherwise serious public people have posed with pigs, gobbled all things fried, grilled or frosted, fought tirelessly for a poll of straw and made their impassioned pleas before the likes of a big red tractor and a 33-foot stainless steel Jesus."[3]

Democrats and Republicans took strikingly different approaches in fielding candidates. For the Democrats, Al Gore, now 51, who made a brief run as a presidential candidate in 1988 and most recently served as Clinton's vice president for eight years, was primed to climb to the top rung on the ladder. His only opponent was Bill Bradley, a Princeton graduate, Rhodes scholar, former professional basketball player and three-term senator from New Jersey who chose not to run for a fourth term in 1996. Both candidates were entrenched Washington liberal politicians. Bradley had been out of the national limelight for a few years and therefore hoped to be considered more of a fresh face to the American people, and in particular to the people of Iowa, than Gore.

The challenge for Bradley was to identify the differences between him and Gore. He said, "Al Gore and I would be very different presidents. We approach leadership in very different ways. In order to go for the best, you sometimes have to take big political risks. It is the risk of leadership. Al is much more cautious."

Gore ran an aggressive campaign in Iowa. Rather than differentiating

Candidates' wives are often active on the Iowa campaign trail. Here, Tipper Gore, wife of Vice President Al Gore, chats with the author during a stop at the Country Kitchen restaurant in Mason City one week before the caucuses in January of 2000 (photograph from author's personal collection).

himself from Bradley, Gore found himself constantly having to distance himself from Clinton, whose sexual escapades and grand jury testimony about them eventually led to his impeachment. The vice president had to walk the political tightrope of defending the president's political record while assuring voters that he, Gore, should be judged on his own moral values.

Gore supporters were inventive in backing their candidate. In Mason City, a group of them, including a man dressed as a corn stalk, picketed outside the public library where Bradley was speaking because they opposed Bradley's agriculture proposals. "They don't bother me," Bradley told the press. "You should have seen what they used to wave at me when I was at the free throw line."[4]

One of the staples of presidential campaigns in Iowa is the obligatory stop at the local newspaper office for a visit with the paper's editorial board. This usually consists of a group of editors who meet regularly to determine topics for future editorials and what stand the newspaper will take on them. Many of them also endorse political candidates — hence the interest of presidential hopefuls in stopping by for a visit.

On one occasion, early in 2000, Gore met with the editorial board of the *Quad City Times* in Davenport, Iowa, a city on the Iowa-Illinois border, across the Mississippi River from Moline, East Moline and Rock Island, Illinois. Politicians like Gore enjoyed the opportunity to talk to one group of editors who would convey his message in two different states.

Sometimes, the editorial board meetings take strange twists that provide some quaintness and levity and serve to remind the candidates they aren't in the offices of the *Washington Post* or *New York Times*. Such was the situation in Davenport when Gore met not only with the newspaper editors but also with Bill Wondram, a crusty, veteran columnist who was not hung up on the usual issues of war and peace, the economy and foreign policy. Wondram later wrote about his encounter with the vice president:

> Not particularly interested in such things as relations with Russia and the problems of health care, I zeroed right in on Vice President Al Gore with relevant questions on everyone's mind.
>
> "You know," I said, "whenever I leave the house in the morning, my wife asks if I have money in my pocket. Do you carry any money in your pocket?"
>
> This was not your everyday type of question and the veep was a bit puzzled. But he broke into a Tennessee smile.
>
> Vice President Gore stood up before God and all the humanity of the *Quad City Times* editorial board. He reached into the pants of his dark blue suit and pulled out his pockets. Empty. Nothing in them. Not even a comb.
>
> Other newsroom types were champing to ask him about important things, like crime and saving the Rock Island Arsenal, but I wanted to know more about this fellow who wants to be the next president of the U.S.A.
>
> He is on the road all the time lately, a hectic pace, so I asked him, "Do you ever call home?"
>
> "Twice today," he answered with a smiling snap. "Tipper's recovering from minor surgery and is doing fine, thank goodness. I have four kids and talk to them daily too."
>
> They're all around the country at the moment but he tries to track them down. Fortunately, he says, some carry cell phones.
>
> "I called my mom, too, down in Tennessee. She's 87." He was going into detail about how Pauline came from a poor family and a Rotary Club loan helped her through college. I did not care to hear about his

mom's history and switched gears to ask him if he ever drives a car any-more.

"Not often, the Secret Service is around," he answered. "But some-times on my own, I go out."

"What kind of car do you drive?" I inquired.

That threw the veep for a moment until he recalled that it was a Mercury, and then one of the news people said it might be a Sable and he agreed and said it was five years old. He told of once having a Ply-mouth van. When he gets back to the Tennessee farm that he and Tipper own, he tools around in a GM pickup truck.

Those serious news people, figuring that their questions were going to change the axis of the universe, wanted to talk about tobacco and the FDA but I kept rambling folksy, about going to the movies.

Vice President Gore pointed a friendly finger at me and said, "I highly recommend 'Mansfield Park.'" He and Tipper like to get rental movies (do they pay for them?) but he admitted rentals can be a gamble. Both of us agreed that we liked "Deep Blue Sea." He laughed when I told him that at first I thought it was going to be a poor man's "Jaws."

"You know, I liked 'Matrix,'" he said in an almost apologetic tone.

We could have chatted all afternoon in small talk, light years distant from the problems of the world. No one else had a chance to get a word in, and at one point he said to me, which made others in the room a bit aghast: "This is the damndest interview I ever had."

Then we got down to important things, like how he has time to eat decently.

"I fly on Air Force Two. I get a lot of chicken, and you know how airplane food is. I think chicken survives better at 10,000 feet." He laughed, held his hands together in pilgrimage and added: "Oh, I really like Iowa pork — and corn."

Finally, I allowed the real reporters to ask questions. After a Secret Service agent came in and said to the real reporters, "Only one more question," the vice president of the United States came over to ask me what I had for lunch.

"Tuna fish and pretzels," I said.

"No mayonnaise?" he questioned.

He signed the legal pad in which I had written his choice quote: "This is the damndest interview I ever had." He signed it "Al Gore, Jan. 3, 1999." That is so — he wrote 1999. (The interview took place three days into 2000).

While the Democrats had an engaging two-man contest, the Repub-lican field was wide open. There were some familiar names — Buchanan, Forbes and Alexander had practically established residencies in Iowa and

Alan Keyes was also back for another run. But several new candidates had emerged, representing a wide spectrum of political philosophies.

Gary Bauer, 43, was a conservative who stressed Christian values. An underling in the education department in the Reagan administration, Bauer formed the Family Research Council, a conservative, religious-oriented think tank in 1987 and headed it for 12 years. He announced his candidacy for the presidency in April 1999. Like Keyes, he was never considered a serious contender, but his candidacy gave his anti-abortion platform a national stage for a few months.

Elizabeth Dole, 63, wife of Senator Bob Dole, the 1996 Republican nominee, had an impressive resume. A one-time Democrat who campaigned for John F. Kennedy in 1960, Dole had served in the Nixon administration as a deputy assistant for consumer affairs, then was a member of the Federal Trade Commission for eight years before joining the Reagan administration as a public liaison adviser. She served as Reagan's secretary of transportation and later as President Bush's secretary of labor. From 1991 to 1999, Dole was president of the American Red Cross.

Orrin Hatch, 65, was a Mormon, a songwriter and a senator for 24 years. He entered the race late, on July 1, 1999, at a time when Texas governor George W. Bush had reportedly already raised $36 million. Hatch said he thought of a way he could catch up. "If one million people can pay $36 — then what?"

Hatch was one of the most conservative members of the Senate and hoped his candidacy would cut into Buchanan's base and into whatever following Bauer had. The *Washington Post* captured Hatch's challenge with the headline, "For Hatch, Nowhere to Go But Up."[5]

John Kasich, 47, a congressman from Ohio, formed an exploratory committee while he considered a presidential bid, and did some campaigning in Iowa. Kasich was a state senator in Ohio when he ran for the U.S. House in 1982. He won and served eight terms before retiring in 1999. He suffered from a lack of name recognition in Iowa, compared to most of the other candidates, but he followed the established protocol of traveling through the state, shaking hands, and talking to whoever would listen.

His lack of recognition was never more obvious than on the day he spoke to a local Kiwanis club in northern Iowa. He brought with him Bob Feller, the Hall of Fame pitcher of the Cleveland Indians who was a native of VanMeter, Iowa. As the two men walked in to the room in the restaurant where the Kiwanians were eating their lunch, the club's piano player struck up a rousing rendition of "Take Me Out to the Ballgame" as the club members sang, cheered and paid little attention to Kasich. He dropped out of the race in July, about the same time Hatch got in.[6]

Another devout Christian who toyed with trying to get the Republican nomination was Senator Bob Smith, 58, of New Hampshire. At six feet, six inches tall, Smith towered over the other candidates in height but not in popular appeal. He espoused the views of the religious right wing

Former vice president Dan Quayle came to Iowa in 1999 to test his political strength for a run for the presidency. He fared poorly and dropped out quickly. Here he shakes hands with spectators at a parade in Clear Lake on July 4, 1999 (courtesy *Mason City Globe Gazette*).

of the party but had little traction in the already conservative Middle West and against such a formidable field of better known candidates. He announced his candidacy in January and, like Kasich, dropped out in July, six months before the caucuses and one month before the Iowa Straw Poll. Smith's candidacy prompted CNN commentator Bruce Morton to muse, "If Bob Smith gets taken seriously, everybody in New Hampshire is going to be mad at him. He'll take all the steam out of the primary there just like Harkin did in Iowa eight years ago."[7]

As early as September of 1997, eight months after President Clinton began his second term, Dan Quayle, vice president under President Bush, started thinking about the presidency. "I'm very serious about it," he told reporters at a Midwest Republican Leadership Conference in Indianapolis. "I'm doing many things in preparation for a possible run in 2000. And one of those things is spending a lot of time in Iowa."

Quayle, 52, had a meteoric rise in Indiana politics. He was elected to the U.S. House in 1976, at the age of 29. In 1980, he ran for the Senate and defeated three-term incumbent Birch Bayh and was re-elected by a wide margin in 1986. In 1988, George H.W. Bush selected the 41-year-old senator as his running mate. Quayle had a difficult time maintaining a positive public image. In an August 1988 debate between vice presidential candidates, Quayle compared himself to a young John F. Kennedy. Lloyd Bentsen, the Texas senator who was the Democratic vice presidential nominee, responded, "Senator, I served with Jack Kennedy. I knew Jack Kennedy. Jack Kennedy was a friend. Senator, you're no Jack Kennedy."

During his vice presidency, Quayle visited a New Jersey school and served as a judge at a spelling bee. He informed a student that he had incorrectly spelled the word potato when in fact the student had spelled it correctly. This flub was widely publicized and was the banter of late night comedians. Hoping all of that was behind him, Quayle formally announced his candidacy in April 1999.

Senator John McCain of Arizona was regarded by many as an American hero for his military service as a Navy pilot who was shot down, tortured and held as a prisoner of war in Hanoi, North Vietnam, for more than five years. The son of a Navy admiral, McCain, 63, was elected to the U.S. House in 1982 and served two terms. He was elected to the Senate in 1986 and was in his third term when he announced his candidacy for the presidency on September 27, 1999. He made the announcement in Nashua, New Hampshire, the first indication that he intended to ignore the Iowa caucuses and concentrate on early eastern and southern primaries.

While the assortment of Republican candidates glad-handed their way across Iowa, an effort was mounted to persuade yet another man to enter the race — Texas governor George W. Bush, the eldest son of former president George Bush. The younger Bush, 53, had been a Texas oilman who later became the owner of the Texas Rangers baseball team. In 1994, he ran for governor and defeated Ann Richards, the sharp-tongued Democratic incumbent who, in a keynote speech at the 1988 Democratic convention, described the senior George Bush as having been born "with a silver foot in his mouth." The younger Bush formally announced his candidacy in June and was immediately tabbed as the front-runner.

Early in his campaign, Bush was asked repeatedly about his reported drinking escapades in his younger days and rumors about drug use during that same time period. Prior to a speech in Clear Lake, Iowa, in April, in anticipation of questions about his past, he scribbled a few lines with a felt pen on the back of a card which had, on the flip side, the names of

Texas governor George W. Bush (hunching in foreground) is surrounded by security and media as he greets supporters after giving a speech in Clear Lake in May 1999 (photograph from author's personal collection).

Texas governor George W. Bush had to field many questions about reports of his heavy drinking in his younger days. Before giving a speech in Clear Lake, Iowa, in May 1999, he scrawled a note on a card as a reminder of what he would say if he was asked about it again. The note read, "Game of gotcha. Chase wild rumors or crazy insinuations" (photograph from author's personal collection).

local dignitaries he was to acknowledge at the start of his talk. In scrawling cursive, he wrote "game of gotcha ... chase wild rumors and crazy insinuations."

In a press conference after his speech, a reporter from Houston traveling with the campaign asked Bush about the reports that had surfaced about his past. Bush remembered his note, telling the newsman he wasn't going to get involved in the media's "game of gotcha" where they "chase wild rumors and crazy insinuations."[8]

Meanwhile, Forbes, who had the financial means to fly across the state in a private jet and dine on lobster or filet mignon at the finest restaurants, instead was whisked from one small town to another in a van driven by one of his aides.

He was professorial in looks and manner, with horn–rimmed glasses, well-pressed suit and well-polished vocabulary but those who worked with Forbes saw an entirely different individual than the man the public saw.

"For a man of his wealth and stature, he was the most unassuming man I've ever met," said Chuck Laudner of Rockford, Iowa, one of the people responsible for shuttling him around.

"He was a baseball fan and he liked to talk about baseball as we drove from one place to another. He liked the New York Yankees. While he was campaigning in Iowa, there was some change in management going on with the Iowa Cubs (the minor league team in Des Moines) and there was some talk of the possibility of the team being sold and possibly moving. That disturbed him. He did not want to see that happen.

"It's tough on the campaign trail," said Laudner. "Many times you'd arrive at an event after everyone had eaten. "He'd give his talk and then we'd be off to the next stop. Sometimes, while he was speaking, we'd sneak over to the salad bar or dessert table and stash away anything we could to take in the van with us so he would have something to eat." So the van was usually stocked with doughnuts and cheese and crackers — "not exactly junk food but pretty close," he said.

Laudner said Forbes never wanted to be a problem for the people working for him. "We'd ask him if he wanted to stop somewhere and get some 'real food' and he'd say anything we wanted to do was fine with him. Well, there was at least one time I remember that we went through a Burger King drive-through with Steve Forbes. He probably didn't do that too often," said Laudner.[9]

The gala Iowa Straw Poll, the fund-raising bonanza for the state

Millionaire magazine publisher Steve Forbes competed in the Iowa caucuses in 1996 and 2000 and delighted Republican crowds with his promise to abolish the Internal Revenue Service. Here he talks to supporters at a picnic in Nora Springs on August 5, 1999 (courtesy *Mason City Globe Gazette*).

Republican Party, was held in Ames on August 14. Party officials had made some changes from previous formats. The biggest change was that this year, only Iowans would be allowed to vote. There would be no busing in of supporters from other parts of the country.

But the carnival atmosphere that had prevailed in the past was not only allowed, it was encouraged. And candidates were spending big bucks to try to win over voters. The overwhelming majority of those who attended the Straw Poll had their $35 ticket already paid for by a candidate.

George W. Bush's campaign had budgeted $750,000 for the Straw Poll but spent $825,000, having given away 10,500 tickets and provided food and beverages for patrons in his tent outside the Hilton Coliseum. Inside the tent, former Dallas Cowboy quarterback Roger Staubach, San Antonio Spurs basketball star Sean Elliott, and Hayden Fry, Iowa football coach and a native Texan, signed autographs and promoted Bush.

Country singer Crystal Gayle entertained folks in Alexander's tent where the specialty was barbecued ribs. Hatch had the Osmond Brothers and Utah basketball star Karl Malone. Forbes provided his food and entertainment in an air-conditioned tent with French doors — accounting for part of the $2 million he spent on his Iowa campaign. Outside his tent, children enjoyed carnival rides that Forbes had shipped in for the occasion. Buchanan, assessing the celebrities in the other tents, told the press, "I invited the pope but he was busy."[10]

Each candidate was given 10 minutes to speak that night. The audience of nearly 20,000 included 600 media representatives from all over the country. One reporter who wasn't impressed was the venerable James Flansburg of the *Des Moines Register* who, 25 years earlier, was one of the few newsmen to follow Jimmy Carter around and report on him.

To Flansburg, the old days represented down-to-earth politics and were worth something. The Iowa Straw Poll was a money-maker that should have little significance, he thought. "It's an absurdity," he wrote. "It's mostly pretense." He admitted that he once wrote extensively about the Straw Poll because he thought it was a big story. His reaction on this day to his earlier exuberance: "Sorry about that."[11]

But Laudner, who, as an activist for Forbes and later the state Republican Party chairman, makes no excuses or apologies for the Straw Poll. "It has its own style," he said. "People make out of it that the campaigns buy you a $35 ticket and put on some entertainment. Well, you can throw me a free ticket to a lot of concerts that I'm not going to go to.... You're dealing with a specific type of Iowan — the political junkie."

Laudner used Forbes as an example of how the Straw Poll can benefit both the candidate and the public. "If he gets 30,000 votes on caucus night, he probably met every one of them." he said. " That's the difference. If you run nothing but TV, bombard them with mail, telephones — that's an insult to the Iowa caucusgoer."[12]

After the long day of partying and the long night of listening to speeches and voting, the results were finally announced:

George W. Bush	7,418	31.3%
Forbes	4,921	20.8%
Elizabeth Dole	3,410	14.4%
Bauer	2,114	8.9%
Buchanan	1,719	7.3%
Alexander	1,428	6.0%
Keyes	1,101	4.6%
Quayle	916	3.9%
Hatch	558	2.4%
McCain	83	0.4%
Kasich	9	0.04%
Smith	8	0.03%

Bush and Forbes had passed the expectations test that had become so crucial in Iowa presidential politics. Buchanan was mystified that three of the top four — Forbes, Dole and Bauer — had never held public office. Buchanan was referring to the four candidates who finished ahead of him. Had he counted himself, the number would have been four out of the top five who never held elective office.

Bush, who had only been an official candidate for two months and spent nearly $1 million on the Straw Poll, nonetheless credited his victory to grassroots politics. "Two months ago, when my Iowa supporters convinced me to participate in the Straw Poll, some pundits said I had nothing to gain and potentially a lot to lose," he told a crowd of supporters. "Well, thanks to you, we gained a lot. We jump-started our grass-roots organization for the main event, the Iowa caucuses."[13]

Alexander was bitterly disappointed. He had spent much of the past six years campaigning in Iowa and had nothing to show for it. "George W. Bush was such a good candidate that the *Washington Post* was writing articles in mid–1995 about how he was the next president," said Alexander years later. "So no one would give money to me. And they wouldn't give it to Quayle, And they wouldn't give it to Elizabeth Dole. And we all got out."[14]

Alexander and Quayle, the biggest losers in the expectations contest, dropped out within days of the Straw Poll. Mrs. Dole hung on for a while but eventually folded because she could not raise enough money. Buchanan also dropped out later and tried unsuccessfully to mount a campaign as a candidate for the Reform Party.

So the Straw Poll, technically a non-binding exercise, had the same winnowing effect as the Iowa caucuses, even though the Straw Poll was supposed to be like a spring training baseball game — entertaining for fans with meaningless results. As of the night of August 14, 1999, that had all changed and another page was turned in the history of the Iowa caucus season.

"Ames demonstrated to many donors that several Republican candidates were not viable. With Mrs. Dole, Alexander, Quayle and Buchanan out of it, it's taken a lot of the surprise out of caucus night," said historian Hugh Winebrenner.[15]

Pat Buchanan, a television commentator and former speechwriter for President Richard Nixon, challenged President Bush for the Republican nomination in 1992 but got in the race after the Iowa caucuses. He sought the nomination four years later and ran as a third party candidate after not faring well in the Iowa caucuses. He is shown at a press conference in Mason City on July 8, 1999 (courtesy *Mason City Globe Gazette*).

Laudner, the Forbes campaign aide who eight years later would be executive director of the state Republican Party, says the Straw Poll is a wake-up call for some candidates and a test of how good their organizations are for all of them.

Lamar Alexander of Tennessee was a familiar face in Iowa for about six years as he competed in two Iowa caucus campaigns. Here he addresses a luncheon gathering on July 20, 1999 (courtesy *Mason City Globe Gazette*).

"Because it has become so big, it pulls the herd, it is a test of strength," he said. "Because the caucus and primary seasons have become so condensed, there isn't much time to reorganize. The Straw Poll lengthens the season. You can't just show up the day before the caucuses and say, 'I'm running for president.' It doesn't work that way," he said. "Sure, it started out as a fund-raiser but it is so much more than that now. It has some impact."[16]

The Democrats went about their business methodically but no less enthusiastically. Gore and Bradley shared the same stage for the first time in October at the Jefferson-Jackson Day Dinner at the Polk County Convention Center in Des Moines. It was the setting where, as *Des Moines Register* columnist David Yepsen, said, "the Democratic Tribe" got together. Comedian Al Franken, who eight years later would enter Minnesota politics as a U.S. senator from Minnesota, was the headliner for the evening, keeping the partisan crowd laughing as he threw one barb after another at the ambitious politicians on hand.

When Gore and Bradley spoke, each for about an hour, they touched on the usual Democratic themes — health care, education, the economy — but offered different views on how the campaigns between the two of them should go. Bradley stressed the importance of positive messages rather than tearing down the opponent. Gore wanted more hand-to- hand com-

bat, suggesting weekly debates between the two of them. Gore supporters in the crowd, well primed in advance, chanted, "Stay and fight."

Rather than appear jointly with Gore, Bradley preferred to take his
case to the people on his own, often scarfing down a chicken sandwich,
bananas, potato chips, yogurt or some combination thereof, while riding
in a van from one appearance to another. He had a soft, mellow voice and
would tell many of the same stories from one place to another. One of his
favorites was recalling the day he spoke to a group of elementary school
children and asked them how many of them hadn't had breakfast that
morning. One little boy raised his hand. "Why not?" asked Bradley.
"Because it wasn't my turn," replied the youngster.[17]

Gore's style was to come into VFW halls or community rooms in small
towns, shake hands with as people as time allowed and then would wow
his audiences with examples of how the Clinton-Gore administration had
helped them over the last eight years and how he was well qualified and
well prepared to carry on. Sometimes, in crowded rooms he would stand
on a table so people could see him as well as hear him.

Bradley spent 63 days in Iowa to Gore's 38, but January 24, 2000,
caucus night, clearly belonged to Gore. The results:

Al Gore	63%
Bill Bradley	35%
Uncommitted	2%

The old Iowa bugaboo — the "exceeded expectations — didn't meet
expectations" syndrome manifested itself in the biggest thumping since
1980 when Carter dismantled Ted Kennedy's presidential aspirations.

On the Republican side, so many would-be candidates were gone
after the Iowa Straw Poll that the caucus results were fairly predictable:

George W. Bush	35,231	41%
Steve Forbes	26,198	30%
Alan Keyes	12,268	14%
Gary Bauer	7,323	9%
John McCain	4,045	5%
Orrin Hatch	882	1%

The front-runner won, the man with the biggest bankroll finished
second, and John McCain, who chose not to campaign in Iowa, got 3,200
more votes than Orrin Hatch.

"We're no longer an asterisk," a gleeful Forbes chirped.

When Bush defeated Gore in a highly-controversial election decided by the Supreme Court later that year, he became only the second non-incumbent to lead the field in the Iowa caucuses and go on to win the presidency. The other was Jimmy Carter who set the table for Iowa presidential politics in 1975 and 1976; he actually finished second to Uncommitted at the caucuses but finished ahead of all other candidates.

CHAPTER ELEVEN

2004

"Don't put all of your begs in one Ask-it."

Gloria Goll, a widowed farm wife, stood on the front porch of her modest farmhouse in Klemme, Iowa, population 532, put her hands on her hips, and said to the man standing next to her, "This state is more interested in pigs than in people."

She pointed to three long, narrow hog confinement buildings about 300 yards from her home. "There are more hogs in there than in all of Hancock County," she said. "Why should I have to worry which way the wind is blowing every day?"

The man beside her was tall, gaunt and Lincolnesque, with a thin face, sad eyes and gray-black hair. He wore blue jeans and boots and had on a blue dress shirt with rolled-up sleeves and perspiration wetness under his arms. John Kerry, a multi-millionaire senator from Massachusetts, was boning up on the problem of corporate hog farms in Iowa because that's what Massachusetts senators do on hot afternoons in August 2003 when they are running for president.

Earlier in the day, Kerry met with supporters in a bar at the back of a bowling alley, then got into a van and took a high-speed ride for 30 miles on mostly gravel roads so he could meet Mrs. Goll, talk about hog confinement smells and other environmental issues, and then head for Des Moines, two hours away, for a dinner and speech that night.[1]

Kerry, 60, was a Vietnam War veteran who became nationally known for his outspoken views against the war when he came home. He was a leader of Vietnam Veterans Against the War and a cofounder of Vietnam Veterans of America. In 1972, he ran unsuccessfully for the U.S. House. He was elected lieutenant governor of Massachusetts in 1982. In 1983, he was elected to the U.S. Senate and was re-elected in 1989, 1995 and 2001.

Knowing something about agriculture and hog lots was helpful for anyone wanting to talk to voters in Iowa — but so was knowing about war — because the most divisive issue in America in 2003 was another war, the one in Iraq in which the United States had the unfamiliar role of being the invader. On September 11, 2001, Islamic terrorists hijacked four American commercial airliners and engineered an attack on the United States by flying the aircraft head-on into symbols of American power. Two struck the twin towers of the World Trade Center in New York. One struck the Pentagon in Washington, D.C. One was believed headed for the White House when passengers fought with the terrorists and, in the havoc, the plane crashed in Pennsylvania. In all, thousands of Americans were killed. The terrorist attacks were linked to a group called Al-Qaeda led by Osama bin Laden, who was thought to be operating out of Afghanistan.

Vice President Al Gore topped former Senator Bill Bradley in the Iowa caucuses of 2000 and went on to get the nomination as well as the popular vote for the presidency. He lost the hotly contested election that was ultimately decided by the Supreme Court. He never ran again but was active in the 2004 campaign, throwing his support to former Vermont governor Howard Dean. Here he campaigns for Dean in Mason City in August of 2003 (courtesy Andrew Hampton).

But the administration of President George W. Bush believed the government of Iraq, led by its ruthless dictator, Saddam Hussein, was also a party to the attacks and, in fact, was hiding weapons of mass destruction that could be used in future attacks. Based on that intelligence, the U.S. invaded Iraq on March 20, 2003. That invasion and its aftermath of a continuous American presence and hundreds of U.S. casualties, laid the groundwork for a heated presidential campaign back home. Senator Kerry supported the war at first but later voted against additional funding for it, a circumstance that political opponents called a flip-flop that he continually had to defend during his campaign.

An "early and often" severe critic of Bush administration policies was Howard Dean, a physician turned politician who, in 2002, had recently completed five two-year terms as governor of Vermont. Dean, 55, was elected to the Vermont House of Representatives in 1982 and rose to be lieutenant governor in 1986. In 1991, Governor Richard Snelling died in office and Dean, next in the line of succession, took over and served for the next 11 years.

In May of 2002, he set up an exploratory committee, the first step toward a possible presidential run. That same month, ABC News ranked him eighth out of 12 possible Democratic candidates that the network had identified. Dean was not the stereotypical careful-what-you-say politician and was not above criticizing many in his own party. One of his standard stump speech lines was, "I represent the Democratic wing of the Democratic Party." He formally announced his candidacy on June 23, 2003, more than a year after he said he intended to run.

By that time, he had already spent 24 days in Iowa. His opposition to the war was his signature issue. Other candidates joined him in their opposition — but Dean was the first to register his indignation and, not being in the House or Senate, had never taken a public vote on it that he had to defend, explain or modify.

"Not since Vietnam had an insurgent Democrat become so identified with a single transcendent issue so early in the presidential campaign cycle."[2]

Congressman Richard Gephardt of neighboring Missouri, who had been a member of the House for 26 years and served as both majority and minority leader, decided to make a second run for the presidential nomination. He had won the Iowa caucuses in 1988 but his campaign fizzled outside of the heartland. Now 62 years old but still with reddish brown hair, an engaging smile and boyish good looks, he hoped to once again capitalize on his Midwest background, his knowledge of agriculture issues and his experience as a congressional leader to win the hearts and minds of the American people, beginning in Iowa.

Another new kid on the block was Senator John Edwards, 50, of North Carolina, who was serving his first term in the Senate and was as unknown to Iowans as Jimmy Carter had been in 1975. But that's about the only comparison that could be made to Carter, the peanut farmer from Georgia. Edwards was the son of a mill worker, a fact he brought up in almost all of his stump speeches, but he made his living as a highly successful trial lawyer who had a reputation for winning millions of dollars in settlements for his clients.

Edwards built a theme of "two Americas" — one in which the rich prospered, the other in which the middle class and poor struggled — and he traveled across Iowa with his message of uniting the two Americas. Behind the scenes, as early as 2002, the Edwards campaign was supplying local Democratic headquarters throughout the state with 100 computers — a goodwill gesture but with the unspoken hope that the goodwill would be returned at caucus time two years later.

Edwards formed an exploratory committee on January 2, 2003, and formally announced his candidacy on September 16, more than two years after he started actively campaigning. By the end of the first quarter in 2003, Edwards had received $7 million in campaign contributions, much of it from people and organizations associated with the legal profession. It was this kind of opportunistic philanthropy that prompted writer Walter Shapiro to muse about the credo of political fund-raising: "Don't put all of your begs in one Ask-it."[3]

Joseph Lieberman, 61, who was Al Gore's running mate in the 2000 presidential election, wanted to run for president in 2004 but would not seek the nomination if Gore wanted to run again. So the 61-year-old senator from Connecticut and his team of advisers waited in the wings until after Gore had taken center stage — whenever that would be. Lieberman, who was Jewish, had decided during his run for the vice presidency that his religion was not a pivotal issue with voters. He was a seasoned politician, having been elected to the Connecticut state senate in 1970 and served 10 years before losing a bid for re-election in 1980, victimized at least in part by the Reagan Revolution.

In 1982, he was elected Connecticut's attorney general and served in that capacity until he was elected to the U.S. Senate in 1988. When Gore announced on a *60 Minutes* television broadcast on December 15, 2002,

that he would not be a candidate, the Lieberman forces mobilized immediately. He announced the next day that he would "probably" be a candidate — and most political observers ignored the "probably." Within a
month, he made it official.[4]

Senator Bob Graham of Florida had thought about running for president for several years. He was said to be on the short list for a vice presidential candidacy when Gore ran for president in 2000; he had served as
chairman of the Senate Intelligence Committee for several years and so
was privy to inside information on some of the darkest problems facing
the United States. Graham was governor of Florida from 1979 to 1986 and
had been in the Senate ever since. So his political background stretched
all the way back to the days when Jimmy Carter was in the White House.
Graham also had the distinction of never having lost an election. He formally announced his candidacy for president on February 27, 2003.

Three other candidates emerged, each with shorter resumes and more
checkered backgrounds than the others in the race. Congressman Dennis
Kucinich, 57, of Ohio was a political maverick who was elected to the
Cleveland City Council in 1969, at the age of 23, and became mayor of
Cleveland eight years later. After losing his bid for re-election, Kucinich
left politics and left Ohio for California where he lived for a while with
actress Shirley McLaine. He returned to Ohio and was elected to the state
senate in 1994 and was elected to Congress two years later.

Two African Americans entered the race. The Rev. Al Sharpton, 49,
of New York was a minister, a talk show host and a civil rights activist.
He was an eloquent, articulate speaker but his focus was almost solely on
issues impacting African Americans. Carol Moseley Braun, 56, of Illinois,
was the first African American woman elected to the U.S. Senate, serving
from 1993 to 1999. Like Sharpton and Kucinich, her candidacy never
gained any traction but she stayed in the fray for nearly a year before dropping out on January 15, 2004, just four days before the Iowa caucuses.

Retired army general Wesley Clark also became a candidate and was
competitive in several primary elections but made the decision early on to
skip the Iowa caucuses. He later said repeatedly that he regretted that decision.

Senators Russ Feingold of Wisconsin and Tom Daschle of South
Dakota each contemplated a run for the presidency but chose not to and
therefore did not participate in the caucuses.

So the Democrats fielded nine candidates in Iowa, some of whom
started their campaigns within six weeks of the Bush inauguration on Jan-

uary 20, 2001. Edwards delivered the keynote address at a Drake University banquet in Des Moines on March 3. Kerry attended a fund-raiser picnic for Iowa governor Tom Vilsack on June 23 in Mount Pleasant. Gephardt attended a social at a private home in Norwalk, Iowa, on July 20 and took part in a pancake breakfast at a UAW hall in Newton and an ice cream social in Des Moines the next day, all on behalf of incumbent Democratic congressman Leonard Boswell, who was up for re-election in November 2002. On February 22, 2002, Dean campaigned for congressional candidate Julie Thomas in Iowa City and Cedar Rapids, had lunch with lawyers in downtown Iowa City, then met with University of Iowa officials in the afternoon and attended fundraisers that night in Iowa City and Cedar Rapids. Four days later, Sharpton came to Des Moines, had breakfast with clergymen in the morning, had lunch with community leaders, spoke to students at Des Moines Area Community College in the afternoon and preached at the Union Baptist Church in Des Moines that night. The pace would be that hectic for three years for most of the candidates.[5]

The Iowa caucuses and the campaigns preceding them draw newsmen and women from all over the country. Here Harry Smith, host of the CBS television program *The Early Show*, enjoys a laugh as he heads for a campaign event in Des Moines in the summer of 2003 (courtesy Andrew Hampton).

The press traveling with the candidates got glimpses of how they acted and reacted when the cameras weren't on them. Dean was glib, confident and frugal. He studied airline schedules to determine how he could get the biggest bang for his buck on Southwest Airlines. He often gave major speeches using only a 3 × 5 card as a reminder of what he wanted to say. He would scribble on the card four or five points that he wanted to make. After each point, he would write a word that reminded him of an anecdote he would tell to illustrate the point. Dean traveled the state, ready to speak at a grand opening of a county campaign headquarters or of a supermarket or anything else that might be opening in his vicinity. Political pundit Shapiro wrote that Dean was prepared to speak at the opening of an envelope.

Kerry was more image conscious than Dean, and once brooded when a newspaperman described him as looking sad. Whereas Dean was often blunt and to the point, Kerry had a reputation for being long-winded with a tendency to drift from the subject being discussed. The fingernails on his right hand were longer than those on his left because he was a novice guitar player (off camera) and plucked the strings with his right hand.

Edwards looked much younger than his 50 years and paid attention to his appearance. Republicans got hold of a videotape showing Edwards getting ready for a television appearance. The tape showed him combing his hair for more than two minutes, peering into a mirror, as if to get every hair on his head in exactly the place he wanted it. A makeup assistant was at his side as he combed. The tape showed up on *YouTube* a popular Internet site, where it was seen by millions of viewers.

Early on in his campaign, Rob Tully, a veteran Iowa politician, warned Edwards to sharpen his message — that image and personality alone would not prevail in the Iowa caucuses. Tully gave him a two-word reminder — "John Glenn" — a reference to Glenn's 1984 candidacy in which his image as an astronaut overshadowed his potential as a national candidate.

Edwards traveled across the state in a campaign bus, often accompanied by his wife, Elizabeth, and their two youngest children. On one campaign stop in northern Iowa, the family went into a bookstore. Edwards chatted with the proprietor while his wife purchased a couple of children's books for the youngsters. As they departed and headed back toward the bus, they were met by a throng of media representatives in front of them, armed with cameras, microphones, tape recorders and notebooks. Edwards' seven-year- old daughter, Emma, had apparently had enough media attention for the day. She surveyed the situation, then marched ahead of her family, waving her arms as if to clear the way for the others, telling the news people, "no questions, no questions."[6]

Lieberman put people around him at ease with his sense of humor and his even temperament. He patiently waited for Gore to decide whether he was going to make a second run for the presidency. When Gore bowed out, Lieberman's reaction was that he thought his chances were now "great," but observers said it wasn't a Tony the Tiger "GRRRREAT," a la the cereal commercial, but more less a just plain, unemotional "great."

Graham's penchant for chronicling every detail of his day in color-coded notebooks was, if not an obsession, an extraordinary habit. His jottings were so detailed that he often noted what he had for breakfast, what time he had it and what he thought of it. Graham had considered running for president for so long that it became part of his natural thought process, so much so that, rather than carefully planning a formal announcement ceremony, he blurted his intentions while being interviewed on a Haitiian radio station in Florida.

Gephardt was a veteran politician who, like Edwards, was blessed with looks that belied his age. His challenge during the campaign was to tout his 26 years of experience as an advantage over other candidates, lest it be considered the liability of a Washington insider.

Kucinich, Sharpton and Moseley Braun were considered vanity candidates on ego trips with little chance of winning.[7]

One of the factors that had emerged in presidential politics since the days of Jimmy Carter's door-knocking was what author Arthur T. Hadley referred to as "The Invisible Primary," the time between the election of one president and the first caucus or primary to determine the next president.

The Invisible Primary takes shape in many ways but the two biggest influences are power and money. Two circumstances involving John Kerry are illustrative of both. In 2001, shortly after George W Bush was inaugurated, Harry Bookey, a Des Moines businessman, went to Kerry's office in Washington, D.C., and asked to speak to Kerry's chief of staff. When the receptionist asked, "Who are you?" Bookey replied, "I'm a prominent Iowa Democrat." Responding to that introduction on that day, nearly three years before the 2004 Iowa caucuses, chief of staff David McKean arranged to have lunch with Bookey.[8]

The other incident is just as telling. As the caucus drew near and the race between the major candidates became highly competitive, Kerry injected $7 million of his own money into the campaign.

Dean, who was so technically challenged that he often had trouble figuring out how to retrieve messages on his cell phone, was responsible for an important technological breakthrough in campaign financing — or, probably more accurately, his people were. The Dean campaign began soliciting donations through the Internet. Initially, they raised $400,000 in five days. Later, when the Internet fundraising was well publicized, the campaign raised $2 million in eight days. That feat "was a moment in political terms, (that) equaled Alexander Graham Bell shouting into a primitive telephone mouthpiece, 'Mr. Watson, come here. I want you.'"[9]

Meanwhile, politics as usual continued. Kerry, Edwards and Dean were the keynote speakers at the Jefferson-Jackson Day Dinner in 2002 and they were joined in 2003 by Gephardt, Kucinich and Moseley Braun. But much of the media attention at the 2003 gathering was on the emcee — Hillary Rodham Clinton, former first lady and now a senator from New York, who wasn't running for anything yet but was on stage more than any of the active candidates.

One of the major media events for Democratic political candidates is a steak fry hosted by Iowa senator Tom Harkin on a farm in Indianola. It is attended by hundreds of potential voters who want to hear what the candidates have to say. Here, in August 2003, former president Bill Clinton addresses the crowd. In the background, left to right, are Harkin's wife, Ruth; Senator Harkin; and presidential hopefuls Bob Graham, Dennis Kucinich and Howard Dean (courtesy Andrew Hampton).

Iowa senator Tom Harkin continued to be a kingpin in the state political process. He held an annual steak fry fundraiser that drew hundreds of
Democrats from all over the state who came to chat and listen to the presidential candidates. In addition, in 2003, Harkin arranged to sponsor nine
forums in nine cities on nine different days, each featuring one of the presidential candidates. Harkin looked back on his own brief presidential run
in 1992, telling reporters he was observing the 11th anniversary of his candidacy by "calling each of the six people in New Hampshire who voted
for me."

Graham, who entered the race in February, withdrew in October.
Moseley Braun continued her ego trip into 2004 and then withdrew on
January 15, four days before the caucuses. Kucinich and Sharpton held on
but their candidacies were little more than causes in search of constituencies. Clark and Lieberman were viable candidates but had made decisions
to bypass Iowa.

Celebrities often come to Iowa to campaign for presidential candidates. Here
Rob Reiner, Hollywood actor and film director, has some fun with a crowd
in Mason City as actor Martin Sheen looks on. They were campaigning for
Howard Dean. At the time, Sheen portrayed a fictional president in the popular television program *The West Wing* (courtesy Andrew Hampton).

In the final weeks of the campaign, the front-runners were clearly Dean, the blunt, outspoken, eastern establishment doctor-turned-politician who was a novice to national politics, and Gephardt, the Washington political pro with the boy-next-door image he was counting on to take the top spot, just as he had done in 1988. Dean and Gephardt bombarded the airwaves with commercials in which they took on each other, virtually ignoring the other candidates.

Celebrities made their way to Iowa to campaign for one candidate or another. Two well-known actors, Martin Sheen and Rob Reiner, traveled together to campaign for Dean. At the time, Sheen was portraying a fictional president on a top-rated television series, *The West Wing.* Reiner gained fame in the 1970s playing Archie Bunker's son-in-law, "Meathead," on a brash television comedy series called *All in the Family* and more recently was a successful director of films.

Sheen took aim at President Bush for his hunt for "weapons of mass destruction" that were reportedly buried somewhere in Iraq. Sheen told audiences across Iowa that "poverty and ignorance are the weapons of mass destruction."

On January 19, 2004, Iowa Democrats went to their caucuses and had the final say. The results:

Kerry	37.6%
Edwards	31.9%
Dean	18.0 %
Gephardt	10.6%
Kucinich	1.3%
Clark	1.0%
Uncommitted	0.1 %
Lieberman	0%
Sharpton	0%

Dean had raised millions of dollars through the Internet and by conventional means and had a strong organization statewide. But the organization failed to get the thousands of Dean supporters to the caucuses on a cold January night — and that is the name of the game in Iowa. Nothing else matters.

"The Dean campaign's failure illustrated the drawbacks of using online discussion as a substitute for outreach to undecided voters," according to Andrew Chadwick and Philip N. Howard, who use the Dean campaign as an example in a handbook they produced on the newest craze or gimmick in Iowa caucus campaigns and campaigns throughout the nation — Internet politics.[10]

Gephardt, devastated by his fourth place finish, withdrew from the race the next day. Once again, a well-worn but accurate political axiom had taken hold because, for all practical purposes, there were only three tickets out of Iowa.

Dean gave a concession speech to hundreds of supporters who gathered in the Val-Air Ballroom in Des Moines. His voice was scratchy from months of campaigning and he was suffering from a cold as he shouted in order to be heard above the din of the crowd. Senator Harkin stood next to him as Dean told the crowd what would happen next.

"Not only are we going to New Hampshire, Tom Harkin, we're going to South Carolina and Oklahoma and Arizona and North Dakota and New Mexico and we're going to California and Texas and New York, and we're going to South Dakota and Oregon and Washington and Michigan — and then we're going to Washington, D.C., to take back the White House." Then, with a cracking voice, he shouted "Yeah!"

Former Vermont governor Howard Dean was the early favorite to win the 2004 Iowa caucuses. His third place finish and what came to be known as his "I Have a Scream" speech on caucus night haunted him for the rest of his campaign (courtesy Andrew Hampton).

The speech was televised on all the major networks. The TV audio carried only Dean's cracking, shouting voice and none of the crowd noise he was attempting to shout over. The result was that he appeared to be out of control. It came to be known as the "I Have a Scream" speech.[11]

People in attendance at the ballroom that night saw nothing unusual in Dean's behavior. He was simply a man raising his voice so he could be heard above the noise of a crowd. But the television image, showing a man who wanted to be leader of the free world seemingly ranting uncontrollably was replayed hundreds of times and dogged him the rest of his campaign.

Frank Lontz, a linguist who has studied the impact of the spoken word, wrote: "The famous Dean Scream in 2004 fixed Dean's image in the public mind in a way that was impossible to undo." Lontz pointed out that a transcript of Dean's remarks showed that he was simply rattling off the list of states that his campaign would take him — not an unreasonable message to tell his supporters.

"But along with it came a sound that had not come from a presidential candidate before — or at least not caught live on every network.... Viewers got a chance to imagine Governor Dean as President Dean — and it frightened them," said Lontz.[12]

Author Matt Bai considered Dean's outburst as that of a desperate man trying to make the best of an incredibly uncomfortable situation while being surrounded by hundreds of guests, all looking at him, anticipating some scintillating words of encouragement. It was, said Bai, "like a man trying his damndest to give an upbeat toast at his ex-wife's wedding."[13]

Iowa had once again done a number on the front-runners. Political writer Shapiro said Dean in particular, the newcomer to presidential politics who raised more money and spent more time in Iowa than any other candidate, got what amounted to a political hazing.

Shapiro said it was ironic that Dean, who hoped to benefit as being a refreshing contrast to the veteran Gephardt, "was himself victimized in Iowa by second thoughts about the front-runner. Such is the price, whether temporary or permanent, that Dean paid for being the first insurgent candidate to rise to the top of the pile before a single vote is cast."[14]

The curse upon the Iowa front-runner had struck once again. But Kerry and Edwards achieved the ultimate distinction in Iowa caucus politics: They exceeded expectations.

A look at the amount of time each of the candidates spent on the campaign trail shows that, when it was all over, the big winner was the

Senator John Kerry of Massachusetts surprised the pundits by winning the Iowa caucuses in 2004 on his way to winning the Democratic presidential nomination. Here Kerry greets supporters in an event at the Music Man Square in Mason City (courtesy Andrew Hampton).

state of Iowa's economy, benefiting from not only the candidates, but their staffs and the newsmen and women following them as they patronized the state's hotels, motels, restaurants, bars, gas stations and retail outlets.[15]

Howard Dean

Year	Visits to Iowa	Days spent in Iowa
2002	11	24
2003	39	72
2004	5	14
Total	55	110

John Kerry

Year	Visits to Iowa	Days spent in Iowa
2001	1	1
2002	2	2

John Kerry (continued)

2003	33	63
2004	3	15
Total	*39*	*81*

John Edwards

Year	Visits to Iowa	Days spent in Iowa
2001	2	3
2002	4	9
2003	23	51
2004	3	14
Total	*32*	*77*

Richard Gephardt

Year	Visits to Iowa	Days spent in Iowa
2001	1	2
2002	2	5
2003	26	51
2004	6	17
Total	*35*	*75*

Dennis Kucinich

Year	Visits to Iowa	Days spent in Iowa
2002	1	2
2003	26	55
2004	3	10
Total	*30*	*67*

Joseph Lieberman

Year	Visits to Iowa	Days spent in Iowa
2001	1	1
2002	1	2
2003	10	15
2004	2	2
Total	*14*	*20*

Bob Graham

Year	Visits to Iowa	Days spent in Iowa
2003	10	31

Carol Moseley Braun

Year	Visits to Iowa	Days spent in Iowa
2003	8	9
2004	4	4
Total	*12*	*13*

Al Sharpton

Year	Visits to Iowa	Days spent in Iowa
2002	1	1
2003	5	6
2004	1	1
Total	*7*	*8*

An isolated incident on the final day of the 2004 Iowa caucus campaign illustrates several aspects of the intensity of it. On the day of the caucuses, Teresa Heinz Kerry, wife of the winning candidate, walked into a local Democratic headquarters in northern Iowa where John Stone, the Cerro Gordo County party chairman, was studying lists of precincts with Jack Ryan, a Kerry volunteer from Boston.

Mrs. Kerry was a familiar sight on the Iowa campaign trail, accompanying her husband sometimes but often appearing without him at events — so the two of them could cover more territory.

Stone and Ryan had been discussing potential troublesome precincts and were strategizing on last-minute efforts to get people to come out on caucus night. When Mrs. Kerry came in, they stopped what they were doing to see if they could be of assistance to her. She apologized for the interruption and told them to continue on with their work.

A few weeks later, at a fundraiser in Las Vegas, Mrs. Kerry saw Ryan and recognized him from that brief encounter in Iowa.

"Hello," she said. "How did things come out in that precinct in Swaledale?"[16]

CHAPTER TWELVE

2008

"Am I running for president or auditioning for American Idol?*"*[1]

When Jimmy Carter ran for president and decided to make Iowa his first testing ground in 1974 and 1975, he benefited from getting off to an early start without any competition for audience or media attention. His success created a political quirk. So many politicians have tried to follow his example in the years to come, all hoping to get the early jump on any competition, that the field of candidates is almost instantly crowded. In other words, so many candidates wanted to emulate the Carter strategy, their sheer numbers make it impossible to happen.

Prior to the 2008 caucuses, 22 Republican and Democratic candidates set their sights on the White House with Iowa as the first leg of the journey. But the times and circumstances had changed dramatically since Carter's forays across the state. Two interlocking factors are the amount of money needed to finance campaigns and the front- loading of primaries and caucuses. No longer can candidates do well in Iowa and New Hampshire and use those successes to raise money for caucuses and primaries in March, April, May and June. In 2008, so many states had moved up their primary and caucus dates, Iowa had to do the same in order to keep the coveted position of being first in the nation. The result was the Iowa caucuses were held on January 3, 2008, the earliest date in history, and by February 5, Super Tuesday, primaries and caucuses had been held in 32 states, including 24 on Super Tuesday.

Having to raise that much money that fast killed the campaigns of at least two candidates — Iowa governor Tom Vilsack and Indiana senator Evan Bayh. Vilsack announced his candidacy on November 30, 2006, but soon realized he could not compete financially with the likes of John

Edwards, who had been campaigning and raising money for six years and Hillary Rodham Clinton, former first lady and senator from New York who, early on, was a front-runner because of her name and her money. Vilsack dropped out on February 23, 2007, ending his candidacy after less than three months. Similarly, Bayh of Indiana, whose father, Senator Birch Bayh, had presidential aspirations 30 years earlier, announced the formation of an exploratory committee on December 3, 2006, and had made several trips to Iowa prior to that. Twelve days later he announced he was not running. Both Vilsack and Bayh had fallen victim to the invisible primary of multi-million-dollar fundraising of other candidates — something that Carter and George McGovern did not have to contend with, at least to that extent, in their day.

Indeed, McGovern, whose second-place finish in the 1972 Iowa caucuses launched his successful bid for the presidential nomination, recalled that he did not clinch the Democratic nomination until he won the California primary in June — six weeks before the national nominating convention. "I am as disturbed as anybody about the front-loading system. I think it's really unhealthy. I liked the system we had when I was running, where it was strung out over six months," he said.[2]

A third potential candidate, retired army general Wesley Clark, who made a run in 2004 but skipped the Iowa caucuses, returned to the state prior to the November elections to campaign for Iowa Democratic legislative candidates, an action Republicans Steve Forbes and Lamar Alexander had done in previous years as a way of building support for their own future candidacies. Clark told Iowans he made a mistake in bypassing the 2004 caucuses. But he too was up against the invisible primary forces of other candidates and decided not to run in 2008.

Clinton, 60, wife of former president Bill Clinton and in her second term as a senator from New York, took a 21st century approach to announcing her candidacy. Rather than standing on her front porch or in front of her old high school with a nostalgic look at the past or about her dreams for the future, Clinton announced her candidacy through her Internet Web site, saying, "I'm in to win."

Edwards, whose presidential aspirations dated back to 2002, formally entered the 2008 race on December 28, 2006. He had the advantages of name recognition from being John Kerry's running mate in 2004 and having an organization in place early in Iowa because of his caucus candidacy four years earlier.

New Mexico governor Bill Richardson entered the race with a resume that included not only experience in state and federal government but in international relations as well. Richardson was elected to Congress in 1980 and was serving his seventh term in the U.S. House when President Bill Clinton nominated him as the U.S. ambassador to the United Nations. He served in that capacity for a little over a year and then was named secretary of energy, a position he held for the remainder of the Clinton administration. He was elected governor of New Mexico in 2002.[3]

Richardson had a jovial nature and punctuated his television advertising and his press conferences with a sense of humor and candor not often seen on the campaign trail. After giving his stump speech and answering questions in a motel dining room on December 30, 2007, one of his aides in the back of the room pointed to his watch and said, "Governor, we have time for one more question." Richardson laughed and said, "I'm at 3 percent in the polls and there's four days before the caucuses. I've got time for a lot more questions."[4]

Delaware senator Joseph Biden, 65, whose 1988 quest for the nomination was short- circuited by allegations of plagiarism, announced his candidacy for the 2008 nomination on January 31, 2007. Biden, like Richardson, touted his foreign policy experience because of his years as chairman of the Senate Foreign Relations Committee and the relationships he had formed with foreign leaders. In his campaign, he said he had often been regarded as someone who would make a great secretary of state. He would ask his audiences, "Wouldn't you want someone like that to be your president?"

Senator Christopher Dodd of Connecticut used the Don Imus radio program, *Imus in the Morning* to announce his candidacy on January 11, 2007. Dodd, 63, the son of a senator, had been in the Senate for 26 years, and appeared frustrated at times that his background was not resonating with voters. "The presidency is the only job in the world where no experience is required," he said. "Gosh, if you call a plumber, you check references, don't you?"[5]

Two candidates who sought constituencies that never materialized were Dennis Kucinich, 61, the maverick congressman from Ohio, who ran unsuccessfully for the nomination in 2004, and Mike Gravel, 67, a former governor and senator from Alaska, who was first to announce a candidacy when he entered the race on April 17, 2006.

Midway through George W. Bush's presidency, some Democrats were searching their ranks for up-and-coming leaders — young, articulate, liberal activists who would someday grab the baton from the old guard of

Clinton, Gore, Kerry, Lieberman and Biden and run with it into a new era of Democratic leadership. Many believed they found just such a person in a legislator from Illinois named Barack Obama, 46, an African American who was intelligent and eloquent but whose only experience in elective office was in the Illinois Senate.

In 2004, Obama, a Chicago lawyer and neighborhood organizer, whose father was black and from Kenya and whose mother was white and from Kansas, decided to make a run for the U.S. Senate. The national Democratic Party, aware of his talent and his potential, decided to take a chance on the energetic but untested state legislator. Party leaders decided to showcase Obama by putting him on center stage as the keynote speaker at their national convention.

His only previous exposure to a national convention had been four years earlier when Gore was nominated. Obama had flown to Los Angeles for the convention but had trouble getting there when the Hertz car

When Barack Obama came to Mason City in April 2007, nine months before the caucuses, he attracted an audience of 1,800 at North Iowa Area Community College. Obama and New York senator Hillary Clinton consistently drew huge crowds, a departure from Iowa's stereotypical grassroots campaign style. Here Obama greets supporters young and old after his talk at the college (courtesy Andrew Hampton).

rental agency at the airport rejected his credit card. When he finally arrived at the convention center, he was denied a floor pass and had to watch the proceedings on a Jumbotron screen outside the arena. In other words, he was a spectator.[6]

Obama was given only 17 minutes to speak on the night of July 27, 2004, but, as the *Washington Post* observed later, it turned out to be "the 17 minutes that launched a political star."[7]

Obama told the delegates — and a national television audience,

> Tonight we gather to affirm the greatness of our nation — not because the height of our skyscrapers or the power of our military or the size of our economy. Our pride is based on a very simple premise, summed up in a declaration made over 200 years ago:
>
> "We hold these truths to be self-evident, that all men are created equal and that they are endowed by their Creator with certain inalienable rights; that among these are life, liberty and the pursuit of happiness."
>
> That is the true genius of America — a faith — a faith in simple dreams, an insistence on small miracles, that we can tuck in our children at night and know that they are fed and clothed and safe from harm; that we can say what we think and write what we think without hearing a sudden knock on the door; that we can have an idea and start our own business without paying a bribe; that we can participate in the political process without fear of retribution; and that our votes will be counted — at least most of the time.
>
> This year, in this election, we are called to reaffirm our values and our commitments, to hold them against a hard reality and see how we're measuring up to the legacy of our forbearers and the promise of future generations.
>
> And fellow Americans, Democrats, Republicans, Independents, I say to you tonight: we have more work to do.[8]

Through that one speech, Obama achieved not only the applause and admiration of those gathered in the Fleet Center convention hall, but he also had instant name recognition and countless invitations to speak at other functions and to be a guest on numerous television programs. Yet he was still just a state senator from Illinois. Obama was favored to win his U.S. Senate race, as most Democrats from Cook County are, but his fledgling political career got another unanticipated boost when it was revealed that his Republican opponent, Jack Ryan, had taken his wife to sex clubs against her will, according to papers filed when she divorced him. Ryan withdrew from the Senate race. Republicans imported Alan Keyes, the east coast radio commentator who had sought the GOP presidential nomination twice, as a new, last-minute candidate, but Obama won easily.

On February 10, 2007, in front of the state capitol building in Springfield, Illinois, Obama, the man who couldn't even get into the convention seven years earlier, and had been a U.S. senator for only two years, announced his candidacy for the presidency.

The stage was set for a vigorous campaign in Iowa. Clinton had a war chest that far outmatched any of her opponents. Edwards had been campaigning in Iowa in one form or another for six years and was well known and well liked. Obama was from a neighboring state, always a plus in the Iowa caucuses, and was a fresh face on the horizon. But he was also an African American, born of a mixed marriage, competing in a state that was 93 percent Caucasian. Biden, Dodd and Richardson all had impressive credentials but were considered to be in the second tier of candidates. Kucinich and Gravel were thought to only go as far as their egos and checkbooks would take them.

Out of this conclave of candidates, Clinton had the dubious distinction of front-runner early on because she already had the funds to overwhelm her opponents. Her strategy was to win Iowa and New Hampshire and then to lock up the nomination with a series of victories on Super Tuesday.[9]

Republicans faced the challenge of picking a successor to George W. Bush. The challenge was to promote Republican principles and ideals and yet to distance themselves from the incumbent president of their own party who was extremely unpopular with voters, primarily because of the ongoing war in Iraq and problems with the economy at home.

Their field of candidates was just as crowded as the Democrats. Leading contenders were Senator John McCain of Arizona, the former prisoner of war who sought the nomination in 2000, and former New York mayor Rudy Giuliani, who became nationally famous for his efforts in restoring tranquility to New York, and, by extension, the rest of the nation after the terrorist attacks on America on September 11, 2001.[10]

The race also featured a former Baptist pastor and a Mormon. Mike Huckabee, 52, had served as governor of Arkansas from 1996 to 2007. He pastored two Baptist churches in Arkansas from 1980 to 1992 during which time he also developed television ministries. In 1992, he ran for the Senate against the incumbent Democrat Dale Bumpers and lost. Arkansas governor Bill Clinton was elected president the same year and Lt. Governor Jim Guy Tucker ascended to the governorship. Huckabee won a special election to become lieutenant governor and then became governor in

In 2008, Iowa was no longer the fertile political landscape where presidential candidates could sneak in early and get a foothold as Jimmy Carter had done in 1975. Here former Arkansas governor Mike Huckabee is surrounded by media on January 2, 2008, the day before the caucuses (courtesy *Mason City Globe Gazette*).

1996 when Tucker resigned because of involvement in a land deal scandal. Huckabee, a favorite among religious conservatives, announced his candidacy for the presidency on January 28, 2007.

Mitt Romney, 60, a Mormon, downplayed his religion but emphasized his business background after he announced his candidacy on February 13, 2007. The son of the late George Romney who had been president of General Motors, governor of Michigan and who sought the Republican presidential nomination in 1968, Willard "Mitt" Romney made a fortune as chief executive officer of Bain & Co., a management consulting firm. When the 1992 Summer Olympics in Salt Lake City fell into dire financial straits, Romney was called on to take over the leadership and guided the events successfully, earning a national reputation for saving the games. In 1994, he ran for the U.S. Senate seat held by Ted Kennedy. Though he lost by a wide margin, he came closer than most of Kennedy's opponents had. He was elected governor in 2002 and did not seek re-election in 2006, choosing instead to run for president.

A late entry into the race was former Tennessee senator Fred Thompson, 65, a former prosecutor and actor who was widely known for his role as a prosecutor on the television program *Law and Order*. Conservative Republicans enticed Thompson to become a candidate. Forty years earlier, Thompson was a political ally of Tennessee senator Howard Baker. He was minority counsel to the Senate Watergate Committee investigating President Richard Nixon in 1973 and 1974, a committee on which Baker served. While remaining in private practice, he maintained his political connections and was named special counsel to the Senate Foreign Relations Committee in 1980 and 1981 and to the Senate Intelligence Committee in 1982. In 1994, he was elected to the U.S. Senate to fill the unexpired term of Al Gore and was re-elected in 1996. In 2000, he was the national co-chair for Senator John McCain during McCain's first bid for the Republican presidential nomination. He chose not to run for re-election to the Senate in 2002 and resumed his successful acting career. He announced his candidacy for president on *The Tonight Show With Jay Leno* on September 5, 2007, less than four months before the Iowa caucuses.

Other candidates were Senator Sam Brownback of Kansas, who appealed to the religious conservative wing of the party; former Wisconsin governor Tommy Thompson, who served as President George W. Bush's secretary of health and human services during Bush's first term; Congressman Tom Tancredo of Colorado, whose campaign focused primarily on one issue — toughening laws and policies on immigration; Congressman Duncan Hunter of California who, like Kucinich among the Democrats, never really found a constituency; and Congressman Ron Paul of Texas.

Paul, 71, who had served 11 terms as a congressman, was an obstetrician by profession and an outspoken, often outlandish spokesman for causes he believed in. In 1988, he was the Libertarian candidate for president. After he announced his candidacy for the 2008 Republican nomination, he became almost a cult figure among a segment of voters who appreciated his candor in espousing limited government, strict adherence to the Constitution, low taxes, free trade and sound monetary policies. While never considered a serious candidate even by members of his own party, he raised millions of dollars through Internet fundraising and outlasted many more viable candidates in the race.[11]

The sheer number of candidates from both parties provided Iowa with two or three years of economic growth as the candidates and their staffs crisscrossed the state, meeting and greeting potential voters but also purchasing millions of dollars in goods and services along the way. It was not unusual for candidates to run into one another, sometimes unexpectedly. Years earlier, Pat Buchanan was walking in a residential area in Des Moines early one morning when a jogger ran by him, huffing and puffing. It was Lamar Alexander. In 2007, Hillary Clinton and Mitt Romney walked in the same parade in Clear Lake, Iowa, though not together.

The influx of candidates' staff members, who are often young, eager, energetic and ambitious, can have comical moments. Frank Smillie, manager of the Holiday Inn in Mason City, Iowa, was badgered at the front desk by a staffer of Senator John Edwards because the young aide was to pick up an important fax and deliver it to the room of one of Edwards' campaign gurus. The staffer made several trips to the front desk, asking if the fax had arrived. Smillie told him it hadn't, but when it came, he would call him and let him know. Apparently not satisfied with that answer, the young man stood for a few moments and stared at the fax machine behind the counter. "If you think it will make it come faster, I'll get you a chair and you can come back here and sit next to the machine," said Smillie.[12]

The Democratic campaign provided a far different scenario than Iowans had ever experienced in pre-caucus politics. The hectic travel schedule, the countless stump speeches and the obligatory trip to the Iowa State Fair to pose for pictures in front of the butter sculpture were still a part of the routine. But Hillary Clinton and Barack Obama added a star quality to the campaign — rock star, according to many observers, because of the huge crowds each of them was attracting. While John Edwards was drawing 100 to 200 on an especially good day and Joe Biden and Chris Dodd and the others were speaking to groups of 40 and 50, Obama and Clinton were getting audiences of anywhere from 1,500 to 4,000, depending on the venue. It was this phenomenon that prompted Dodd to ask, "Am I running for president or auditioning for *American Idol?*"

Former four-term Iowa governor Terry Branstad, Lamar Alexander's state campaign chairman in 2000 was amazed at the changes he was seeing. "There's more money, more media and bigger crowds," he said. "But Iowans are kind of spoiled. They're used to meeting the candidates one-on-one and talking with them.

"One thing hasn't changed." said Branstad. "On caucus night, the winners are still the ones who get their supporters there."[13]

The Clinton campaign strategy was clear from the beginning. Win Iowa. Win New Hampshire. Wrap it up on Super Tuesday. She had $35 million in the bank before some of her rivals had raised their first million.

Barack Obama's road to the White House began with his win in the Iowa caucuses on January 3, 2008, 10 months before the election. He often engaged his audiences in give and take that would result in laughter, as in this appearance in Mason City in 2007 (courtesy Andrew Hampton).

And she had Bill Clinton, her husband, the popular former president and an outstanding fundraiser. Obama campaigned on the premise that he represented change, and that change was what was needed in Washington. He incorporated the phrase "Yes we can" into many of his speeches and it became a familiar chant from his audiences. Edwards had an immediate goal. He had to win Iowa or he might be swept aside like yesterday's news. For Obama, while race was never mentioned publicly as an issue in the campaign, if he could win in lily-white Iowa, it would send a powerful message to the rest of the country. Biden, Richardson, Dodd and the others realistically hoped to emerge in the top tier of candidates because as Branstad and others often said, "There's only three tickets out of Iowa."

Edwards made elimination of poverty a central issue in his campaign. So he ran into a credibility problem when it was discovered in April 2007 that he had a Beverly Hills stylist flown in to Dubuque, Iowa, to cut his hair for $400, and charged the expense to his campaign. It was first reported on the Fox television network but was quickly picked up not only by other media but by late-night television comedians as well. In July, the *Washington Post* published a feature story on the stylist, Joseph Torreneau, in which he disclosed that Edwards had him flown to many locations to give him a haircut.[14]

The disclosure of the Edwards haircut also brought references to the 2003 incident in which the candidate was captured on the YouTube Internet site primping his hair for more than two minutes. But the bigger picture in 2007 was the amount of money all of the candidates were spending. By the middle of April, more than $169 million had been raised. Hillary Clinton was the leader with $26 million. Barack Obama, who had started with little or no name recognition or background compared to Clinton, had raised $25 million — a clear indication that he was a serious player. Republican Mitt Romney had $21 million in campaign contributions, Rudy Giuliani had $15 million, John Edwards $14 million and John McCain $13 million.[15]

Former President Bill Clinton chats with the author while participating in the Fourth of July parade in Clear Lake in 2007. Clinton campaigned hard for his wife, Senator Hillary Clinton, and made many appearances throughout Iowa (photograph by Arian Schuessler from author's personal collection).

Meanwhile, Clinton also had problems to overcome. In May, an internal memo was leaked to the press in which Mike Henry, her deputy campaign manager, suggested that she skip Iowa altogether and concentrate on the Super Tuesday states, which Henry referred to as the "national Democratic primary." His memo said, in part, the campaign should embrace a new approach. "This approach involves shifting the focus away from Iowa and running a campaign that is more focused on other primary states and winning the new national primary. More specifically, I propose skipping the Iowa caucuses"[16]

Clinton's handlers were quick to point out that the Henry memo was one of dozens of suggestions put forward by advisers and that Clinton had no intention of

Senator Hillary Clinton of New York makes a point during a speech in Clear Lake in October of 2007. Her presidential aspirations were set back by her third place finish in the Iowa caucuses (courtesy Andrew Hampton).

skipping Iowa. But the story of the memo made headlines in daily newspapers throughout the state so, despite the disclaimers, the genie was out of the bottle.

Much later in the campaign, more trouble erupted when it was disclosed that Clinton staffers were planting questions for audience members to ask at some of her public appearances. The revelations came to light after Clinton toured a biodiesel plant in Newton, Iowa, and talked about her energy plan with a crowd that had gathered there. After her speech, she asked if anyone had questions. Muriel Gallo-Chasanoff, a Grinnell College student, raised her hand. She told Clinton she was worried about global warming to which Clinton quickly replied, "You should be."

Later, the student told reporters she had been approached by a Clinton staffer before the speech who requested that she ask a question about global warming. After that incident, it was reported that there had been other instances of question planting which is not illegal and, in the minds of many, not even unethical, but certainly going against the grain of the grassroots, spontaneous nature of Iowa pre-caucus campaigns. Clinton staffers acknowledged their error in judgment and promised it would not happen again.[17]

One of Hillary Clinton's biggest assets early on was her husband, Bill, the former president, who was immensely popular in Iowa. The Clintons could cover twice as much ground by campaigning separately. But sometimes they saw the need to double-team a community. Such was the case on July 4, 2007, when they made a joint appearance in the Fourth of July parade in Clear Lake, Iowa, a city of 8,000 about 30 miles south of the Minnesota border.[18]

The annual parade, part of a daylong festival that ended with a spec-

Hillary and Bill Clinton walk hand in hand in the Fourth of July parade in Clear Lake in 2007. In a town of 8,000 residents, the crowd at the parade was estimated at 40,000, most of whom came to see the Clintons and Mitt Romney, a Republican presidential hopeful who also participated in the parade (courtesy Andrew Hampton).

tacular fireworks display at night, usually drew about 10,000 spectators. On this day, not only the Clintons but Mitt Romney also had agreed to walk the parade route of several miles, and 40,000 people from all over northern Iowa and southern Minnesota lined the streets to see them.

The Clintons, with bands and baton twirlers and fancy farm vehicles ahead and behind them, walked on each side of the streets waving, shaking hands and exchanging pleasantries, then each crossing and working the other side of the streets. Sometimes they would walk hand in hand and wave as they walked down the middle of the street. A few blocks back in the parade route, Romney also walked and worked the crowd.

Afterward, Clinton relaxed with a group of local Democrats and reflected on her day in the parade. "People were waving to me," she said, "and they were using all of their fingers."[19]

On the Republican side, a more traditional campaign was being waged, with emphasis on raising money and delivering a compelling message, without the rock star presence of a Clinton or an Obama. The closest thing to celebrity was Giuliani but he made a decision early on to make token appearances in Iowa and to concentrate his resources in Florida, which held its primary a month later and a state that Giuliani's backers believed would be a firewall, stopping others' campaigns in their tracks. McCain had name recognition and the experience of competing in the 2000 presidential campaign. But he bypassed Iowa that year and his consistent view of believing ethanol should not be subsidized did not endear him to Iowa voters. Romney campaigned hard in Iowa and set his sights on winning the Iowa Straw Poll in August to help catapult him to winning the caucuses in January.

Huckabee, the former Arkansas governor and preacher, had little money compared to the other candidates but he had a sense of humor and a homespun, conservative, family-values message that resonated with Iowans. As the Iowa Straw Poll on August 11 approached, Huckabee and his staff faced decisions that would shape the rest of his campaign.

Reflecting on it later, Huckabee wrote, "The big question was whether we should dedicate our meager resources to that event — more than a year ahead of the election — or save our pennies for later, especially the actual Iowa caucuses on January 3 and the New Hampshire primary on January 8."

Huckabee and his staff weighed the pros and cons of what it would take in money and stamina to compete in the Straw Poll. He thought about what many candidates before him had thought about. "It was grueling traveling from town to town across Iowa, speaking to maybe 15 or 20 people at one event, then making another long haul to speak to 15 or 20 more," he wrote.

Senators McCain and Thompson as well as Giuliani had all decided to skip the Straw Poll, all for different reasons. "Thompson had just started his campaign, Giuliani put all his eggs in the Florida basket and McCain evidently didn't want to go up against Mitt Romney's huge publicity machine and knew that he had some serious issues with Iowa voters on ethanol and agricultural legislation," wrote Huckabee.

He determined that if he did poorly, the national media and potential donors would leave him for dead — and if he did well, they would say it was only because McCain, Giuliani and Fred Thompson weren't in it.

"I wasn't all that pumped up about the long drives and the small crowds during a brutal summer when it might not do little more than spend the last of what little money we had," wrote Huckabee. But he talked to his friend, fellow former governor and fellow candidate Tommy Thompson who had decided to compete in the Straw Poll.

In the end, so did Huckabee but not with high expectations. Part of his concern was what he called the pecking order of the candidates' campaign finance reports which had Romney leading, followed by Giuliani, Fred Thompson, Brownback and Huckabee who thought that was also the order of importance that the national media placed on candidates.[20]

So he came to Hilton Coliseum in Ames, set up his tent in 90-degree heat and tried to woo voters with barbecue, beverages and banter, hoping for, if nothing else, respectability. The venue and the atmosphere were much the same as in previous Straw Poll settings. It was a political carnival in which Iowa residents, 18 and older, had to have a $35 ticket to get in — and the candidates paid for most of them as well as the bus fare to get them there in many cases. In Huckabee's tent, supporters ate barbecue and watermelon and got a chance to see the candidate pick up his bass guitar and play along with Capitol Offense, a rock band of which he was a member. He joked that he couldn't afford to bring in bigger name entertainment. "I can't buy you," he told his audience. "I can't even rent you."[21]

Across the way from the Huckabee tent, Brownback had a much larger tent that was air conditioned. Outside the tent, he had inflatable slides, a rock-climbing wall and a Dunk the Democrat dunk tank in which the person being dunked wore a Bill Clinton mask.

The other candidates' environs paled compared to what one reporter called Camp Romney that had several tents, an inflatable slide called The

Screamer, a stage and a jumbo, stadium style television screen. Romney staff members were easy to spot in their bright yellow T-shirts emblazoned with Team Mitt on them. The campaign also had a fleet of golf carts on hand to give his backers a ride to the polling places.[22]

As expected, Romney won the Straw Poll. But as *Time* magazine reported in its next edition, "If Romney's first-place finish was just the logical next step in his mechanical push toward January, the genuine surprise of the day was Mike Huckabee's runner-up status."[23]

The results were:

Mitt Romney	4,516	31.6%
Mike Huckabee	2,587	18.1%
Sam Brownback	2,192	15.3%
Tom Tancredo	1,961	13.7%
Ron Paul	1,305	9.1%
Tommy Thompson	1,039	7.3%
Fred Thompson	203	1.4%
Rudy Giuliani	183	1.3%
Duncan Hunter	174	1.2%
John McCain	101	0.7%
John Cox	41	0.3%

Huckabee hadn't won the Straw Poll but he won the all-important expectations game — by exceeding them. He called it the turning point in his campaign. An ironic twist to the outcome was that Huckabee stayed in the Straw Poll after talking with Tommy Thompson, who dropped out of the presidential race the day after he finished sixth in the Straw Poll voting.

Senator Tom Harkin held his annual steak fry for Democrats in Indianola on September 16 and 15,000 party faithful attended including candidates Obama, Clinton, Edwards, Biden, Richardson and Dodd. Clinton staffers had lined the highway to the site of the steak fry with Clinton signs but the media moment occurred when Obama and about 1,000 supporters marched into the event en masse.[24]

Democrats held their annual Jefferson-Jackson Day dinner in Des Moines on November 10 with 9,000 Democrats attending. House Speaker Nancy Pelosi was master of ceremonies and six candidates — Obama, Clinton, Edwards, Richardson, Biden and Dodd — spoke, but the spotlight was clearly on Obama and Clinton who sparred with one another in back-to-back speeches without ever mentioning the other's name.

Obama implied that Clinton's stands on issues were based on polls showing how she would do against the Republicans. "Poll-driven positions because we're worried about what Mitt and Rudy might say about us just won't do it," he said. Clinton, who touted her experience, implied Obama was too new on the scene to be effective in creating the change in government that he promised. "Change is just a word if you don't have the strength and experience to go with it," she said.

No teleprompters were allowed so speakers had to be well prepared. Obama memorized his speech and he used one of his proven crowd-pleasers — a story about having to go to an early morning breakfast rally in South Carolina when he was dead tired and had difficulty getting motivated. Hardly anybody showed up, he said, and those who did were not enthusiastic — except for one older woman. At one point she began shouting, "fired up, ready to go," and pretty soon she had everyone chanting along with her, he said.

As Obama told that story in an amusing way to the Jefferson-Jackson dinner audience in Des Moines, he suddenly switched gears and, raising

In 2008, Barack Obama became only the second Democratic candidate to be the leading candidate in the Iowa caucuses who went on to win the presidency. The other was Jimmy Carter (courtesy Andrew Hampton).

his voice, said to the crowd, "So I've got one thing to ask you: Are you fired up, ready to go?" The Obama supporters reacted as if on cue: "Fired up! Ready to go!"[25]

The proceedings started late and ended late, as usual, prompting Senator Dodd, who was among the last speakers, to say, "Welcome to breakfast in Des Moines." Edwards, who was one of the first speakers, actually left the event for a while and returned at the end to stand on the platform with the other candidates in a show of unity.[26]

Christmas week and the week after were busy for all the candidates, their staffs and the media because of the earliest ever caucus date of January 3. The results provided plenty of fodder for expectations analysts. For the Democrats:

Barack Obama	37.6%
John Edwards	29.7%
Hillary Clinton	29.5%
Bill Richardson	2.1%
Joseph Biden	0.9%
Uncommitted	0.1%
Christopher Dodd	0.0%
Dennis Kucinich	0.0%
Mike Gravel	0.0%
Others	0.0%

Biden and Dodd withdrew as candidates shortly after the results were in but the biggest loser of the night was Clinton, the early front-runner with the biggest campaign war chest who not only could not stop the momentum of Obama but finished behind Edwards as well. Her game plan all along had been to win the Iowa caucuses and ride that wave of success through Super Tuesday on February 5 when she hoped to wrap up the nomination. But she failed to meet those expectations.

A big obstacle for her turned out to be one of the unusual wrinkles in the Democrats' caucus procedures in Iowa — the requirement for caucusgoers to regroup if one or more of the candidates at a caucus site is deemed not viable because supporters don't represent at least 15 percent of everyone attending.

So, for example, at any caucus site, if candidates Biden, Richardson, Dodd, Kucinich or Gravel failed to have 15 percent support, the call would go out to realign, as Cerro Gordo County chairman John Stone refers to it, at which time supporters of candidates still in the mix try to woo the others over to their side. This is where Obama and Edwards gained on Clinton.

Authors T.J. Walker and Jess Todtfeld explain her dilemma in their analysis of the 2008 Iowa caucuses. They wrote: "Clinton is nobody's second choice. Her negatives are just too high. If you weren't for her at the beginning of the night, you weren't going to support her at all."[27]

During the past year, the Obama campaign had waged a massive voter registration campaign and it apparently paid off. Nearly 240,000 Democrats participated in the 2008 caucuses, compared to 124,000 in 2004, according to figures compiled by the Iowa Democratic Party.

Republicans drew about half as many to their caucuses, still a respectable number compared to other years. The Republican results:

Mike Huckabee	40,841	34.4%
Mitt Romney	29,944	25.2%
Fred Thompson	15,904	13.4%
John McCain	15,559	13.1%
Ron Paul	11,817	10.0%
Rudy Giuliani	4,097	3.5%
Duncan Hunter	524	0.4%
Tom Tancredo	5	0.0%

Huckabee, the candidate whose second place finish in the Iowa Straw Poll gave him an instant credibility boost, had defeated the front-runner, Romney, and, in fact, stayed in the presidential race longer than Romney even though Romney far outspent him. McCain defied the "three tickets out of Iowa" by becoming only the second candidate since 1972 to finish fourth in Iowa and to go on to win the nomination. The first was Bill Clinton in 1992 when favorite son Tom Harkin won his home state caucus.

Delaware Senator Joseph Biden competed in the Iowa caucuses twice — in 1988 and in 2008 — and did poorly both times. Yet Biden has praised the caucuses as being "a level playing field" for candidates. Barack Obama picked Biden as his running mate and he was elected vice president in the November 2008 elections (courtesy Andrew Hampton).

Former Arkansas governor Mike Huckabee won the Republican caucuses in 2008. Here he is shown playing with his band, Capital Offense, at the Surf Ballroom in Clear Lake in November of 2007 (courtesy *Mason City Globe Gazette*).

Huckabee did not go on to win the nomination as Obama did, but he and the Democratic winner each received something from the Iowa caucus results that served them well with voters and potential donors — momentum — that quality that is hard to define but history has proven that those who have it advance; those who don't go home. They had won the all-important expectations game, the hallmark of victory in the Iowa caucuses.

There is another statistic from the 2008 caucuses that is noteworthy. The state of Iowa estimates that the political campaigns generated $51.6 million in revenue for the state economy from television, radio and newspaper ads and campaign costs for hotels and motels, food, car rentals and other transportation and assorted other costs.[28]

CHAPTER THIRTEEN

The Media Influence

"If you do surprisingly well in the Iowa caucuses and the media aren't there to report it, does it make a noise?"

In the fall of 1975, when former Georgia governor Jimmy Carter was contemplating a run for the presidency, he received a memo from Hamilton Jordan, one of his trusted assistants who had helped shape and guide Carter's political career.

Candidates' political aides have the unenviable task of thinking of everything so that the candidate does not stumble along the way because he didn't know something or wasn't told something in advance that could have prevented an embarrassing moment.

Jordan's memo zeroed in on a key element of the upcoming campaign that had nothing to do with issues such as Soviet aggression abroad, rising inflation at home or President Ford's pardon of Richard Nixon.

His memo stated simply, "We would do well to understand the very special and powerful role the press plays in interpreting the primary (and caucus) results for the rest of the nation."[1]

One of the great paradoxes concerning the influence of the Iowa caucuses is the attitude of the national media. Some in that genre criticize, even mock Iowa's unique caucus format as being archaic, undemocratic, inconvenient and producing misleading results. Yet it is the immense media attention that has given the caucuses their distinctive place in the history of American presidential politics.

As Richard Bender, one of the creators of the caucus system points out, in 1972, when caucus results were coming in, there were only about 12 news people on hand to report on them. Now, says Bender, there are that many just from Japan.

Walter Shapiro, a political columnist for *USA Today*, is eloquent in his disdain for Iowa and the caucuses. He makes fun of the Iowa State Fair, a favorite campaign site for candidates because of the thousands of people gathered there, calling it a "hot-diggety-corn dog" event and says more people in Iowa are interested in the sculptures made out of butter than in what the candidates have to say. As for the caucuses, Shapiro is blunt.

"Unlike voters who make a five-minute trip to the voting booth or cast absentee ballots in a primary, caucus-goers must personally show up on a wintry Monday evening, listen to their neighbors debate party resolutions on everything from hog lots to whaling boycotts (and) declare their candidate allegiances in public...."[2]

Political commentator Jeff Greenfield has this assessment: "Iowa's vaunted precinct caucuses — especially those of the Democratic Party — violate some of the most elemental values of a vibrant and open political process." For openers, he points out, there's no secret ballot. For another thing, there's no absentee voting.

Greenfield says the caucus suppresses rather than encourages turnout because a participant has to show up at 7 P.M. on caucus night; no other time will do. "So, if you work the night shift — if you're a cop, a firefighter, an emergency room nurse, a waitress — and you can't change your hours, you're shut out."[3]

Robert Thompson, a county Democratic chairman in the 1980s, and later a political science professor in Pennsylvania, expresses disgust for the system he participated in. "The procedures are indeed arcane, and as print and electronic journalism hungers after concrete results, the Iowa parties have been happy to supply meaningless straw polls and conglomerations of delegate counts to keep the media happy."[4]

Drake University professor Hugh Winebrenner says this: "At its worst, media exploitation of the Iowa caucus process (1) disrupts the normal functioning of the local political process (2) may give a false image of the national political appeal of the candidates involved and (3) subjects the national electoral process to the influence of a contrived event."[5]

R.W. "Johnny" Apple, the late veteran political reporter for the *New York Times*, observed how the crush of media attention on the candidates made it virtually impossible in today's politics for an unknown like Jimmy Carter to sneak into Iowa to get a jump on his opposition.

"The national news organizations come to Iowa so early now that candidates who could once find their themes and hone their skills in blessed obscurity find themselves scrutinized closely from the start. There is no longer an exhibition season in presidential politics; every inning counts now," he wrote.[6]

It was Apple's coverage of the 1972 Democratic caucuses, won by Senator Edmund Muskie of Maine, that displayed another way the press has been accused of manipulating public opinion through a process known as gatekeeping. Muskie was the Democratic leader in the caucuses that night, as he was expected to be. What wasn't expected is what Apple referred to as the "surprisingly strong showing for George McGovern."

Apple was one of the most respected political reporters of his day and, in the view of many of his colleagues, if Apple was trumpeting McGovern's showing, it must be worth trumpeting. Apple was the unwitting gatekeeper who opened the door (or gate in this case) to a flood of positive publicity for McGovern, at the expense of Muskie, the actual winner.[7]

Winebrenner contends, "Since media interest centers around who is winning and who is losing the game, the candidates' strategies and tactics are emphasized at the expense of the substance of the campaigns: the public problems, the policy debates and the candidates' leadership qualities."[8]

Presidential election researcher E.D. Dover contends the media creates a front-runner and then often also creates an adversary and plays one off the other in news coverage even when there is no basis for it.

The late historian Theodore H. White contended that as early as 1960, when there wasn't the intense scrutiny on either the presidency or the press as developed in years to come, the media treated John F. Kennedy as the front-runner. It often reported the news by leading with Kennedy's words or actions and followed with how or what his adversaries had done during the same news cycle. The drawing of comparisons between one candidate and another was enhanced by the creation of the front-runner and his adversaries, according to White.

The front-runner attains that status, according to Dover, by getting the most votes early on or achieving high standings in the polls "even though the differences between this candidates' accomplishments and those of his rivals may be quite small." He cites the example of Jimmy Carter in 1976. In 1980, Ted Kennedy was Carter's adversary in Iowa and he didn't succeed. For Republicans in that same year, George H.W. Bush was the adversary to the front-runner Ronald Reagan — and he overtook him when Reagan ran a lackluster campaign in Iowa.

In 1984, Walter Mondale was clearly the front-runner among the Democrats and Gary Hart emerged as the adversary in the press. Though

Mondale got the most support in the caucuses, the outcome was closer than some in the press had predicted and therefore Hart won the all-important expectations game. [9]

Not everyone in the national press is critical. Mark Manoff, former reporter for the *Philadelphia Daily News*, acknowledges that the Iowa caucuses are far different than the usual methods of a representative democracy but sees some value in them nonetheless. "The caucuses give the average guy a chance to stand up and tell what he believes. It may be in a church basement in front of his friends and neighbors. And everybody gets that chance."

Manoff believes the caucus process has been one of the last bastions of grassroots politics. "In Iowa, just because you have a lot of money didn't really mean anything. Iowa is small but the people there listen to what the

Candidates make good use of airports in Iowa during the caucus campaign season. Here members of the media wait for President George W. Bush to depart from *Air Force One* at the Mason City Municipal Airport in 2004 (photograph from author's personal collection).

candidates say and they've proven over the years that they're not swayed by the pundits. They're able to penetrate through all of the hype."[10]

Howard Kurtz, media critic for the *Washington Post*, says the winning candidate in Iowa will benefit from "an immutable law of political physics" which will propel him or her into New Hampshire with "bulked up poll numbers" and "blinding momentum." But the chief reason, says Kurtz, is the bombardment of media coverage that creates superstars and also-rans.

"Without that massive media boost, prevailing in Iowa would be seen for what it is: an important first victory that amounts to scoring a run in the top of the first inning."[11]

Candidates and their handlers offer their own unique perspective on the media's impact on the caucuses. Jim Hightower, radio commentator and former congressman from Texas, was a supporter of Senator Fred Harris when Harris challenged Jimmy Carter in the Iowa caucuses of 1976.

"Our task ... was not to beat Carter but only to beat the 'media expectations,' he said, "to run better than the media pundits thought we would."

But he said their problem was that the national press operates on East Coast time, so there was a 9 o'clock deadline to get any news into the *New York Times*, the *Washington Post* and other East Coast media strongholds.

"So we faced the age-old question," said Hightower. "If you do surprisingly well in the Iowa caucuses and the media aren't there to report it, does it make a noise?"[12]

Four years later, Ronald Reagan, who didn't spend much time in Iowa, was not impressed with how he was treated by some in the media. He said the goal of many reporters traveling with him was to catch him making a flub in a speech or trapping him by asking a question about some obscure, inconsequential detail.

"Then, satisfied, most would run off in a pack and report the identical story about a minor goof while ignoring other important things ... and neglecting the kind of beneath- the-surface digging that could have shed more light on the ... differences between the various candidates."[13]

In 1984, Walter Mondale easily won the Iowa caucuses, as he was expected to, and therefore, in his estimation, did not get the bounce he deserved. "The expectations games are a farce but believe me they're real," said Mondale. "I won in Iowa but Gary Hart finished second — and the press reported that Hart was the guy to watch. The press does this because the press wants a fight. Without a fight, there's no story. The press establishes the expectations game and thrives on it."[14]

Senator John Glenn finished far down in the pack in the Iowa Democratic caucuses. New Hampshire voters, who went to the polls eight days later, learned of the Iowa results through media coverage, and the coverage, rather than the results themselves, might have influenced New Hampshire voters, according to some observers.

Herbert P. Asher, in a study of voter attitudes, wrote, "The media coverage of the Iowa results stressed how badly the Glenn campaign was hurt there. Glenn's New Hampshire survey showed that interviews completed before reports of his poor finish in Iowa had him running much stronger in New Hampshire than did interviews completed after the reports of the Iowa results."[15]

Paul Simon ran well in Iowa in 1988 but wrote in his autobiography about the problems with media interpretations of results.

"Before the networks went off the air on caucus night, CBS and ABC declared Gephardt the winner, NBC stating it was too close to call," wrote Simon.

He said when the networks went off the air, tabulating results slowed down in many counties so final results weren't known until much later.

The networks reported Gephardt with 31 percent, Simon with 27 percent, Dukakis 22 percent, Jackson 9 percent, Babbitt 6 percent, uncommitted with 5 percent and Hart and Gore with less than 1 percent.

"The next day Tom Brokaw reported on NBC that Gephardt had won by less than ½ of one percent. The headline in the *Des Moines Register*: 'Gephardt Beats Simon in Squeaker.' But he won."[16]

Author Alexandra Pelosi offers a simple, secondary goal of what all candidates hope to achieve in Iowa: "If they can manage to win the Iowa caucuses, they will attract enough media respect to fill the seats on the press plane to New Hampshire."[17]

David Yepsen, political reporter and columnist for the *Des Moines Register* for more than 30 years, covered nine caucuses, starting with the days of eating grapes with Jimmy Carter in an empty hotel banquet hall to being part of the hundreds of news people following Barack Obama, Hillary Clinton, John McCain, Mitt Romney and the others in 2008.

Yepsen, who now works for Southern Illinois University, may show a little Iowa bias in his thinking but he contends the flaws in the Iowa caucus system are overblown by outside observers. The presidential selection process has to start somewhere — and there would be complaints if it started in Kansas or Oregon or North Carolina or any of the other states, he said.

Whether (critics) are right or not, the caucuses exist and they're first in the nation. People complain about their disproportionate influence.

Whereever you start, there would be disagreement on whether the state was representative of the rest of the country.

A lot of this is just plain envy. If the country wants to come up with a better system, Iowans cannot be parochial enough to be against it. But just moving it to another state will not solve anything.

If you want to improve the process, allow independents to vote, have same-day voter registration and spread things out. Iowa wouldn't be so important if these things were spread out. If someone stumbles or gains in Iowa, everyone would have a chance to recover. But with everything so close together, Iowa takes on even more importance.

One change being considered is having regional primaries. If you love money and television advertising, you'll love regional primaries.[18]

CHAPTER FOURTEEN

Thirty-Six Years of High Expectations

"To become President of the United States, you have to want it almost more than anything else in the world. You must possess the dedication of a martyr ... the precision of a heart surgeon and the fortitude of a guerrilla commando."[1]

The Iowa precinct caucuses are a fascinating facet of American presidential politics for what they mean and what they don't mean, for what they portray and what they betray, and for the roller coaster ride of expectations that most every candidate who ever entered them has experienced.

The caucuses launched Jimmy Carter and Barack Obama to the presidency. Many historians believe that without wins in Iowa, both would have had trouble even getting their party's nominations. (Carter actually finished second to "uncommitted" but defeated all other challengers.)

Ted Kennedy finished second in 1980 and it killed his campaign. Yet Michael Dukakis finished third in 1988 and it launched his. Bill Clinton finished fourth in 1992 with 3 percent of the vote and went on to win the presidency. Hillary Clinton finished third in 2008 and had to reshape her whole campaign strategy. John McCain finished fourth in 2008 and yet won the nomination.

There are eight lessons to be learned from 36 years of history and they are full of paradoxes.

1. It doesn't pay to be the front-runner in Iowa.
2. Despite the perception of importance, only three non-incumbents have won the Iowa caucuses and gone on to win the presidency.
3. Though Iowans have not picked many winners, candidates who

have chosen to bypass the Iowa caucuses or treat them lightly have never won the presidency.

4. History has shown that for the most part, a candidate must finish in the top three in Iowa to have much of a chance at the nomination — hence, the expression "there are only three tickets out of Iowa."

5. Jimmy Carter's strategy has been tried by so many other candidates that it can't possibly work any more.

6. The caucus dynamics are no longer just grassroots politics as they were in the beginning.

7. The media has treated the Iowa caucuses as a game that has a final score to be reported to the rest of the nation, all of which is a misconception.

8. A candidate's success or failure in the Iowa caucuses depends on how well he lives up to media expectations.

It is useful to examine each of these points in more detail.

1. Woe betide the candidate who earns the label of front-runner, an honor usually bestowed by the national news media or from public opinion polls. From Ed Muskie in 1972 to Ronald Reagan in 1980 to Howard Dean in 2004 to Mitt Romney and Hillary Clinton in 2008, the distinction of being at the head of the pack in Iowa can be a kiss of death or at least a bad omen.

2. The eyes of the political world have been on Iowa ever since its caucuses became the first test of presidential strength in 1972. Yet since 1972, in elections where an incumbent was not running, the leader in the Iowa caucuses has won the presidency only three times — Jimmy Carter in 1976, George W. Bush in 2000 and Barack Obama in 2008. And Carter actually finished second to "uncommitted" but received the most support of any individual candidate.

3. While the importance of winning the Iowa caucuses may seem overblown, it is also noteworthy to examine the fate of candidates who chose to ignore them:

> — Al Gore in 1988, who not only withdrew but chastised opponents who pandered to Iowa voters.
>
> — Pat Buchanan in 1992, who chose to enter the race in New Hampshire rather than spar in Iowa.
>
> — John McCain in 2000, whose straight talk about not favoring federal subsidies for ethanol antagonized Iowa farmers.
>
> — Joseph Lieberman in 2004, who chose to use his resources in primaries further on down the line.

— Retired army general Wesley Clark, who announced his candidacy later than the others in 2004 and essentially made the same decision as Lieberman.

— Rudy Giuliani in 2008, who made a few token appearances in Iowa but chose to concentrate instead on winning the Florida primary a month later, which he failed to do.

Each of these candidates decided to bypass Iowa on the campaign trail and all of their campaigns faltered.

4. Those who say "there are only three tickets out of Iowa" have proven to be right most of the time. David Yepsen, longtime political columnist for the *Des Moines Register* says the three tickets are "first class, coach and standby."

Whatever they may be called, the fact is that since 1972, only two candidates who finished out of the top three in Iowa went on to win the nomination of their party — Bill Clinton in 1992 and John McCain in 2008 — and Clinton was up against Iowa senator Tom Harkin who was the easy winner. So Clinton finished third among those running against the favorite son candidate.

5. Jimmy Carter was the trailblazer for future candidates by coming to Iowa well in advance of other candidates — to be "the only candidate campaigning that day in Sioux City," as he put it. So many candidates have tried to follow that approach since then, that, by their very number, it is now impossible to accomplish. In early 2007, a year before the caucuses, 22 men and women had been to Iowa to either actively campaign or to publicly announce they were thinking about it.

6. The dynamics of the caucuses have changed over the years. The caucus and primary season used to stretch from January into June. Indeed, in 1972, the first year that Democratic reforms created the more open nominating procedures and Iowa's caucuses became the first test, George McGovern did not wrap up the Democratic nomination until he won the California primary in June.

The spreading out of caucuses and primaries over a period of several months gave lesser-known candidates an opportunity to gain recognition in places like Iowa and New Hampshire. It also gave them time to raise money so they could be competitive in other states. The advent of Super Tuesday in February, where usually more than 20 states hold primaries and caucuses, has made it virtually impossible for candidates with limited funds to compete. George McGovern in 1972 and Jimmy Carter in 1976 didn't have that problem.

In 2007, Iowa governor Tom Vilsack was a candidate for about a month before dropping out, conceding he did not have the financial wherewithal to carry on. Indiana senator Evan Bayh formed an exploratory committee but decided against running for the same reasons as Vilsack. The odds are overwhelmingly against candidates who do not have a huge war chest that will carry them through Iowa and beyond.

"It's a money race," says Tennessee senator Lamar Alexander, who twice competed in Iowa as he sought the Republican presidential nomination. He cited John Kerry's Democratic campaign in Iowa in 2004 as an example. "He got to a stage in the Iowa race, where I have been before," said Alexander, "and where (Dan) Quayle was and where Elizabeth Dole was and where many candidates have been, when he was out of money. And he got $7 million of his own money, he and his wife's, put it in the campaign, and won."[2]

7. America is a sports-oriented society in which its citizens determine outcomes of events in terms of winners and losers and the lexicon of sports makes its way into many other areas of life, including politics. The Iowa caucuses are therefore considered a game in the eyes of the media and the public. Everything leading up to them is an increasingly longer exhibition season. In actuality, in terms of the political game, the caucuses are just the first inning and therefore there is no final score.

The Democratic Party in Iowa recognized this game mentality early on, and how it could capitalize on it. Republicans eventually caught on. So both parties eagerly feed the news media results on caucus night so they can report to the public who won and who lost, despite the fact that the caucuses are just the first step in Iowa's complicated delegate-selection process and that nobody has officially won or lost.

There's no guarantee that the winners on election night are going to have the same delegate strength after the state conventions. As Robert Thompson, the former county chairman, puts it, the caucuses are "not an election with winners and losers and the results may vary between precinct caucuses and the state convention."[3]

Senator John McCain, who bypassed the Iowa caucuses in 2000 and therefore received scant support, told reporters afterwards, "As we all know, the definition of 'win' is in the view of those who judge who winners and losers are. Yes, we have to 'win' in the view of those who judge these things."[4]

Despite all of the apparent faults in the Iowa caucus system, the candidates keep coming. Vice President Joseph Biden, who fared poorly in the caucuses of 1988 and 2008, nonetheless, says, "Iowa is the last level playing field in presidential politics."[5]

Former Vice President Walter Mondale says,

> You know, after Iowa with its face-to-face campaign style, you kind of go from one television station to another. It's not that way in Iowa. It's open. It's real. In Iowa, people want to be asked. They don't want to be assumed. And it's possible to go from Dubuque to the White House. Jimmy Carter did it. Barack Obama did it.
>
> There are weaknesses in the Iowa caucuses. If you're a soldier serving overseas or the mother of three caring for your children at home or if you're at work in the evening, you can't go to the caucuses. But there's a

A typical scene on caucus night in Iowa is one in which supporters of one candidate cajole backers of other candidates, hoping to win them over. Here a supporter of former North Carolina senator John Edwards waves an Edwards sign in the midst of Howard Dean backers in a middle school cafeteria in Mason City in 2004 (courtesy *Mason City Globe Gazette*).

strength to them. They are meetings. People are there together. It's a debate. It's tangible. It's real. And it's not manipulative. In Iowa, by the time you get to the caucuses, people really know the candidates. It is a hallmark in American politics.[6]

The Iowa precinct caucuses, flawed as they are in the eyes of many, have drawn more than 100 men and women to the state in the past 36 years, all with dreams of making a difference, of achieving the pinnacle of political power, of having an impact on the destiny of millions of people. More than 70 of them survived long enough to get at least a modicum of support in the caucuses, to have their names called out in church basements and school rooms and VFW halls by truck drivers and lawyers and salesmen and housewives, all of whom believed in them.

The caucuses have brought in millions of dollars, not only to Iowa's economy but to the coffers of the two major political parties whose major fundraising events, the Jefferson-Jackson Day Dinner for the Democrats and the Iowa Straw Poll for the Republicans, are now broadcast for the entire nation to see.

The candidates do what they can to polish their images, whether it be trying to mask a southern accent, dyeing one's hair to hide the gray, spending $400 on a haircut, wearing checkered wool shirts to look more like the average guy or posing for pictures in front of big, green John Deere tractors.

When the results are tallied on caucus night, as misleading as they may be, they will be reported to the nation and the world by the hundreds of news media representatives who have descended on Des Moines, and who view Des Moines as an otherwise rather unexciting city where, as one eastern writer observed, "every meal served after 8 P.M. is called breakfast."

Christopher Hull, a researcher who did a thorough study of the Iowa caucuses, concluded that critics are right when they say that media coverage of the caucuses is way out of proportion to what it should be, considering the caucuses are but the first lap in a long race.

He agrees also with those who say the caucuses have become increasingly more a haven for big-time television advertising and less of a venue for retail politics although grassroots campaigning is still an important element.

Further, Hull is in accord with those who say the Democrats' 15 percent viability rule eliminates candidates and flies in the face of the reforms of 1972 that was supposed to make the process more inclusive. Also, Hull sides with critics who say the delegate selection process at the caucuses should be binding and not subject to change further down the line.

But the overall conclusion of his study, which weighs the strengths and weaknesses of the process, is that "Iowa is doing exactly what it's supposed to be doing. On a high, prominent, well-lit stage, it is forcing presidential candidates to engage in a personal effort to meet and persuade voters."[7]

8. It is in this setting that something far more meaningful than results are registered. For ambitious politicians, Iowa is the land of expectations and on caucus night, the candidates and the nation learn who exceeded expectations and who failed to meet them.

"The Iowa caucuses are a collaborative effort between the state parties, presidential candidates and the media in which perception, rather than reality, is enough to send one candidate packing and another to the White House.... Failing to meet expectations can be deadly, even for candidates who 'win' Iowa."[8]

Exceeding expectations or failing to meet them is the story of Jimmy Carter in 1976 and Barack Obama in 2008 taking the first steps toward the presidency.

It is the story of the Howard Dean scream in 2004, the Ted Kennedy tumble in 1980, the Pat Robertson surge in 1988 — and of Ronald Reagan providing a serious challenge to an incumbent president in 1976 but being told to get off his ass and work a little harder after the caucuses of 1980.

It is a story that Fanny Lou Hamer had a part in but didn't live long enough to see it fully unfold. In 1964, the poor, uneducated black woman went to a national convention and begged white political leaders for the right to vote and to participate in the presidential process. Hamer died on March 14, 1977, almost 32 years before Barack Obama became the first African American to become president of the United States.

Only time will tell how the next chapter will be written in 2012. But there are some hints. On November 22, 2008, less than three weeks after the presidential election and more than three years before the next Iowa caucuses, Bobby Jindal, Louisiana's young Republican governor, was in Cedar Rapids, Iowa, apparently getting a feel for the territory, like so many other politicians before him have done.

That same week, almost four years before the next election, Mike Huckabee was in the state promoting his new book. The first chapter is entitled "I Love Iowa."

Appendix A:
The Record Book

.

Bob Dole is the only candidate to receive support in caucuses in three different years.

Jimmy Carter and Bob Dole are the only candidates to be leading candidates in caucuses in two different years.

Bill Clinton and John McCain are the only two candidates to finish fourth in the Iowa caucuses who have gone on to receive their party's presidential nomination.

Shirley Chisholm was the first woman and the first African American to receive support in the caucuses.

Shirley Chisholm and Hillary Clinton are the only two women to receive support in the caucuses.

Shirley Chisholm, Jesse Jackson and Barack Obama are the only African Americans to receive support in the caucuses.

Bill Clinton and Hillary Clinton are the only husband and wife to each receive support in the caucuses, though in different years.

George H.W. Bush and George W. Bush are the only father and son to each receive support in the caucuses, though in different years.

Jimmy Carter, George W. Bush and Barack Obama are the only leading candidates in the Iowa caucuses who have gone on to win the presidency.

Since 1972, 71 candidates have received support in the caucuses — 41 Democrats and 30 Republicans; 69 men and two women.

Appendix B:
The Participants

indicates winner

Democrats

Reuben Askew 1984
Bruce Babbitt 1988
Birch Bayh 1976
Joseph Biden 1988, 2008
Bill Bradley 2000
Jerry Brown 1992
Jimmy Carter 1976*, 1980*
Shirley Chisholm 1972
Wesley Clark 2004
Bill Clinton 1992
Hillary Clinton 2008
Alan Cranston 1984
Howard Dean 2004
Christopher Dodd 2008
Michael Dukakis 1988
John Edwards 2004, 2008
Richard Gephardt 1988*, 2004
John Glenn 1984
Albert Gore 1988, 2000*
Mike Gravel 2008

Tom Harkin 1992*
Fred Harris 1976
Gary Hart 1984, 1988
Ernest Hollings 1984
Hubert Humphrey 1972
Henry Jackson 1976, 1972
Jesse Jackson 1984, 1988
Ted Kennedy 1980
Bob Kerrey 1992
John Kerry 2004*
Dennis Kucinich 2004, 2008
Joseph Lieberman 2004
Eugene McCarthy 1972
George McGovern 1972*, 1984
Walter Mondale 1984*
Edmund Muskie 1972*
Barack Obama 2008*
Bill Richardson 2008
Sargent Shriver 1976
Paul Simon 1988
Paul Tsongas 1992
Morris Udall 1976

Republicans

Lamar Alexander 1996
John Anderson 1980
Howard Baker 1980
Gary Bauer 1996
Sam Brownback 2008
Pat Buchanan 1996
George H.W. Bush 1980*, 1988
George W. Bush 2000*
John Connally 1980
Phil Crane 1980
Bob Dole 1980, 1988*, 1996*
Robert Dornan 1996
Steve Forbes 1996, 2000
Gerald Ford 1976*

Rudy Giuliani 2008
Phil Gramm 1996
Orrin Hatch 2000
Mike Huckabee 2008*
Duncan Hunter 2008
Alan Keyes 1996, 2000
Richard Lugar 1996
John McCain 2000, 2008
Ron Paul 2008
Ronald Reagan 1976, 1980
Mitt Romney 2008
Tom Tancredo 2008
Maurice Taylor 1996
Fred Thompson 2008
Tommy Thompson 2008

Appendix C:
Year-by-Year Results

1972

Democrats

Uncommitted	36%
Muskie	36%
McGovern	23%
Humphrey	2%
McCarthy	1%
Chisholm	1%
Jackson (Henry)	1%

1976

Democrats

Uncommitted	37%
Carter	28%
Bayh	13%
Harris	10%
Udall	6%
Shriver	3%
Jackson (Henry)	1%

Republicans
(random straw poll)

Ford	264
Reagan	248

1980

Democrats

Carter	59%
Kennedy	31%

Republicans

Bush (George H.W.)	32%
Reagan	30%
Baker	15%
Connally	9%
Crane	7%
Anderson	4%
Dole	2%

1984

Democrats

Mondale	49%
Hart	17%
McGovern	10%
Cranston	7%
Glenn	4%
Askew	3%
Jackson (Jesse)	2%

Republicans

Reagan (unopposed)

1988

Democrats

Gephardt	31%
Simon	27%
Dukakis	22%
Babbitt	6%

Republicans

Dole	37%
Robertson	25%
Bush (George H.W.)	19%
Kemp	11%
DuPont	7%

1992

Democrats

Harkin	76%
Uncommitted	12%
Tsongas	4%
Clinton	3%
Kerrey	2%
Brown	2%

Republicans

Bush (George H.W.) (unopposed)

1996

Democrats

Clinton (unopposed)

Republicans

Dole	26%
Buchanan	23%
Alexander	18%
Forbes	10%
Gramm	9%
Keyes	7%
Lugar	4%
Taylor	1%

2000

Democrats

Gore	63%
Bradley	37%

Republicans

Bush (George W.)	41%
Forbes	30%
Keyes	14%
Bauer	9%
McCain	5%
Hatch	1%

2004

Democrats

Kerry	38%
Edwards	32%
Dean	18%
Gephardt	11%
Kucinich	1%

Republicans

Bush (George W.) (unopposed)

2008

Democrats

Obama	38%
Edwards	30%
Clinton (Hillary)	29%
Richardson	2%
Biden	1%
Dodd	0%
Gravel	0%
Kucinich	0%

Republicans

Huckabee	34%
Romney	25%
Thompson	13%
McCain	13%
Paul	10%
Giuliani	4%
Hunter	1%

Chapter Notes

Introduction

1. Christopher C. Hull, *Grass Roots Rules: How the Iowa Caucus Helps Elect American Presidents* (Stanford, CA: Stanford University Press, 2008), p. 39.

2. U.S. Census Bureau, 2005.

3. Ken Dychtwald and Joe Flower, *The Age Wave: How the Most Important Tool of Our Time Can Change Your Future* (New York: Bantam, 1990), p. 62.

4. The basketball fans didn't miss anything at the political rally. Dole was an hour late.

Chapter One

1. Joshua Zeitz, "Democratic Debacle," *American Heritage* 55, No. 3 (June-July 2004).

2. Examples of literacy test questions were contained in a television interview between correspondent Mike Wallace and Senator James Eastland that was broadcast July 28, 1957.

3. Audio and text versions of the Kennedy civil rights speech can be found on the Web site americanrhetoric.com.

4. The account of Dirksen's efforts is recounted in a *Peoria* (Ill.) *Journal Star* article published June 10, 2004, the 40th anniversary of the vote.

5. Eventually, arrests were made but no one was convicted until the case was reopened in 2004. On June 21, 2005, Edgar Ray Killen, then 79 years old, was convicted on three counts of manslaughter and sentenced to three 20-year prison sentences. Killen, an ordained Baptist minister, was also head of the local Ku Klux Klan unit and, with the compliance of sheriff's deputies, set up the killings of Chaney, Goodman and Schwerner. The story of the deaths and the search for the murderers was the basis for the film *Mississippi Burning*.

6. Moses said his work in Mississippi consisted of driving around and asking business leaders, ministers and others if they would support efforts to mount a voter registration drive. Soon, blacks in neighboring towns heard about his efforts and wanted him and his volunteers to come to their communities. They couldn't refuse, said Moses, even though they knew they would experience violent protests. "The problem is that you can't be in a position of turning down the tough areas because the people then, I think, would simply lose confidence in you; so, we accepted this," he wrote in the January issue of *Liberation* magazine. Moses dropped out of the Student Non-Violent Coordinating Committee (SNCC) in 1966 and returned to teaching. He later headed the Algebra Project, an effort to help inner-city school children to achieve mathematics literacy and to teach them higher level problem-solving skills.

7. The text of Fanny Lou Hamer's testimony is widely circulated. It is on file at the Lyndon Baines Johnson Presidential Library in Austin, Texas, and is available online, in both text and audio, at americanrhetoric.com.

8. Theodore H. White, *The Making of the President 1964* (New York: Athenium, 1965), p. 279. White wrote detailed accounts of the presidential campaigns of 1960, 1964, 1968 and 1972, all of which were published as books with identical titles except for the change in year.

9. George McGovern, *Grassroots: The Autobiography of George McGovern* (New York: Random House, 1977), p. 132.

10. White, *The Making of the President 1964*, p. 279.

11. Zeitz, "Democratic Debacle." Johnson reportedly dangled the vice presidency in front of Humphrey in exercising his powerful persuasive style to get what he wanted. Humphrey reportedly mentioned what was at stake for him in the course of the negotiations. Hamer, whose stirring testimony put the issue in the national spotlight, was unhappy with the results, telling the press she hadn't come all the way from Mississippi to get just two delegates seated.

12. Interview with author on March 11, 2009.

13. Ibid.

14. Mondale, speaking on Minnesota Public Radio on February 11, 2000, 36 years after the Mississippi compromise that he helped broker, said, "All of it was very hard to come by. So when you hear people say that citizens can't do anything, that it is foolish to become involved, that nobody listens, please tell them to take a hard look at American history, and while you're at it, take a look at Fannie Lou Hamer as well." At the Democratic National Convention in 2008, on the night Senator Barack Obama was nominated as the first African American to be the presidential candidate of a major political party, Mondale reflected on the event in a television interview with Jim Lehrer on National Public Television. He took pride in how far the country had come in 40 years — a long way from the time when a deal had to be made to get blacks seated as delegates.

Chapter Two

1. McGovern, *Grassroots: The Autobiography of George McGovern*, p. 109.

2. Nixon made the comment at a press conference on November 7, 1962, in which he told reporters it was his last press conference. Nixon was elected president in 1968 and re-elected in 1972, resigning from office in 1974 when he faced impeachment for obstructing justice in the investigation of the break-in of the Democratic National Headquarters in the Watergate office building in Washington. The irony was that the Watergate scandal that led to Nixon's political demise was uncovered by the press—reporters Bob Woodward and Carl Bernstein of the *Washington Post*.

3. Interview with the author on March 11, 2009.

4. David Mixner, writing on the Huffington Post blog, posted February 4, 2007. Mixner was later to serve on the McGovern-Fraser Commission, a group that set new rules for delegate selection, a process that laid the groundwork for the Iowa caucuses to take on national prominence.

5. McGovern, *Grassroots: The Autobiography of George McGovern*, p. 130.

6. White, *The Making of the President 1968*, pp. 272–273.

7. McGovern, *Grassroots: The Autobiography of George McGovern*, p. 130.

8. Ibid., 149.

9. Rhodes Cook, *The Presidential Nominating Process: A Place for Us?* (New York: Rowman & Littlefield, 2004), p. 43.

10. Christopher, a former deputy attorney general, would later become secretary of state under President Bill Clinton. Three members of the commission,

Senators George McGovern, Birch Bayh and Harold Hughes, as well as Senator Fred Harris, who named the members of the commission, all later sought the Democratic presidential nomination, participating in the wide-open primary and caucus system their commission helped create. Mitchell, the national committeeman from Maine, later was elected to the U.S. Senate and became Senate majority leader.

11. "Reform or Die," *Time* magazine, June 27, 1969.

12. McGovern, *Grassroots: The Autobiography of George McGovern*, p. 153.

13. "How a little-known task force helped create Red State/Blue State America," *Boston Globe*, November 23, 2003.

Chapter Three

1. Hugh Winebrenner, *The Iowa Precinct Caucuses: The Making of a Media Event* (Ames: Iowa State University Press, 1998), p. 25.

2. R.W. Apple, Jr., "The Election Process: Iowa's Weighty Caucuses; Significance by Accident," *New York Times*, January 25, 1988.

3. Winebrenner, *The Iowa Precinct Caucuses*, p. 26.

4. Interview with author, September 13, 2008.

5. Apple, "The Election Process."

6. A mimeograph machine, forerunner to today's copiers, was a mechanical duplicator that produced copies by pressing ink onto paper through openings cut in a stencil. Whatever was to be copied was typed, usually via a manual typewriter, onto a special sheet, called a stencil, which was then run through the machine. It was a slow, labor-intensive process.

7. "Super Complicated Tuesday," *The Nation*, February 4, 2008.

8. Larsen's comments are taken from a transcript of a broadcast of *Iowa Journal* on Iowa Public Television, posted December 31, 2007.

9. Interview with author, September 13, 2008.

10. Winebrenner, *The Iowa Precinct Caucuses*, p. 45.

11. Mark Stricherz, *Why the Democrats Are Blue: Secular Liberalism and the Decline of the People's Party* (New York: Encounter Books, 2007), p. 189–190.

12. Walter Shapiro, *One-Man Caravan: On the Road with the 2004 Candidates Before America Tunes In* (New York: Perseus Books, 2003), p. 147.

13. africanamerican.com

14. McGovern's speech in Des Moines was covered by The Associated Press and the story was published in newspapers throughout the country. This excerpt was taken from the *Mason City* (Iowa) *Globe Gazette*, January 13, 1972.

15. Gary Hart. *Right from the Start: A Chronicle of the McGovern Campaign* (New York: Quandrangle/ New York Times Book Co., 1973), pp. 112–113.

16. Ibid., p. 115.

17. Ibid., p. 113.

18. Ed Tibbetts, "So Why Do We Caucus, Anyway?" *Quad City* (Iowa) *Times*, December 15, 2007.

19. Hart, *Right from the Start*, pp. 114–115.

20. Winebrenner, *The Iowa Precinct Caucuses*, p. 9.

21. Timothy Crouse, *The Boys on the Bus* (New York: Random House, 1973), p. 79.

22. Hart, *Right from the Start*, p. 115.

23. Hart, interview with the author, January 14, 2000.

24. Pete W. Schramm, American National Biography, Volume I (Oxford: Oxford University Press, 1999), p. 47.

25. Winebrenner, *The Iowa Precinct Caucuses*, p. 55.

26. Interview with author, September 13, 2008.

Chapter Four

1. According to the *Congressional Record*, Agnew first used the expression in

referring to the press during a speech at the California state Republican convention in September, actually coining the phrase.

2. Louis W. Liebovich, *The Press and the Modern Presidency: Myths and Mindsets from Kennedy to Election 2000* (New York: Praeger, 2001), p. 104.

3. In an August 7, 2007, interview with the Center For Public Integrity, Gary Hart, McGovern's campaign manager, said Carter used a book Hart wrote, *Right from the Start: A Chronicle of the McGovern Campaign*, as a handbook for his own campaign.

4. Jimmy Carter, *Why Not the Best?* (Nashville: Broadman Press, 1975), pp. 139–140.

5. Jules Witcover, *Marathon: The Pursuit of the Presidency 1972–1976* (New York: Viking Press, 1977), p. 194.

6. Martin Schram, *Running for President 1976: The Carter Campaign* (New York: Stein and Day, 1977), p. 6; Peter G. Bourne, *Jimmy Carter: A Comprehensive Biography from Plains to Post Presidency* (New York: Scribner, 1997), p. 264.

7. Interview with author, February 11, 2009.

8. Winebrenner, *The Iowa Precinct Caucuses*, p. 60.

9. Ellen Weiss and Mel Friedman, *Jimmy Carter: Champion of Peace.* (New York: Aladdin, 2003), p. 50.

10. Interview with author on September 6, 2008. Mrs. Garst said Carter called her on Thanksgiving Day 1980, three weeks after he lost his bid for re-election to express his thanks to her. "He didn't have to do that," she said. "I have a nice little corner of my heart saved for Jimmy Carter."

11. Bourne, *Jimmy Carter*, p. 277.

12. Winebrenner, *The Iowa Precinct Caucuses*, p. 63

13. Interview with the author on March 11, 2009.

14. Witcover, *Marathon: The Pursuit of the Presidency 1972–1976*, p. 51

15. Reston's column was published in *The New York Times* on November 21, 1975, and is quoted in Witcover's *Marathon: Pursuit of the Presidency 1972–1976* on pages 91–92.

16. Winebrenner, *The Iowa Precinct Caucuses*, p. 74–75.

17. Alexandra Pelosi, *Sneaking Into the Flying Circus: How the Media Turn Our Presidential Campaigns into Freak Shows* (New York: Free Press, 2005), p. 34.

Chapter Five

1. George Herbert Walker Bush, a Republican candidate for the presidential nomination in 1980, as quoted in *Time* magazine, January 21, 1980.

2. *Washington Post* staff, *The Pursuit of the Presidency 1980.* (Washington: Washington Post, 1980), p. 124.

3. Interview with the author, January 18, 2009.

4. *Washington Post* staff, *The Pursuit of the Presidency 1980*, p. 66.

5. Burton Hersh, *The Education of Edward M. Kennedy: A Family Biography* (New York: Dell, 1980), p. 610.

6. William E. Leuchtenburg, *In the Shadow of FDR: From Harry Truman to George W. Bush* (Ithaca, NY: Cornell University Press, 2001), p. 202.

7. *Washington Post* staff, *The Pursuit of the Presidency 1980*, p. 121.

8. Herbert S. Parmet, *George Bush: The Life of a Lone Star Yankee* (New York: Scribner: 1997), p. 224.

9. Washington Post staff, *The Pursuit of the Presidency 1980*, p. 121.

10. *Time* magazine, January 21, 1980, p. 28.

11. Winebrenner, *The Iowa Precinct Caucuses*, pp. 84–86.

12. *Washington Post* staff, *The Pursuit of the Presidency 1980*, 208.

13. Years later, reflecting on the quirkiness of the Iowa caucuses, Kennedy observed that he finished second in 1980 and it killed his chances while Michael Dukakis finished third in 1988 and it launched him on his way to the Democratic nomination.

14. Interview with the author, January 18, 2009.

15. Interview with the author, March 11, 2009.

16. *Washington Post* staff, *The Pursuit of the Presidency 1980*, p. 125.

17. Ibid., 138

18. Roger Ailes and Jon Kraushar, *You Are The Message* (New York: Doubleday, 1989), p. 93.

19. Frances Fitzgerald, *Way Out There in the Blue* (New York: Simon & Schuster, 2001), p. 104.

20. Ed Rollins, *Bare Knuckles and Back Rooms: My Life in American Politics* (New York: Broadway, 1997), p. 117.

21. Lee Edwards, *To Preserve and Protect.* (New York: Heritage Foundation, 2005), p. 35.

22. T. J. Walker and Jess Todtfeld, *Media Training A–Z* (New York: Media Training Worldwide, 2008), p. 138.

23. Parmet, *George Bush*, p. 226.

24. Theodore H. White, *America in Search of Itself* (New York: Harper & Row, 1982), p. 339.

Chapter Six

1. Gillis Long testimony before the Hunt Commission on November 6, 1981.

2. Excerpt from Hunt speech at the Institute of Politics, John F. Kennedy School of Government, Harvard University, December 15, 1981.

3. Ari Berman, "Not So Superdelegates," *The Nation*, February 18, 2008.

4. Rhodes Cook, *The Presidential Nominating Process: A Place for Us?* (New York: Rowman & Littlefield, 2004), p. 56.

5. Tom Curry, "What Role for Democratic Superdelegates?" MSNBC.com, April 26, 2007.

6. Interview with author, March 11, 2008. Harkin's comments were made during a time when presidential candidates Barack Obama and Hillary Clinton were in a tight race both in popular vote and in delegates, with Obama leading in both. At the time of the interview there

was widespread speculation that Clinton could seize the nomination because of her support among superdelegates who might have the power to negate Obama's strength at the polls. That did not turn out to be a factor.

7. *Newsweek*, May 24, 1982, p. 31.

8. There are many references to the orange color of Cranston's hair. The author's primary source is *Wake Me When It's Over: Presidential Politics of 1984* (New York: Macmillan, 1985), p. 126. Authors Jack Germond and Jules Witcover call the hair-dying one of Cranston's "ludicrous attempts at downplaying his age and elderly appearance."

9. Lynch recalled his days with Hart in an interview with the author on September 29, 2008. He said when Hart made a second run for the Democratic nomination prior to the 1988 Iowa caucuses, the two men teamed up again. Lynch drove Hart to the Des Moines airport after a campaign stop in Iowa in 1987. Within days after that, the scandal involving Hart's relationship with a model named Donna Rice hit the headlines, causing his campaign to come to an abrupt end.

10. Russell Baker, "The Handicappers," *New York Times Magazine*, February 6, 1983.

11. Former KIMT-TV staffers Bill Schickel and John Jaszewski recalled the incident in an interview with the author on April 29, 2008. Interestingly, both Schickel and Jaszewski entered politics after their television days. Schickel was elected mayor of Mason City, Iowa, three times and served three terms in the Iowa legislature. At this writing, Jaszewski is serving his third term on the city council in Mason City.

12. Author interview with Schickel on October 1, 2008.

13. Germond and Witcover, *Wake Me When It's Over*, p. 135.

14. Winebrenner, *The Iowa Precinct Caucuses*, p. 120.

15. Hull, *Grassroots Rules: How the Iowa Caucus Helps Elect American Presidents*, p. 57.

16. Michael Nelson, *The Presidency and the Political System* (Washington: CQ Press, 2005), p. 209.

17. John Glenn and Nick Taylor, *John Glenn: A Memoir* (New York: Bantam, 1999), p. 348.

18. Winebrenner, *The Iowa Precinct Caucuses*, pp. 121, 126.

19. Germond and Witcover. *Wake Me When It's Over: Presidential Politics of 1984*, p. 244.

Chapter Seven

1. The fact that du Pont had trouble generating any excitement in the Midwest is demonstrated by an incident involving the author. In March 1987, the author interviewed candidate du Pont in a conference room of the *Mason City Globe Gazette* in Mason City, Iowa. CNN taped the interview for broadcast later as part of its series on presidential candidates. Two weeks later, the author received a call from CNN that the interview was going to be broadcast that day, a Friday. In fact, it would be on in about 15 minutes and would be rebroadcast two days later. Hurriedly, the author called his father, a widower in Illinois, to tell him his son was going to be on television with Pete du Pont in 15 minutes and again on the following Sunday. "I think I'll catch it Sunday," said the father. "I'm in the middle of watching *Days of Our Lives* right now."

2. Rumsfeld served a second stint as secretary of defense from 2001 to 2006 in the administration of President George W. Bush, the son of President George H.W. Bush. Rumsfeld was considered the architect of America's military involvement in Iraq. When that became a politically and publicly unpopular war, he resigned.

3 Winebrenner, *The Iowa Precinct Caucuses*, p. 139

4. Witnessed by the author in August 1987.

5. First reported in *Washington Post,* February 15, 1987, and cited in many newspapers, magazines and books thereafter.

6. *Des Moines Register*, May 8, 1987.

7. Jack Germond and Jules Witcover. *Whose Broad Stripes and Bright Stars: The Trivial Pursuit of the Presidency 1988*. (New York: Warner Books, 1989), pp. 178–179.

8. Ibid., p. 211.

9. Biden faced other pressures when the alleged plagiarism charges emerged. As chairman of the Senate Foreign Relations Committee, he was preparing for the upcoming confirmation hearings of Supreme Court nominee Robert Bork, a jurist generally loved by conservatives and despised by liberals. Biden staffers said the distraction of trying to get ready for what were sure to be contentious hearings may have been why Biden neglected to mention Neil Kinnock in his Des Moines speech. Also, not long after he dropped out of the presidential race, Biden was hospitalized with two brain aneurisms. He suffered from bad headaches during the campaign, a prelude to the aneurisms and perhaps a reason he did not think clearly on some occasions. The account of the plagiarism problems is covered in depth in Germond and Witcover's *Whose Broad Stripes and Bright Stars: The Trivial Pursuit of the Presidency 1988.*

10. David Maraniss and Ellen K. Yakashima, *The Prince of Tennessee: Al Gore Meets His Fate* (New York: Simon & Schuster, 2001), p. 218.

11. Germond and Witcover, *Whose Broad Stripes and Bright Stars*, p. 218.

12. Ailes later founded the Fox News Network. The exchange between Rather and Bush is widely quoted from many sources.

13. Winebrenner, *The Iowa Precinct Caucuses*, p. 158.

14. *Washington Post*, September 14, 1987.

15. Winebrenner, *The Iowa Precinct Caucuses*, p. 150.

16. *New York Times*, February 9, 1988.

17. Parmet, *The Life of a Lone Star Yankee*, p. 327.

18. John P. Cobb, *Progressive Christians Speak: A Different Voice on Faith and Politics* (New York: Westminster John Knox Press, 2000), p. 319.

19. Terry McAuliffe, *My Life Among Democrats: Presidents, Candidates, Donors, Activists, Alligators and Other Wild Animals* (New York: Thomas Dunne Books, 2007), p. 79.

20. Michael Deupree, *Is It Weird Out There or Is It Just Me?* (New York: Authorhouse, 2006), p. 115.

Chapter Eight

1. Bush encountered opposition after the Iowa caucuses. Conservative commentator Patrick J. Buchanan, a former Nixon speechwriter, got into the race in time for the New Hampshire primary but did not present a serious challenge to President Bush's nomination.

2. *MacNeil-Lehrer NewsHour*, April 10, 1991.

3. Winebrenner, *The Iowa Precinct Caucuses*, p. 189.

4. Jerry Brown's father, Pat Brown, defeated Richard Nixon for the California governorship in 1962. Nixon, the former vice president who lost his bid for the presidency to John F. Kennedy in 1960, thought his loss in California was his political obituary. It was in that concession speech that Nixon uttered his famous line to the press that they wouldn't have Dick Nixon "to kick around any more." Six years later, he was elected president.

5. Center for Public Integrity interview with Harkin, August 1, 2007.

Chapter Nine

1. This was part of the stump speech of presidential contender Lamar Alexander, but he also said it in an interview with the author on August 18, 1995.

2. *New York Times*, February 25, 1996.

3. Candidates typically have recurring themes or images that they use in speeches as they travel around. So reporters who cover a candidate on a regular basis have heard many of the stories before. The author covered Gramm's visits to Iowa many times in 1995 and 1996 and could accurately predict what he was going to talk about at campaign events. In fact, just for amusement, he developed a checklist of Gramm's speech topics and would cross them off, one by one, as the senator mentioned them. Dickie Flatts was always on the list and was always crossed off it.

4. The line was part of Forbes' stump speech in two unsuccessful runs for the Republican presidential nomination, first used in campaign speeches in 1995 and again as late as August 1998.

5. Winebrenner, *The Iowa Precinct Caucuses*, pp. 215–218.

6. Ibid., p. 226.

7. *New York Times*, February 13, 1996.

8. Ibid., February 14, 1996.

9. Interview with Center for Public Integrity, July 12, 2007.

Chapter Ten

1. U.S. Senator Charles Grassley of Iowa, watching activities at the Iowa Straw Poll festivities in Ames, Iowa, in 1999, as quoted in the *Washington Post*, August 16, 1999.

2. Interview with the author, January 20, 2000.

3. *Quad City Times*, January 9, 2000.

4. *Mason City Globe Gazette*, January 11, 2000.

5. *Washington Post*, August 16, 1999.

6. The incident occurred at the Royal Fork restaurant in Mason City and was witnessed and reported by Peggy Senzarino, a reporter for the local newspaper who was assigned to cover the Kasich speech that day.

7. Interview with the author, April 18, 1998.

8. Bush left the card on the podium

after he spoke and was retrieved by the author after the event was over. An aide later confirmed it was Bush's handwriting on the card.

9. Interview with author, January 12, 2009.

10. There are many written accounts of the extravagant 1999 Iowa Straw Poll. The source used here was the *San Francisco Chronicle* of August 15, 1999, which ran a story under the headline, "Iowa Straw Poll is Hog Wash."

11. Flansburg's comments appeared in a guest column for the *Washington Post* and were quoted in the *San Francisco Chronicle*, August 15, 1999.

12. Interview with CBS News, August 10, 2007

13. Bush's comments were broadcast on ABC News on the night of August 14, 1999.

14. Interview with Center for Public Integrity, March 28, 2007.

15. Interview with author, January 14, 2000.

16. Interview with author, January 12, 2009.

17. Reporters traveling with the Bradley campaign said that little boy's hometown had a tendency to change, depending on where Bradley was speaking on any given day.

Chapter Eleven

1. *Mason City Globe Gazette*, August 13, 2003.

2. Walter Shapiro, *One-Car Caravan: On the Road with the 2004 Democrats Before America Tunes In* (New York: Public Affairs, 2003), p. 123.

3. Ibid., p. 63.

4. Lieberman's entry into the race provided an expansion of a footnote in American presidential politics. It meant that every vice presidential candidate since 1976, with the exception of Geraldine Ferraro, had also sought the presidency. The breakdown is as follows: 1976 — Bob Dole, Republican (sought presidency in 1988 and 1996), Walter Mondale, Democrat (sought presidency in 1984; 1980 — George Bush, Republican (elected president in 1988), Walter Mondale, Democrat (sought presidency in 1984; 1984 — Bush (elected president in 1988); 1988 — Dan Quayle, Republican (sought presidency in 1996), Lloyd Bentsen (sought presidency in 1976); 1992 — Dan Quayle, Republican (sought presidency in 1996), Al Gore, Democrat, (sought presidency in 1988 and 2000); 1996 — Jack Kemp, Republican (sought presidency in 1996), Al Gore, Democrat (sought presidency in 1988 and 2000); 2000 — Dick Cheney, Republican (sought presidency in 1996), Joseph Lieberman, Democrat (sought presidency in 2004). As of this writing, the string is still in place. The 2004 vice presidential nominees were Cheney, the incumbent Republican, who sought the presidency by participating in the Iowa caucus campaign prior to the 1996 election and Senator John Edwards, Democrat, who sought the presidency in 2004 and 2008.

5. Attending political fundraisers for local candidates is a time-honored part of the pre-caucus campaign cycle. It provides grassroots politicking opportunities for the presidential candidates as well as the local candidates. It also builds a base of support for the presidential candidates because at caucus time, the locals will remember who came to Iowa to support them when they needed it. Information on the candidates' daily schedules came from their campaign staffs and were compiled as part of a study done by George Washington University.

6. Witnessed by the author on July 9, 2003.

7. Descriptions of the candidates are gleaned from many sources, including the author's own observations and from the writing of Walter Shapiro, *USA Today* columnist, in his book about the 2004 campaign, *One-Car Caravan: On the Road with the 2004 Democrats Before America Tunes In.*

8. Shapiro, *One-Car Caravan*, p. 105

9. Ibid., p. 70.

10. Andrew Chadwick and Philip N. Howard, *Routledge Handbook of Internet Politics* (New York: Routledge, 2008), p. 17.

11. Many who were in the audience in the ballroom that night saw nothing unusual about Dean's speech. Later, when they saw replays of it in their hotel room, they were shocked by how distorted the image of Dean was on the television screen. Among those who registered disbelief at the television image was Senator Harkin, who was standing next to Dean as he spoke.

12. Frank Lontz, *Words That Work: It's Not What You Say, It's What People Hear* (New York: Hyperion, 2008), p. 140.

13. Matt Bai, *The Argument: Billionaires, Bloggers and the Battle to Remake Democratic Politics* (New York: Penguin Press, 2007), p. 161.

14. Walter Shapiro, "Hype and Glory," *USA Today*, January 20, 2004.

15. The figures are taken from candidates' daily records, compiled for a study done by George Washington University.

16. Stone recalled the incident at the county Democratic headquarters and told of Flynn's conversation in Las Vegas in an interview with the author on October 12, 2008.

Chapter Twelve

1. Senator Christopher Dodd of Connecticut, in an interview with the author on December 27, 2007, expressing frustration over trying to compete with the media attention being given to Senator Barack Obama of Illinois and Senator Hillary Rodham Clinton of New York, as all three sought the Democratic presidential nomination.

2. Interview with the Center for Public Integrity, June 11, 2007.

3. When Richardson withdrew from the 2008 presidential race, he was wooed by Bill Clinton to endorse Hillary Clinton. Richardson held off making an endorsement for weeks, prompting Bill Clinton to reportedly complain, "Wasn't two presidential appointments enough?" When Richardson eventually endorsed Barack Obama, James Carville, a top adviser to Bill Clinton, publicly compared Richardson to Judas Iscariot, the biblical figure who betrayed Jesus Christ.

4. Witnessed by the author on December 30, 2007.

5. Interview with the author, December 15, 2007.

6. Eli Saslow, "The 17 Minutes That Launched a Political Star," *Washington Post*, August 25, 2008.

7. Ibid.

8. The full text of the Obama convention speech, in both audio and script can be found at www.americanrhetoric.com.

9. The Clinton strategy was widely discussed in the media but was confirmed by her campaign manager, former Democratic national chairman Terry McAuliffe in an interview on the *Meet the Press* television program on May 11, 2008. Within a few days of Clinton suspending her campaign and endorsing Obama, *Meet the Press* moderator Tim Russert asked McAuliffe what derailed the campaign. McAuliffe replied, "I did think it would probably be over after February 5. I think once we had Iowa — Iowa was a key determinant."

10. Democrat contender Joe Biden thought Giuliani put too much emphasis on his experiences during and after the terrorist attacks. Biden often told his audiences, "There are three things in every Rudy Giuliani sentence: a noun, a verb and 9/11."

11. Though Paul had a national following, as shown by his fundraising, he was not invited to participate in several debates among candidates, evidence that GOP leaders did not consider him a viable candidate.

12. Interview with author, June 11, 2007.

13. Interview with author, March 16, 2007.

14. Fox News reported the haircut story on April 27, 2007. The *Washington*

Post story, written by John Soloman under the headline, "Splitting Hairs: Edwards' Stylist Tells His Side of Story," was published on July 5, 2007.

15. The figures, rounded off, come from campaign finance reports filed with the Federal Election Commission.

16. *New York Times,* May 23, 2007.

17. There are many published accounts of the Clinton question-planting, including in the *Los Angeles Times,* November 7, 2007.

18. Clear Lake is widely known as the place it all happened on "the day the music died"— February 3, 1959, when singers Buddy Holly, Richie Valens and J.P. Richardson (better known as "The Big Bopper") were killed in a plane crash shortly after performing at the Winter Dance Party at the Surf Ballroom in Clear Lake.

19. Stone recalled the incident in an interview with the author on October 12, 2008.

20. Mike Huckabee, *Do The Right Thing: Inside the Movement That's Bringing Common Sense Back to America* (New York: Sentinel, 2008), p. 99.

21. *Quad City Times,* August 12, 2007.

22. Ibid.

23. "What Iowa Straw Poll Tells the GOP," *Time* magazine, August 11, 2007.

24. *Des Moines Register,* September 17, 2007.

25. Evan Thomas, *A Long Time Coming* (Washington: Public Affairs, 2009), p. 16.

26. *New York Times,* November 12, 2007.

27. T.J. Walker and Jess Todtfeld, *Media Training A-Z* (New York: Media Training Worldwide, 2008), p. 138.

28. Figures were compiled by Enlighten Technologies Inc. and posted on iowacaucus.com.

Chapter Thirteen

1. Robert J. Donovan and Raymond L Sherer, *Unsilent Revolution: Television News and the America Public Life* (Washington, DC: Woodrow Wilson Center, 1992), p. 231.

2. Shapiro, *One-Car Caravan,* p. 109.

3. Jeff Greenfield. "The Brigadoon Complex: Where the Iowa Caucuses Went Wrong," *Slate,* December 31, 2007.

4. Letter to editor, *New York Times,* January 24, 1988.

5. Winebrenner, *The Iowa Precinct Caucuses,* p. 9.

6. *New York Times,* January 24, 1988.

7. Gerald Stone, Michael Singletary, Virginia P. Raymond, *Clarifying Communication Theories: A Hands-On Approach* (New York: Wiley-Blackwell, 1999), p. 177.

8. Winebrenner, *The Iowa Precinct Caucuses,* pp. 8–9.

9. E.D. Dover, *The Presidential Election of 1996: Clinton's Incumbency and Television* (New York: Praeger, 1998), p. 27.

10. Interview with author, January 18, 2009.

11. Howard Kurtz, "Media Notes," *Washington Post,* November 26, 2007.

12. Jim Hightower, *There's Nothing in the Middle of the Road but Yellow Stripes and Dead Armadillos* (New York: Harper Paperbacks, 1995), p. 140.

13. Ronald Reagan, *An American Life* (New York: Simon & Schuster, 1990), p. 198.

14. Interview with author, March 11, 2009.

15. Herbert P. Asher, *Polling and the Public: What Every Citizen Should Know* (Washington, DC: CQ Press, 2007), p. 161.

16. Paul Simon, *P.S.: The Autobiography of Paul Simon* (New York: Bonus Books, 2003), p. 215. The margin of victory cited by the next day's newscast, cited by Simon, makes the outcome much closer than are shown in the official results

17. Pelosi. *Sneaking Into the Flying Circus,* p. 34.

18. Interview with the author, February 11, 2009.

Chapter Fourteen

1. Hart, *Right from the Start*, p. 29.
2. Interview with Center for Public Integrity, March 28, 2007.
3. *New York Times*, January 24, 1988.
4. *Washington Post*, January 16, 2000.
5. Interview with the author, December 30, 2007.
6. Interview with the author, March 11, 2009.
7. Hull, *Grassroots Rules*, pp. 151–153.
8. "About the Caucuses: Perception Becomes Reality," iowapresidentialpolitics.com, January 27, 2008.

Bibliography

Books

Ailes, Roger, and Jon Kraushar. *You Are the Message.* New York: Doubleday, 1989.

Asher, Herbert P. *Polling and the Public: What Every Citizen Should Know.* Washington: CQ Press, 2007.

Bai, Matt. *The Argument: Billionaires, Bloggers and the Battle to Remake Democratic Politics.* New York: Penguin Press, 2007.

Bourne, Peter G. *Jimmy Carter: A Comprehensive Biography from Plains to Post Presidency.* New York: Scribner, 1997.

Broder, David, Lou Cannon, Haynes Johnson, Martin Schramm, and Richard Harwood. *The Pursuit of the Presidency 1980.* New York: Berkley Books, 1980.

Cannon, Lou. *President Reagan: The Role of a Lifetime.* New York: Touchstone/ Simon & Schuster, 2000.

Carter, Jimmy. *Why Not the Best?* Nashville: Broadman Press, 1975.

Chadwick, Andrew, and Philip N. Howard. *Routledge Handbook of Internet Politics.* New York: Routledge, 2008.

Cobb, John P., Jr. *Progressive Christians Speak: A Different Voice on Faith and Politics.* New York: Westminster John Knox Press, 2000.

Cook, Rhodes. *The Presidential Nominating Process: A Place for Us?* Lanham, MD: Rowman & Littlefield, 2004.

Crouse, Timothy. *The Boys on the Bus.* New York: Random House, 1973.

Dallek, Robert. *Flawed Giant: The Years of Lyndon Johnson.* New York: Oxford University Press, 1999.

Deupree, Michael. *Is It Weird Out There or Is It Just Me?* New York: Authorhouse, 2006.

Diamond, Sara. *Not by Politics Alone: The Enduring Influence of the Christian Right.* New York: Guilford Press, 2000.

Donovan, Robert J., and Raymond L. Sherer. *Unsilent Revolution: Television News and the America Public Life.* Washington: Woodrow Wilson Center, 1992.

Dover, E.D. *The Presidential Election of 1996: Clinton's Incumbency and Television.* New York: Praeger, 1998.

Dychtwald, Ken, and Joe Flower. *The Age Wave: How the Most Important Trend of Our Time Can Change Your Future.* New York: Bantam, 1990.

Edwards, Lee. *To Preserve and Protect.* New York: Heritage Foundation, 2005.

Fitzgerald, Frances. *Way Out There in the Blue.* New York: Simon & Schuster, 2001.

Freddoso, David. *The Case Against Barack Obama: The Unlikely Rise and Unexamined Agenda of the Media's Favorite Candidate.* New York: Regnery, 2008.

Germond, Jack W., and Julies Witcover. *Blue Smoke and Mirrors: How Reagan*

Won and How Carter Lost the Election of 1980. New York: Viking, 1980.

___. *Mad as Hell: Revolt at the Ballot Box 1992.* New York: Warner Books, 1993.

___. *Wake Us When It's Over: Presidential Politics of 1984.* New York: Macmillan, 1985.

___. *Whose Broad Stripes and Bright Stars: The Trivial Pursuit of the Presidency 1988.* New York: Warner Books, 1989.

Glenn, John, and Nick Taylor. *John Glenn: A Memoir.* New York: Bantam, 1999.

Hart, Gary. *Right from the Start: A Chronicle of the McGovern Campaign.* New York: Quandrangle/New York Times Book Co., 1973.

Hersh, Burton. *The Education of Edward Kennedy: A Family Biography.* New York: Dell, 1980.

Hightower, Jim. *There's Nothing in the Middle of the Road but Yellow Stripes and Dead Armadillos.* New York: Harper Paperbacks, 1995.

Huckabee, Mike. *Do the Right Thing: Inside the Movement That's Bringing Common Sense Back to America.* New York: Sentinel, 2008.

Hull, Christopher C. *Grassroots Rules: How the Iowa Caucus Helps Elect American Presidents.* Stanford, CA: Stanford University Press, 2008.

Kaplan Critical Reading Notebook. New York: Kaplan, 2008.

Kaufman, Burton I., and Scott Kaufman. *The Presidency of James Earl Carter, Jr.* Manhattan, KS: University Press of Kansas, 2006.

Kovach, Bill, and Tom Rosenstiel. *The Elements of Journalism: What Newspeople Should Know and the Public Should Expect.* New York: Three Rivers Press, 2007.

Leuchtenburg, William L. *In the Shadow of FDR: From Harry Truman to George W. Bush.* Ithaca, NY: Cornell University Press, 2001.

Liebovich, Louis. *The Press and the Modern Presidency: Myths and Mindsets from Kennedy to Election 2000.* New York: Praeger, 2001.

Lontz, Frank. *Words That Work: It's Not What You Say, It's What People Hear.* New York: Hyperion, 2008.

Maraniss, David, and Ellen Y. Nakashima. *The Prince of Tennessee: Al Gore Meets His Fate.* New York: Simon & Schuster, 2001.

McAuliffe, Terry. *What a Party: My Life Among Democrats, Presidential Candidates, Activists, Alligators and Other Wild Animals.* New York: Thomas Dunne Books, 2007.

McGovern, George. *Grassroots: The Autobiography of George McGovern.* New York: Random House, 1977.

Meyer, Peter. *James Earl Carter: The Man and the Myth.* Kansas City: Sheed Andrews & McMeel Inc., 1978.

Nelson, Michael. *The Presidency and the Political System.* Washington: CQ Press, 2005.

Nessen, Ron. *It Sure Looks Different from the Inside.* Chicago: Playboy Press, 1978

Parmet, Herbert S. *George Bush: The Life of a Lone Star Yankee.* New York: Scribner, 1997.

Pelosi, Alexandra. *Sneaking Into the Flying Circus: How the Media Turn Our Presidential Campaigns Into Freak Shows.* New York: Free Press, 2005.

Reagan, Ronald. *An American Life.* New York: Simon & Schuster, 1990.

Rollins, Ed. *Bare Knuckles and Back Rooms: My Life in American Politics.* New York: Broadway, 1997.

Rudell, B.J. *Only in New Hampshire: My Journey on the Campaign Trail.* Concord, NH: Plaidswede, 2003

Schramm, Martin. *Running for President 1976: The Carter Campaign.* New York: Stein and Day, 1977.

Schramm, Peter W. *American National Biography,* Volume I. Oxford: Oxford University Press, 1999.

Shapiro, Walter. *One-Car Caravan: On the Road with the 2004 Democrats Before America Tunes In.* New York: Public Affairs, 2003.

Simon, Paul. *P.S.: The Autobiography of Paul Simon.* New York: Bonus Books, 2003.

Stricherz, Mark. *Why the Democrats Are Blue: Secular Liberalism and the De-*

cline of the People's Party. New York: Encounter Books, 2007.

Stone, Gerald, Michael Singletary, and Virginia P. Richmond. *Clarifying Communication Theories: A Hands-on Approach*. New York: Wiley-Blackwell, 1999.

Sytek, Donna. *Further Ado: Practical Protocol for New Hampshire*. Concord, NH: Plaidswede, 2003.

Thomas, Evan. *A Long Time Coming*. Washington: Public Affairs, 2009.

Thompson, Hunter S. *Fear and Loathing: On the Campaign Trail '72*. New York: Grand Central, 1973

Walker, T.J., and Jess Todtfeld. *Media Training A-Z*. New York: Media Training Worldwide, 2008.

Weiss, Ellen, and Mel Friedman. *Jimmy Carter: Champion of Peace*. New York: Aladdin, 2003.

Wheelan, Charles. *Naked Economics: Undressing the Dismal Science*. New York: W.W. Norton, 2003.

White, Theodore H. *America in Search of Itself*. New York: Harper & Row, 1982.

___. *In Search of History*. New York: Warner Books, 1978.

___. *The Making of the President 1964*. New York: Athenium, 1965.

___. *The Making of the President 1968*. New York: Athenium, 1969.

___. *The Making of the President 1972*. New York: Athenium, 1973.

Witcover, Jules. *Marathon: The Pursuit of the Presidency 1972–1976*. New York: Viking Press, 1977.

Winebrenner, Hugh. *The Iowa Precinct Caucuses: The Making of a Media Event*. 2nd ed. Ames: Iowa State University Press, 1998.

Wright, Stephen J. *The Road to the White House 2000—The Politics of Presidential Elections*. New York: Bedford-St. Martin's, 2000.

Media

"About the caucuses." *Iowacaucus.org*.

"About the Caucuses: Meaningful Test," *iowapresidentialpolitics.com*.

"A Complete History of the Iowa Caucuses." *Cedar Rapids Gazette*, December 27, 2006.

Apple, R.W. "Iowa's Weighty Caucuses: Significance by Accident." *New York Times*, January 25, 1988.

"A Second Place Finish Gives Heart to Buchanan." *New York Times*, February 13, 1996.

Baker, Russell. "Handicapppers." *New York Times Magazine*, February 6, 1983.

Balz, Dan. "Expect the Best, Spin the Rest." *Washington Post*, January 16, 2000.

Beinert, Peter. "Rethinking Iowa." *Washington Post*, January 14, 2005.

Berman, Ari. "Not So Superdelegates." *Nation*, February 18, 2008.

"Bradley Shares a Ride, Some of His Philosophy." *Mason City Globe Gazette*, January 12, 2000.

Broder, David. "Reform or Die." *Time*, June 27, 1969.

"Bowing Out: Poor Showing in 2 Contests Leads Gramm to Withdraw." *New York Times*, February 14, 1996.

"Buchanan: A Little Older but Same Conservative Message." *Mason City Globe Gazette*, March 29, 1999.

"Buchanan Blasts U.S. Actions in Kosovo." *Mason City Globe Gazette*, March 24, 1999.

"Bush Image, Forbes Cash Barriers to Buchanan's Goal." *Mason City Globe Gazette*, June 25, 1999.

Curry, Tom. "What Role for Democratic Super-Delegates?" *MSNBC.com*, April 26, 2007.

"Dean Has a Little Fun While Courting the Uncommitted." *Mason City Globe Gazette*, December 6, 2003.

Duffy, Brian, "The Seven Dwarfs." Cartoon. *Des Moines Register*, May 8, 1987.

"Everett McKinley Dirksen's Finest Hour." *Peoria Journal Star*, June 10, 2004.

"Forbes Flays the Feds." *Mason City Globe Gazette*, August 6, 1999.

"Forbes: It's Time to Cut Spending." *Mason City Globe Gazette*, June 9, 1999.

"For Hatch, Nowhere to Go but Up." *Washington Post*, August 16, 1999.

"Gary Hart and the Iowa Caucuses." *Mason City Globe Gazette*, January 17, 2000

Greenberg, David. "After the Assassination: How Gene McCarthy's Response to Bobby Kennedy's Murder Crippled the Democrats." *Slate*, June 4, 2008.

Greenfield, Jeff. "The Brigadoon Complex: Where the Iowa Caucuses Went Wrong." *Slate*, December 31, 2007.

"Harkin Promises Effort to End Super Delegates." *Mason City Globe Gazette*, March 11, 2008.

"Hatch Braves Snow to Spread Message." *Mason City Globe Gazette*, January 20, 2000.

Henderson, O. Kay, "Hart Claims He Invented Iowa Caucuses." *Iowa Public Radio*, January 25, 2003.

Hirshberg, Meg Cadoux, "What I Saw in Iowa: It's Not N.H. but It's Exuberant and Good for Democracy." *Concord (N.H.) Monitor*, January 20, 2008.

"History of the Iowa Caucus," *Iowa Public Television*, December 31, 2007.

"Iowa Caucus: Winners and Surprises." *history.com*.

"Iowa Caucuses." *Des Moines Register*, January 14, 2008.

"Iowa Envy: How Did an Undersized, Atypical Farm State Get Such an Oversized Role?" *minnpost.com*, January 3, 2008.

"Iowa Straw Poll Is Hog Wash." *San Francisco Chronicle*, August 15, 1999.

Karmack, Elaine. "A History of Superdelegates in the Democratic Party." John F. Kennedy School of Government, Harvard University (op-ed), February 14, 2008.

"Kerry Touts Farm Reform." *Mason City Globe Gazette*, August 13, 2003.

"Lamar Alexander Here." *Mason City Globe Gazette*, August 19, 1995.

"McGovern Visiting State." *Mason City Globe Gazette*, January 13, 1972.

"Meet the Press" television broadcast, May 11, 2008.

"Mississippi and Freedom Summer." *Watson.org*, June 29, 1998.

Mixner, David. "Citizen Participation Endangered in Democratic Primary." *huffingtonpost.com*, February 4, 2007.

"Next Stop in the Democratic Presidential Race: Iowa." *Mason City Globe Gazette*, March 12, 2008.

Olinger, David, and Chuck Plunkett. "In Tight Race, Super Delegates Super Important." *Denver Post*, February 6, 2008.

Page, Susan. "The Importance of Iowa." *USA Today*, January 19, 2004.

"President Kennedy's Civil Rights Speech." *CNN.com*, August 16, 2008.

Purdum, Todd S. "Carter Put It on the Political Map and Iowa Hasn't Budged Since." *New York Times*, January 19, 2004.

"Quayle Continues Call for Clinton Resignation." *Mason City Globe Gazette*, September 19, 1998.

Reeves, Richard. "It's 1972 Again in Presidential Politics." *Los Angeles Times*, March 23, 2007.

"Robertson Victory Shocks Rivals." *Washington Post*, September 14, 1987.

"Romney Wins Straw Poll." *Quad City Times*, August 12, 2007.

Rudin, Ken. "History May Not Help Figure Out Iowa." National Public Radio, December 12, 2007.

Saslow, Eli. "The 17 Minutes That Launched a Political Star." *Washington Post*, August 25, 2008.

Shapiro, Walter. "Hype and Glory." *USA Today*, January 20, 2004.

"Slain Civil Rights Workers Found." *history.com*.

Soloman, John. "Splitting Hairs: Edwards' Stylist Tells His Side of Story." *Washington Post*, July 5, 2007.

Squire, Peverill, "The Iowa Caucuses, 1972–2008: A Eulogy." *The Forum*, University of Missouri, 2008.

"Steve Forbes at NIACC." *Mason City Globe Gazette*, June 13, 1999.

Stricherz, Mark. "Primary Colors: How a Little-Known Task Force Helped Create Red State/Blue State America." *Boston Globe*, November 23, 2003.

"Stunning Result Carries a Grim Message for Bush." *New York Times*, February 9, 1988.

"Super-Complicated Tuesday." *Nation*, February 4, 2008.

Swarns, Rachel. "A Contender Struggles to Protect His Image." *New York Times*, February 25, 1996.

Tapper, Jake, "Political Punch: Power, Pop and Probings." *abcnews.com*, February 14, 2008.

"The Mondale Lectures: Atlantic City Revisited." *minnesotapublicradio.org*, February 11, 2000.

"Tonight's the Night (At Last)." *Mason City Globe Gazette*, January 24, 2000.

Tierney, John. "Gary Hart's Strengths Vie With Embarrassing Past." *New York Times*, January 24, 2003.

Thompson, Robert R. "In Iowa Caucuses, Uncommitted Did Better Than Jimmy Carter." Letter to the editor. *New York Times*, January 24, 1988.

Tibbetts, Ed. "So Why Do We Caucus, Anyway?" *Quad City Times*, December 15, 2007.

Wehrman, Jessica. "A Brief History of the Iowa Caucuses." *Atlanta Journal-Constitution*, January 2, 2008.

"What Iowa Straw Poll Tells the GOP." *Time*, August 11, 2007.

Witcover, Jules. "Candidates are Dreaming the Jimmy Carter Iowa Dream." *Columbia* (Mo.) *Tribune*, November 5, 2007.

Zeitz Joshua. "Democratic Debacle." *American Heritage*, June/July 2005.

Index